The Real Estate Investor's Survival Guide

The Real Estate Investor's Survival Guide

Stuart M. Saft

John Wiley & Sons, Inc.
New York • Chichester • Brisbane • Toronto • Singapore

*This book is dedicated to my wife Stephanie,
and my sons Brad and Gordon, without whose
support it could not have been written.*

In recognition of the importance of preserving what has been
written, it is a policy of John Wiley & Sons, Inc., to have
books of enduring value published in the United States
printed on acid-free paper, and we exert our best efforts
to that end.

Library of Congress Cataloging-in-Publication Data

Saft, Stuart M.
   The real estate investor's survival guide / by Stuart M. Saft.
      p.   cm.
   Includes bibliographical references.
   ISBN 0-471-55229-1
   1. Real estate business.   2. Recessions.   I. Title.
HD1375.S226   1992
333.33—dc20   91-30088

Printed in the United States of America

10 9 8 7 6 5 4 3 2 1

Printed and bound by Courier Companies, Inc.

Foreword

Real estate has long been one of the most common investments for millions of Americans. Unfortunately, whether it's a small rental vacation home purchased with friends, or a more substantial commercial property such as an apartment building or shopping center, real estate investors are in the midst of a very challenging time. Economic weakness has hurt many real estate markets. Vacancies are high. Banks, and other traditional real estate lenders, have adopted restrictive lending policies. The result is that many real estate investors are facing, often for the first time, financial difficulties, mortgage defaults, work-outs and debt restructuring, foreclosures, and even bankruptcy. Stuart Saft, one of the country's foremost real estate attorneys, has written not only an authoritative guide, but an understandable one. This indispensable book will serve as your guidebook through these troubled times, providing practical advice and invaluable insights of a seasoned real estate expert.

The preferable approach to addressing real estate problems is avoidance. Saft provides considerable insight into the real estate investment process and specific advice on how to avoid, to the extent possible, the problems plaguing so many real estate investors. This includes prudent use of financing, proper maintenance, bidding, contracts, leases, and other aspects of properly managing your property.

Where avoidance isn't possible, you must take action to protect your investment. The most important step in addressing real estate adversity is acknowledging that problems exist and deciding to confront them. Saft identifies realistic warning signs that can help you identify problems at the earliest time. You must then assess your situation and evaluate all potential options. Details for both residential and commercial property are provided.

Every cloud is said to have a silver lining. The current real estate difficulties also spell opportunities for future real estate moguls. Saft provides important perspective with insights into the historical trends of real estate investments.

Stuart Saft's outstanding book, *The Real Estate Survival Guide* will guide you through the current real estate difficulties, and prepare you for the coming upturn in the market.

MARTIN M. SHENKMAN

Preface

Historically, the owners of real estate have survived periods of boom and bust, overbuilding and absorption, inflation and recession, loose credit and tight money policies, war and peace, bank expansion and bank failures. Notwithstanding the good times and bad times, the one constant has been that real estate has maintained its value as an investment; thus, those who can survive the downturn will be in the best position to prosper when the market improves.

The market is presently experiencing a serious downturn, caused by many of the same factors that have created problems in the past—bank failures, abrupt changes in tax policy, tight credit, overbuilding (which is another way of saying underutilization), optimism, and recession. Nevertheless, since the end of World War II, the value of real estate has gone through an unprecedented period of growth that has continued virtually unabated for over 40 years. During this period, there have been temporary downturns; however, in every instance, the value of real estate has recovered and then accelerated. The issue becomes how to survive the bad times in order to be prepared to achieve an immediate benefit when the situation begins to improve.

Survival entails three components: avoiding problems, minimizing the effect of the downturn, and benefiting from the problems of those who have failed to be prepared for the downturn. The purpose of this book is to provide the real estate investor with a guide for preparing for, and then navigating through, the unchartered waters of a real estate downturn. Reading the eleven chapters in the book will enable the real estate investor to function effectively to survive and prosper during this period. The book is written for both the neophyte and the experienced investor and was written because, although real estate downturns occur periodically, they do occur. Therefore, an experienced owner may not have had to previously deal with the problems or, if he or she has, may not remember what had to be done to survive. In this respect, it is interesting to note that, when asked about his bank's inept response to the first waive of defaults, one banker commented that none of the current officers were around during the last downturn, so they did not have experience in dealing with the problems.

Each of the eleven chapters is self-contained, enabling the reader to use the book either to develop an understanding of the entire process or as a reference source in dealing with a particular problem as it develops or a particular kind of property. Property is categorized in this book by its use, since the different uses result in different problems for the owners. To facilitate its use, this book is divided into four sections:

1. Chapters 1 and 2 provide an understanding of real estate cycles to give the reader the historical context in which the cycles occur. It also provides a detailed discussion of the actions that an owner can take to avoid being affected by the downturn.

2. Chapters 3 through 5 provide the reader with guidelines as to the nature of problems with which owners of particular kinds of properties may have to deal, methods of preventing the problems, and techniques for dealing with the problems if they do occur. This section also provides warning signs for owners of passive investments, those that are managed or operated by a third party who merely sends periodic statements to the owner.

3. Chapters 6 through 10 discuss the actions that can be taken by the owner in attempting to minimize the effects of the downturn on his or her property and the things that must be considered by the owner in taking various actions to save the property or the investment. Because most problems involve financing, this section analyzes financing, restructuring and refinancing a property's debt, and methods that might be necessary to weather the storm. This section also includes the elements of foreclosure and bankruptcy, and the tax consequences of any of these actions. Although this material provides a generic understanding of these highly complex areas and will enable the owner to understand his or her options in dealing with the property, it does not obviate the need for sound legal advice.

4. Chapter 11 discusses the things that a purchaser must consider and the protection he or she must have before purchasing distressed property. Everyone knows that Olympia & Yorke, the Canadian real estate

firm, purchased what turned out to be several billion dollars worth of prime Manhattan real estate in the late 1970s for a fraction of its value, at a time when New York City was teetering on the brink of bankruptcy. Interestingly, during this same period, a young Donald Trump began putting deals together on property previously owned by successful entrepreneurs who had fallen on hard times. He obviously failed to grasp the lesson learned by his predecessors.

Certainly, there is no guaranty that the owner of a property (or a lender for that matter) can survive an economic downturn or avoid the consequences of past mistakes. However, this book should, to a great extent, remove the element of surprise and increase the likelihood that the diligent owner can withstand these negative forces. This book also provides advice to the new wave of investors as to how they can avoid trouble during the next downturn.

I intentionally refer in the text to the owner, the lender, and the tenant as "it" or as "he or she" depending on whether the entity in each situation is more likely to be a company or an individual.

Acknowledgments

It is unfortunate that this book had to be written, but I am grateful to those who made it possible to write. The current real estate recession has turned multimillionaires into paupers faster than anyone thought possible. The downturn has struck the unsuspecting and the comfortable with incredible speed and has ignored the fact that these same people were considered brilliant deal makers only months before. What is all the more tragic about what is happening is that it was all foreseeable and, in many cases, could have been avoided or the consequences minimized, if preventive measures were taken.

It is heartening, however, to see that those who have lost fortunes have not lost hope and expect to rebuild them—and they will. The real estate industry has even been able to make fun of itself by a prayer that has been faxed from office to office for the last few months, stating "Lord, grant me one more real estate boom and the intelligence not to overleverage my position or waste the profit."

Every book is a collective effort involving those who were directly and indirectly responsible for its production. In this regard, I would like to thank Deborah Cohen Brunell, who has worked with me for the last five years on this and my other books, and who has continuously demonstrated incredible patience under extremely adverse conditions. I would also like to thank my partners at Wolf Haldenstein Adler Freeman & Herz, who provide me a wonderfully congenial and sophisticated atmosphere in which to work.

I would also like to thank my editor, Michael Hamilton, who recognized the seriousness of the real estate problems, got the book approved in record time, and was quite supportive while it was being written.

Finally, I would like to thank my colleagues and clients who, on a daily basis, are proving that you can survive in a hostile real estate environment just as easily as when things were great. Yes, it was more fun before, but now we are getting to prove how creative and resilient we can be in adverse circumstances.

Contents

1

Understanding Real Estate as an Investment

REAL ESTATE CYCLES

People have been investing in real estate for hundreds of years, and more fortunes have been quickly made and lost in real estate than in virtually any other form of investment. One of the attractions of real estate is its limited supply despite the constantly increasing need. Will Rogers, the humorist, once said, "Buy land; they're not making any more of it." Although modern methods enable the development of land that was once considered unusable, those processes will increase the supply by only a limited amount, which will soon be exhausted. Therefore, unless the laws of supply and demand are repealed, all real estate should become more valuable as the population increases and the resource becomes less available. The issue, then, is not whether real estate is a good investment, but whether the investor can protect his or her investment, once acquired, and make certain that it appreciates in value with the rest of the market.

There is no sure formula for selecting the right property or the correct method of protecting the investment to benefit from the ultimate increase in value. However, there are ways to reduce the risks that the property will depreciate in value or that the owner will lose the ability to retain the property in difficult times. Just as it is almost impossible not to benefit from an appreciating market or to have a property increase in value during inflationary periods, making one mistake or overlooking a single potential problem can cause the property's value to be reduced significantly in difficult times, which can cause the owner to lose the property.

It must always be remembered that real estate is a cyclical investment. There are periods of boom and bust, overbuilding and underutilization, scarcity and oversupply. To some degree, the cyclical nature of real estate is affected by the demands of an economy that fluctuates between expansion and contraction, as well as a constantly changing money supply and government policies relating to conceptions of what is best for the general welfare of the citizens. Real estate values are also affected by the lengthy lead time required to plan, finance, construct, and utilize new buildings and the inability of owners to accurately predict the demand for a particular project several years in advance of its construction. Moreover, not only must the need for the property be identified long before the building is ready, but society's future needs must match the locale of the property, the costs of construction or renovation, and the planned use of the property. Considering all the variables involved, it is surprising that there are very many successful properties.

In some situations, the sudden increase in the construction of new buildings creates problems for the older, less up-to-date properties, whereas in other situations, the real estate cycle is affected by general economic conditions. Moreover, even if new buildings are not being developed, existing older buildings can have difficulties surviving. Older properties can develop problems if they are located in deteriorating areas or fail to meet current demands, or if the income generated by the property is insufficient to cover the cost of operating and maintaining the property, the payment of debt service to the holders of mortgages on the property, and the profit to the owner to cover the overhead.

Each real estate cycle adversely affects all real estate regardless of its age, location, condition, and use. However, the cautious owner can act to limit the adverse impact of an economic contraction on a particular property, and thereby increase the likelihood that the property and its owner will survive and prosper. Unfortunately, existing properties can also be adversely affected by the loss of a major tenant, wars, oil embargoes, changes in a neighborhood, changing consumer tastes, the region's economy, and other factors. One problem for real estate investors is that, to a large degree, neither the demand nor the supply of buildings is fixed, and therefore the owners can suffer from the effect of too many variables. Nevertheless, the cycles control events just as events cause the cycles.

To a large extent, each real estate cycle goes through an almost identical life as the previous ones. At the beginning of each real estate cycle, there are shortages of space, causing prices to appreciate and convincing owners, developers, and investors that the time is right to buy more property and develop or refurbish existing properties or rent additional space on the speculation that prices will appreciate. This activity creates additional upward pressure on rents and prices, which creates a greater demand that further reduces the supply of property. The owners of undeveloped and underdeveloped property then start the lengthy process of obtaining and clearing a site, seeking municipal approvals, having plans and specifications prepared, obtaining construction and permanent financing, commencing construction, and then leasing, using, or selling the finished space. Meanwhile, renters, seeing this activity, start analyzing whether the rents will escalate to such a degree that it makes economic sense to buy space rather than rent. The vacant space is leased, the first properties that are completed are usually quickly absorbed into the market, and the properties initially offered for sale are quickly sold.

There then follow several years during which the properties that are completed are absorbed, the properties that are marketed are rapidly sold, and the local vacancy rates remain low. It is a sellers' and landlords' market. The initial absorption is due to the lengthy lead time in developing a project and the fact that it usually takes at least three years between the time the investor recognizes the need for another building and the time the space is available. The key element to the start of a real estate craze is the profit made by the initial owners, developers, and purchasers. Those who have guessed correctly that the real estate cycle was about to begin or were lucky or were able to survive the last downturn, realize a relatively sudden and rapid appreciation of their investment. The publicity generated by this sudden change in fortune creates the frenzy. Overnight, owners who had a difficult time surviving are depicted as geniuses. They are followed into the craze by the investors who are sufficiently liquid to take advantage of the situation and are able to invest quickly. The second group of investors are the ones who generate the largest and fastest profit, who become the conspicuous spenders, and who cause everyone else to want to invest in real estate.

Unfortunately, because many investors recognize the need for additional buildings at the same time, several similar buildings may be completed and enter the market simultaneously. The new buildings compete with existing properties that had been struggling to survive in the previously contracting economy. The owners of existing space whose resources are already depleted then decide to sell their properties in the appreciating market rather than compete with the newer properties. This results in the older properties' becoming highly leveraged while being operated by inexperienced owners. When the new owners are unable to maintain the building and pay the debt service, they begin to reduce expenses in a way that they believe is imperceptible.

As the cycle continues, more and more space becomes available for rent or sale to users, and vacancy rates slowly begin to increase. However, it is then too late for buildings that are in an advanced state of planning or construction to be aborted. This increases the supply and causes the vacancy rates to increase further. Initially, the vacancies occur in the older, secondary space that is being abandoned for the new, more modern space. However, as the process continues, the newer space becomes more and more expensive because of the increasing construction and carrying costs for buildings that lease or sell more slowly than originally projected. Meanwhile, as the real estate cycle continues, investors see that the experienced developers and investors are making a substantial profit from the initial demand and make capital available to finance further development and to purchase existing properties at inflated prices. Neophyte investors, deciding that it is an opportune time to invest in real estate, begin to borrow substantial amounts of money to acquire property. Properties are quickly sold, with the prices of each sale increasing dramatically and most of the money being covered by larger amounts of debt. The experienced investors, not wanting to be closed out of the market, then pay unrealistic prices for properties in anticipation that the income will appreciate significantly and the prices will continue to accelerate.

To a large extent, real estate successes and failures are caused by leveraging (i.e., borrowing against the owner's projected equity in the property). As each real estate cycle continues, more and more investors are carrying larger amounts of debt, which they assume will be paid from increased income or inflation, and they act based upon projections of ever-increasing income being generated by the property. The investors also believe that, even if the income does not continue to appreciate significantly, they will always be able to sell their property, liquidate their indebtedness, and keep their profit.

Eventually, the day of reckoning arrives. Suddenly, vacancy rates begin to increase substantially, the economy softens, and interest rates increase dramatically by a government attempting to control inflation or otherwise effectuate a change in monetary policy. There may also be a sudden change in tax policy to reduce the attractiveness of real estate as an investment. As the debt service on the property's mortgage becomes too much for the owners to continue to pay, the tenants and purchasers, realizing that there is a price adjustment coming in the real estate market, are no longer interested in committing themselves to lease or purchase property at the inflated rents or prices. The owners, suddenly aware that they are unable to either pay their expenses or liquidate their investments, begin to reduce their expenses to maintain their cash flow. These actions taken in the name of efficiency result in more tenants leaving or negotiating to pay a lower rent, which eventually cause the properties to deteriorate further. Loans begin to go into default as more and more owners find it impossible to meet the ever-increasing operating expense and debt service demands of the property.

The cycle ends when the lenders, realizing that their loan portfolios are not producing the revenues that had initially been projected, have to decide whether to foreclose their mortgages and risk a bankruptcy by the owner, or force the owner to file for bankruptcy, or agree to meet with the owner and work out a solution to the property's problems. The most successful investors are those whose actions make them immune to the lender's control because they take steps to minimize the effect of the cycle. Of course, as each cycle ends, every investor swears to avoid excessive leveraging during the next cycle. They only pray that they can make it to the next cycle.

However, this scenario does not have to be the case for an investor. It is possible to acquire property at any stage of the real estate cycle and not risk losing one's investment. Success is not a miracle, although sometimes it seems that it is! A successful real estate investment requires an understanding of the real estate process, a good choice of property, and caution throughout the acquisition, ownership, and disposition of the property. Nevertheless, caution does not require the investor to move so slowly that opportunities are lost. A cautious investor can act aggressively, if he or she understands the manner in which the investment works and how to survive the problems that will invariably develop.

RISKS OF REAL ESTATE INVESTMENT

The essence of real estate ownership and one of its more beguiling features is the owner's ability to finance many times more than the owner's actual investment in the property, by being able to borrow against his or her perceived equity in the property. Real estate is an attractive security for a loan because its value is relatively stable and, unlike other investments, it cannot be moved or hidden from lenders. For these reasons, lenders agree to kinds of financing that stock and bond investors at the height of purchasing on margin would never consider possible. Excessive borrowing is also caused by the fact that there is no real market for real estate with posted prices similar to the stock exchanges, so owners are able to borrow based upon perceived value and anticipated sales, rather than on publicly available information.

Unfortunately, because neither the property's income nor its expenses are usually fixed, owners frequently find themselves in financial difficulties because of overly optimistic income and expense projections. Income projections usually are based upon the owner's anticipation that both the value of the property and the cash flow from the property will continue to increase, providing the owner with the means to meet the property's operating expenses, taxes, and debt service obligations. When times are good, the projections are achieved, and when times are not good, the properties are lost because they cannot carry themselves.

The biggest problem with real estate and the one that causes the most difficulty for owners when the market begins to soften is the fact that real estate is an illiquid investment. Real estate is unsaleable at any price when there is no market for a property. Stocks and bonds purchased on margin can usually be readily liquidated to meet margin calls, if necessary. The sale of real estate is a long, painstaking, and unscientific process in which a property may find a purchaser on the day it is listed or may sit for years without anyone showing an interest in acquiring it.

The real estate market is the last totally free market, and sometimes it is a free-for-all. It is unlike the securities markets, where the exchanges make certain that as long as the security can be traded, someone will be available to purchase it, even if it is an exchange's specialist in a particular stock. Moreover, real estate investors do not have available the extensive public information available to securities investors or the protection against insiders trading on material nonpublic information. However, there is little doubt that far more money has been made by real estate investors over shorter periods of time than through any other investment vehicle. Additionally, unlike an investment in stocks or bonds, where the company can go into bankruptcy and disappear overnight, in real estate, if an investor has the ability to maintain the investment, there is a reduced likelihood that the entire investment will be lost for reasons beyond the owner's control.

Because real estate values seem to invariably increase and the ownership of real estate is one of the surest ways of making a great deal of money, leveraging the real estate investment, by borrowing a large percentage of the purchase price or borrowing against one's equity in the property, is one of the surest ways of losing a great deal of money when the market turns downward. Owners of real estate are usually overly optimistic as to the likely success of their properties. Only when the failure of a property becomes inevitable does the owner finally become realistic as to the problems the property is having. At that moment, the owner begins to look for an easy solution to the property's problems. One solution the owner may consider is to stop making debt service payments on the mortgage and real estate tax payments in order to conserve cash and be able to continue to make payments toward the property's operating expenses. However, this only makes matters worse and increases the likelihood that the property will ultimately be lost.

The mortgage is frequently one of the first expenses to be paid last and to then be omitted because the debt service payment is usually the single largest expense the property owner is required to make. Additionally, the owner's failure to pay operating expenses provides the tenants and users of the property with an excuse not to pay their rent. Furthermore, the tenants and other users of the property will not be initially aware of, or affected by, the owner's failure to pay the mortgage. Only after the payments have not been made for several months does the lender even realize that the owner or the property is having a serious problem and then slowly pursue its remedies. By the time the lender reacts to the default, the borrower has failed to make payments for several months and the lender has to deal with a serious deficiency. Hopefully, during this time, the owner has continued to make tax, insurance, and other operating expense payments so that the property will not be jeopardized. Unfortunately, if the owner is seriously short of funds, those payments also have not been made, and the lender will find itself with a property that is in serious trouble and at risk of suddenly losing its security. Alternatively, the owner may continue making mortgage payments to avoid foreclosure, but stop paying taxes and deferring repairs and maintenance in hopes of buying time.

The most dreaded situation for the lender is when there is a default by the borrower and the security is placed at risk. At such times, the borrower has the biggest risk of losing the property. Lenders are most likely to deal reasonably with a defaulting borrower if he or she has acted prudently and protected the security for the loan and the lender's interest in the property. A lender can understand a soft real estate market, but cannot forgive having its security placed at risk.

Loan defaults also occur during the construction of a property due either to the developer's underestimation of the cost of construction or to the overestimation of the likely market for the finished product. In either event, the developer can find itself unable to make the debt service payments on its construction loan, or the permanent lender uses the developer's failure to complete the project or adequately lease the project on schedule as an excuse to terminate the permanent loan commitment. Default during or immediately after construction is serious because there are no existing tenants or users whose payments can be used to offset the property's costs. Additionally, once a property develops a reputation for having problems, the problems become much more difficult to resolve.

Even if there are tenants or purchasers for all or part of the property, they may refuse to fulfill their obligations out of fear that the developer did not build the property carefully in order to reduce its costs. The tenants or purchasers may also feel that if they proceed with their occupancy of the property, the developer might not return to finish the property or other tenants or purchasers might refuse to become involved with the property.

THE CAUSE OF A PROPERTY'S PROBLEMS

One of the best ways of dealing with the problems that can beset a property is to examine the reasons that a property is having problems in the first place. In every instance, the cure for a property's problems depends in large part on the reason for the problems. The causes of problems include the following:

- An unruly or disreputable tenant causing other tenants to leave
- Excessive deferred maintenance
- Excessive leveraging
- Financial difficulties among the principal owners
- Changes in the public's tastes or interests
- No market for the space due to local or national economic conditions
- Market for the space exists, but at an income level that is inadequate to pay the operating expenses and service the debt
- Unanticipated competition
- Change in demand, which eliminates the market for the property
- Expenses increasing at a faster rate than income
- Investors stop contributing
- An anchor tenant terminates a lease or files for bankruptcy protection
- Significantly higher than anticipated rent concessions to tenants
- Higher than projected development or renovation costs due to site conditions or other reasons
- Anticipated public interest not generated
- A contractor's job not completed due to excessive costs of a fixed-price contract or internal company problems
- Incomplete plans and specifications due to errors by the architect or engineer or the developer's attempt to convince the lender that the project could be built for less then the actual sum

- Labor disputes that delay the project and increase the costs substantially
- A delay in commencing or proceeding with the project, which upsets the schedule for various subcontractors
- Delay in off-site improvements precludes completion on time
- Labor shortages slow completion of the project
- Technical problems in the development slow completion
- Interest costs increase substantially due to an interest rate that is tied to the prime lending rate or another variable factor
- Lender refuses to fund the loan due to technical difficulties or changes in the lender's financial condition
- Estimates of the cost of completing or renovating the property are inadequate to complete the job and no additional funds are available
- Property damaged by a casualty, such as a fire or collapse of part of the project, causing extensive delays
- Inadequate property insurance for the project to proceed after a casualty
- Owner uninsured or underinsured for liabilities
- Zoning or subdivision approvals or building permit withdrawn after commencement of development
- Property has a title defect
- Property loses access to public roads
- A change in the local, state, or federal regulations regarding the property
- All or part of the property taken by condemnation
- Litigation by third parties
- Disagreement among principal owners
- Identification of an on-site environmental hazard
- Unsatisfactory or unsafe construction
- Imposition of government controls over some aspect of the property
- Inability to have utilities connected
- Increase in the scope of the work without additional financing
- Violation of local zoning laws
- Change in the surrounding area
- Wrong location

- Misuse of funds
- Faulty administration
- Extensive building code violations
- Inability to obtain special use permits
- Design defects
- Construction defects
- Waste
- Diversion of funds
- Theft
- Bad luck.

Frequently, upon realizing that the project is having financial difficulties, the owner looks for ways to reduce costs or increase income. There is no reason to object to the owner's taking defensive actions to protect the investment, providing that the effect of such steps does not exacerbate the problem. Nothing is wrong with making the operation of the property more efficient, but that does not mean reducing the operating expenses in such a way as to anger the current tenants, decreasing the likelihood that additional tenants will be identified, or impeding the sale of all or portions of the property.

DEALING WITH PROBLEMS

One of the most important things a property owner can do when a problem develops is to recognize that a problem has developed and deal with it. All too often, a small problem that could be easily resolved is allowed to grow, which makes it more difficult to resolve. A problem rarely resolves itself or goes away. A problem usually does not worsen significantly, but a problem occasionally increases in magnitude if not handled. Although problems come in many different varieties and are generated from different sources, they all have two things in common: Every problem comes at a terrible time and it is a surprise. Therefore, a cautious owner should expect the unexpected and be prepared for it.

If the owner decides to reduce expenses by not paying real estate taxes or insurance premiums, this places the property at great risk and should be avoided at all costs. The owner should also carefully consider changing the use and the marketing of the property to solve a short-term financial problem. However, the owner must never lose sight of the larger, more important issue relating to the property—its long-term viability. The owner's concern should be less on the potential short-term benefit from the owner's entering into leases with noncredit or nonrespectable tenants paying high rent, and more on the long-term effect of changing the reputation of the property or its economic basis. Nothing should be more important to the owner than the property's future and its ability to produce enough cash flow to support itself. The concern should be the likelihood that the property will survive and prosper and that the entire loan can be repaid over its term, rather then the receipt of current cash flow. Therefore, the owner's primary concern in safeguarding the property is to make certain that the owner's short-term needs for cash do not adversely affect the long-term potential income.

A different problem arises when a property has been built or purchased on speculation, and the tenants, users, or purchasers do not appear, leaving the owner with an empty, unused property. This is one of the worst problems. The owner must initially consider a change in the building's marketing strategy, such as changing the group to whom the property is appealing. If the owner can reduce the amount needed from tenants and still make the property viable, the market for potential tenants, purchasers, or users will increase dramatically.

In any event, once an owner realizes that there are problems, the owner should immediately review the options and may want to approach the mortgagee to discuss a uniform approach to solving the problem. Naturally, both the owner and the lender should consider their other options, such as selling the property or finding investors or filing for bankruptcy protection. The lender should also try to determine the reason for the owner's difficulties and whether it should assist the owner by restructuring the indebtedness or proceed to accelerate and foreclose its mortgage as soon as the default exists. From the lender's perspective, a great deal depends on the owner's integrity and the other collateral the lender is holding as security for this loan. The lender also wants to be certain that the income received by the borrower is properly applied and that the troubled borrower does not make matters worse by misapplying the income from the property. At some point in this process, the owner should analyze the manner in which the problem developed and the best way of alleviating it.

2

Avoiding Problems

A number of old sayings, such as "An ounce of prevention is worth more than a pound of cure" and "A stitch in time saves nine," are relevant to a real estate investment. The cautious investor can avoid the most troublesome and expensive problems by maintaining a watchful eye on the property and making certain that simple matters are handled before they become more complex, difficult, and expensive to handle. Virtually all problems that can adversely affect a property can be perceived before they become problems. Usually, a problem is caused either by the owner's action or inaction or by the owner's ignoring the warning signs.

It is impossible to generalize as to the different kinds of problems that can affect a property or the amount of time that the owner can consider alternative courses of action prior to acting. However, regardless of the nature of the problem, if the owner fails to act expeditiously, the problem could quickly overwhelm the owner. This chapter examines how to avoid a number of the fundamental problems. The next chapter advises the investor on the best manner of supervising the managing agent. Because real estate is frequently a passive investment, the owner's first line of defense and the cause of many problems is the independent managing agent.

Avoiding or minimizing problems requires constant vigilance. The owner must initially recognize the potential problem, and then be able to select the correct course of action to resolve the problem before it explodes out of control. *Explodes* is probably an accurate word to use, because serious problems rarely develop gradually; they usually start with an insignificant detail and suddenly become overwhelming.

The most difficult problems with which to deal are usually physical or financial, or a combination of the two. The solutions are varied because each problem frequently takes on a life of its own, and two similar problems can require different solutions based upon the facts involved in each situation. Certainly, many, if not most, problems can be resolved with money. However, most owners do not have an endless supply of money with which to handle problems and, even if they do, most would prefer to resolve a problem as inexpensively as possible.

PREVENTIVE MAINTENANCE

Although no building lasts forever, preventive maintenance can postpone the inevitable almost indefinitely. Every component of a building and each improvement to a property has a finite useful life. All improvements need constant maintenance and repair to ensure that they will achieve their anticipated useful life. A property that is allowed to deteriorate, or one in which the owner is not willing to invest additional capital to maintain and upgrade it, will have to be replaced at a higher cost sooner than projected. It is therefore in the owner's best interest to make certain that the property is operating at peak efficiency. Undoubtedly, the longer an owner can postpone replacing a building or a major component of the building, the larger the owner's return on investment will be. Although preventive maintenance is an expenditure, it is actually a savings over the cost of replacing the entire improvement.

Preventive maintenance has several components, including finding and curing potential problems before they get worse. No structural or mechanical problem cures itself. Thus, the owner should have an engineer or other construction professional periodically (i.e., at least annually) inspect the various components of the property. Then the owner can make repairs before the entire component has to be replaced. Preventive maintenance is similar to the old story that for want of a nail, a horse was lost, which caused the message to be lost, which led to the war being lost and the kingdom being lost. A small expenditure when the problem first appears will usually prevent a larger expense later.

Physical inspections of the property should be performed by professionals trained in the particular area they are investigating. It makes little sense for the electrician to inspect the plumbing or the parking lot contractor to inspect the roof. Probably the last person an owner would want to hire to do an inspection would be a contractor, especially the contractor who would be hired to repair or replace the component being inspected. For instance, if a roofing contractor is asked to examine a roof, it is likely that he is going to recommend replacing the roof. Thus, it is significantly more efficient for the owner to retain for inspections an independent engineer who is not affiliated with a contractor who might be asked to make the repair. In this way, there is no motivation for the inspector to recommend more work than is absolutely necessary.

However, there is also a caveat to using an independent engineer: Do not accept his or her recommendation that excessive work be done. Occasionally, an engineer or other construction professional who wants to be protected from future liability for providing the wrong advice, will recommend excessive work. This protects the engineer if his or her original estimate was incorrect and a greater degree of work is actually required. In such an event, the owner pays an increased amount for work that may not be needed in order to protect the engineer from his or her mistakes. In a sense, the owner is providing the engineer with insurance that the engineer's recommendation was accurate. Thus, if an engineer makes a recommendation that seems outrageous, the owner should seek a second opinion. How does an owner know if the recommendation is outrageous? By asking questions. Unfortunately, many people are too embarrassed to thoroughly question professionals, or the professionals have an attitude of "How can you question my judgment?" There is no reason to feel embarrassed or browbeaten, because even professionals make mistakes, and sometimes their opinions are based on something less than all the facts. If the owner can be made to understand the reason for the advice, the owner might be able to improve upon it. After all, no one knows the property better than the owner.

Of course, the owner must utilize a certain degree of logic and not seek independent engineers and second opinions for jobs that are relatively inexpensive. The question of where the line should be drawn between different solutions must be separately analyzed in each case and cannot be generalized. However, when in doubt, the owner would be wise to spend several thousand dollars to utilize the services of an independent engineer to make recommendations or review proposals.

It is also important to understand that the professional's report should be in writing and the professional should be available to answer questions after the owner reviews and analyzes the report. The owner must be given an opportunity to digest the report before questioning the engineer. In a sense, the property owner must become an expert with regard to every component of the building, regardless of its complexity. This may entail becoming a nuisance to the professional, but it will be a significant benefit to the owner in the long run. Every owner must consider that he or she is not an owner of merely a building, but of a small, multimillion-dollar business.

The components that need to be regularly inspected and repaired include the roof and exterior walls; the parking and other common areas; the electrical, plumbing, heating, ventilating, and air conditioning systems; and the windows and floors. The engineer should check that each is free of leaks and that the systems are operating at peak efficiency. Each of these things will prolong the life of the building and its components, and reduce operating costs.

BIDDING

If work is required, the owner should seriously consider having several contractors bid to do the required work. Although the bidding process is more time-consuming and does have an element of cost, it provides the owner with significant benefits in the long run. If the property requires significant physical work, the bidding process facilitates the owner's selecting the best possible contractor to do the work at the *lowest reasonable* price. In selecting the contractor, it is frequently better to pay more to have the work done by someone who is qualified, than to have the work done by the least expensive, least competent bidder. However, only through an understanding of the bidding process can an owner get the best possible result from bidding.

Obtaining bids for work to be done at the property is important to the owner because a review of the bids, as well as the plans and specifications on which the bids are based, facilitates having the work done in the most economical and efficient manner. Bidding also enables the owner to identify individuals who can replace one or more of the hired contractors, professionals, or other suppliers, who do not perform pursuant to their agreements.

Competitive bidding is utilized in the construction industry as the basis for awarding most contracts for the supply of labor, material, and services to projects. This may seem surprising since, unlike government contracts, the construction or rehabilitation of commercial property does not usually require the use of bidding before contracts are awarded. If done properly, however, bidding provides the owner with an opportunity to obtain a specified job or material at the lowest possible price.

The owner's architect or engineer should prepare the bid documents and divide the work to be done into its component parts, thereby requiring the contractor to bid on each portion of labor, material, or service, as well as to make an aggregate bid for the entire project. A cost is incurred in utilizing the engineer to prepare the bid documents, but the cost is small in relation to the benefit of having the work done at the most competitive price by someone independent from the engineer. Bidding permits the engineer and the owner to compare the individual elements of each bid and enables them to determine if the successful bidder is underbidding on a particular part of the contract. Although conceptually nothing is wrong with an underbid, it might demonstrate ambiguities in the plans and specifications for the work or the bid documents. It could also represent a determination by one bidder that the required work is less extensive than the other bidders think. Moreover, such ambiguities could raise questions as to the entire bidding process. It is therefore imperative that the engineer is certain that the bids clearly specify the work to be done. If the bids are incomplete, the owner must pay for changes in the contract after the work commences. If the bid documents do not include all the necessary work, the cost could increase significantly because the extra work cannot be separately bid and because any delay slows the completion.

Bidding entails several steps, beginning with the preparation and distribution of an invitation to bid, which can be published in a newspaper and delivered to a number of qualified bidders. Those interested in bidding for the job then contact the owner or the project engineer and receive copies of the bid documents. The owner should review the engineer's list of contractors sent invitations to bid to make certain that a cross-section of contractors is represented, and not several unqualified bidders and one friend of the engineer, which would result in selection of the friend.

The bid documents include the following:

- A list of requirements that must be satisfied by the successful bidder
- Copies of the relevant portion of the plans and specifications describing the project
- General information about the job, the owner, the engineer or architect, and the other parties involved
- The requirements for a bid bond
- A copy of the proposed contract or a summary of its terms
- The form that the bid must take.

An interested contractor or supplier responds by submitting to the owner a bid that is irrevocable for a specific limited period of time. The bid is made irrevocable to protect the owner from spending time and money reviewing the bids and awarding the contract, and then learning that the winning bidder cannot or will not proceed with the project. The time and location of the bid opening is described in the bid documents so that all the participants are aware of the time limitations involved. The bids are opened at one time and reviewed together by the owner and the project's engineer or architect. This process protects the owner and the other bidders from one bidder's being able to bid based upon information leaked from earlier bids.

Although the contract is usually awarded to the lowest bidder, this is not mandatory. In reviewing the bids, the owner must also consider the bidders' qualifications to be certain the work will be done in an expert manner by a qualified and experienced contractor and not by someone who is prepared to bid any amount to get the contract. Therefore, the owner should consider the bidders' experience, financial ability to perform, physical ability to satisfy the contract, and reputation for satisfactorily completing prior jobs. Moreover, the owner must be certain that the bid is for the exact work that has to be done and that there are no discrepancies between the winning contractor and the engineer as to the work to be performed under the contract. Thereafter, the engineer reviews all the bids and prepares a schedule indicating the amount bid by each contractor for the whole contract and each component of the work to be done under the contract (see Example). As part of due diligence, the owner should also examine the bidding instructions and each of the bids to be certain that the work will be done properly, efficiently, and as inexpensively as possible.

EXAMPLE: BID ANALYSIS

Project address	123 Main Street, Anytown, USA 00000
Project	Exterior Renovations
Specifications	Drawings dated 1/1/00 by John Architect

Bidders	Jones Const Co.	Smith Const Co.	Doe Const Co.
Total bid	$324,874	$376,451	$295,987
Replace roof	84,550	91,980	76,189
Replace windows	43,980	55,760	41,678
Replace lintels	86,350	84,975	72,190
Rebuild parapet	24,280	31,285	23,150
Replace bricks	21,375	25,550	19,350
Repair terraces	19,365	24,675	18,980
Waterproofing	21,690	27,155	22,350
Scaffolding	11,350	14,285	9,850
Security services	6,550	7,850	5,750
Repair entryway	5,384	12,936	6,500

Nevertheless, mistakes happen in the bidding process, due to the speed with which bids must be submitted and the complexity of the work being bid upon. This is especially true in complex contracts that require the bidder to obtain supporting bids from suppliers and subcontractors. If a bidding mistake is obvious, the bidder is usually given the opportunity to rescind the bid rather than permit the owner to gain from an honest mistake. Nevertheless, the erring bidder must advise the owner that a mistake has occurred as soon after realizing the mistake as possible and must be able to demonstrate that the mistake was made in good faith. The owner can then award the contract to the second lowest bidder. If the owner refuses to permit the bid to be withdrawn, then the bidder can either sue to have the contract rescinded or lose its bid bond.

Whether the bid or the contract that arises from it can be rescinded due to a bidding mistake usually depends on the reason for the mistake. If the mistake was due to ambiguities in the bidding documents, then the bid will be allowed to be withdrawn. If the mistake was caused by a mechanical error, such as a mathematical or typographic error, or was so out of line with the other bids that the mistake should have been obvious to the owner, it is likely that the bidder will be given the right to rescind the bid. However, if the mistake was due to errors of judgment, was grossly negligent, or was made in bad faith, then it is less likely that the bidder will be allowed to withdraw the bid.

The winning bidder then executes the construction contract that is either attached to or described in the bid documents. If the bid documents required a bid bond to be submitted and it was not included with the bid, then it must be supplied with the execution of the contract. If, during the construction, any issues arise as to what is included within the contracted work, the parties will refer back to the bid documents to determine whether the requested work was originally included within the specifications.

CONSTRUCTION CONTRACTS

If construction work is required at the property at a significant cost, a construction contract must be executed by the owner and the contractor. No job costing more than $20,000 should be undertaken based on the contractor's invoice that is devoid of any terms, conditions, representations, or warranties. An owner contracting for a significant amount of work at the property must have the protection afforded by a carefully prepared construction contract.

Frequently, an owner will think that arranging for construction work at a property is similar to purchasing a finished product, which merely requires placing an order for the specific item. That is not the case! To be certain that the work will be properly completed for the anticipated cost and during the projected time frame, the owner and the contractor must execute a construction contract. If the parties did not execute such a contract, then many critical conditions of the relationship between the owner and the contractor would be left to chance. Considering the extraordinary amount of money involved in even minor property modifications and the almost infinite things that can go wrong during construction, not having a construction contract is a risk that no owner should consider taking.

The negotiation of the construction contract should involve participation by the owner, the contractor, and the architect or engineer. The architect or engineer should assist in the negotiation because this contract may include interpretations of the plans and specifications, which were prepared by the architect or engineer, who may also be required to supervise the construction, administer the construction contract, and interpret the contract provisions. The size and scope of the construction contract should bear a direct relationship to the size, cost, and complexity of the job being undertaken by the contractor. This section assumes a massive job requiring a thorough agreement; however, a detailed agreement may not be required in every instance. The owner, with the engineer's assistance, must determine on a job-by-job basis, whether a short form or long form agreement is required.

Instead of being a single document, the construction contract might include a series of documents that are cross-referenced to each other, including the agreement between the owner and the contractor, the general and supplemental conditions of the contract, the plans and specifications, and any modifications and change orders that are issued after the contract is executed. The plans and specifications are included in the contract to preclude the contractor from contending that certain work was not included in the contract.

Construction contracts differ based upon how the contractor is to be paid and whether the contractor is required to design and construct the improvement or facility or to construct it based upon a set of plans and specifications supplied by the owner or the architect. Typically, the construction contract refers to the drawings, the plans and specifications, and the modifications and revisions, which describe the improvements being constructed. Accordingly, the construction contract includes all the work required to be performed in completing the improvements, including all labor, material, and equipment necessary to complete the improvements being constructed by a particular contractor.

The construction contract should also require that the contractor supervise and direct the work described in the construction contract, and the contractor should be responsible for the acts and omissions of the contractor's employees and the subcontractors. Frequently, the contractor is required to maintain a superintendent or project manager on the construction site. To ensure that the work is properly completed, the contract might also require the posting of a performance bond. The construction contract should also indicate the dates when construction is to commence and when the improvements must be completed. The owner should retain the right to require the contractor to pay overtime to its employees to ensure that the work will be completed on time. Alternatively, the owner can assume responsibility for the completion of the work, in which event the contractor is responsible for all financial damages sustained by the owner.

The construction contract should also provide for the method and timing of payment for the construction, including the initial payment, the conditions for the progress payments, and the final payment. Thus, the owner can verify that the work is properly done and fully completed before payment is made. The construction contract should also provide for the manner in which the contractor will be compensated for change orders and modifications, thus avoiding the delay caused by separate negotiations for change orders or modifications. Additionally, the construction contract should provide for each party to have the ability to terminate the contract in the event of a breach or an anticipatory breach by the other party.

Basically, there are three kinds of construction contracts—the fixed-price or cost-plus contract, the fast-track contract, and the design–build contract. The fixed-price and cost-plus contract, the ones most often utilized, require the architect to prepare a set of plans and specifications upon which the contractor bids and is then awarded the contract. Fast-track contracts require the contractor to bid on incomplete plans and specifications. The architect prepares basic design documents for the structural components of the building and the utilities and, based upon the incomplete drawings, the contractor estimates the cost of construction. The owner and the contractor then enter into a cost-plus or fixed-price contract, or a combination of the two, relying on the integrity of the contractor and the architect's ability to properly supervise the job while maintaining quality and speed and minimizing the cost. However, in fast-track construction, cost is a secondary consideration because the benefit of quickly completing the improvement is far more important than the excess costs in utilizing this procedure. The rationale behind a fast-track contract is that by simultaneously designing and constructing the improvement, the construction time can be significantly reduced. Fast-track contracts are usually used only for very large projects being constructed by experienced owners. Excessive cost is the biggest disadvantage of fast-track construction, because the costs can exceed all projections when the contractor says that many aspects of the project are extras and were not included in the original bid.

The contractor in a design–build contract is obligated to both design and construct the improvement. The work is completed either through a joint venture of the architect and the contractor or through an architect who arranges for the designed improvement to be constructed. The relationship between the architect and the contractor eliminates the conflicts between the two, which speeds completion of the improvements. The biggest disadvantage of the design–build contract is the elimination of the competition between the architect and the contractor, which provides information for the owner regarding the project. Moreover, in the design–build contract, the architect is the contractor's partner, and is no longer the owner's agent in protecting the owner from the contractor's actions.

The payment provisions are one of the most important parts of the construction contract because the entire relationship between the owner and the contractor is based upon how the contractor is paid and whether the method of payment ensures the most cost-efficient completion of the project. The three methods of payment are:

1. *Fixed-price contract,* in which the contractor is paid a specific amount for completing the project, so that the contractor's profit is the difference between the actual cost of completion and the amount of the contract.

2. *Cost-plus contract,* in which the contractor is paid for the actual costs of construction plus an amount that is either fixed or a percentage of the amount that is spent toward the contractor's profit and overhead.

3. *Unit-price contract,* in which the contractor is paid a specific amount for each unit constructed.

The fixed-price contract is usually selected because it enables the owner to determine the price of the project in advance. The disadvantage of using the fixed-price contract is that the contractor's profit increases in direct proportion to the contractor's ability to minimize the costs of construction. This could lead to a badly constructed project. Although this problem can be overcome by strict on-site supervision of the construction, as well as frequent testing of the work that has been done, the additional supervision places an extra burden and cost on the owner and the lender. Nevertheless, the contractor may object to the fixed-price contract because there is a risk that, because of inflation or shortages, the cost of labor and material could increase significantly between when the job is bid and when the work has to be done.

During times of inflation and fluctuating costs, contractors prefer the cost-plus method of payment because it passes the risk of higher prices to the owner. The disadvantage of the cost-plus contract to the owner is that it is impossible to determine how much the project will cost to complete. There is no motivation for the contractor to reduce construction costs. In fact, if the contractor's profit is a percentage of the construction cost, the contractor has a reason to maximize the cost. When the cost-plus payment method is utilized, the owner should be certain that the contract contains a cap on the cost of the project. Alternatively, the owner might provide the contractor with an incentive for keeping the construction costs within certain specified limitations by agreeing in the contract to pay an additional fee, or to split with the contractor whatever savings are obtained. The contractor would then have an incentive to complete the project as inexpensively as possible.

The other issue regarding payment that the owner should consider is the manner in which payments are made. Usually, the contract requires a downpayment on execution of the contract equal to 10 to 20 percent of the amount of the contract, followed by progress payments during the construction, with a certain amount retained until after completion of the improvements. Progress payments protect both the owner and the contractor. The contractor would object to not being paid until completion of the project, because he or she would have to finance the total cost of the construction and, upon completion, may have to deal with an owner who was unwilling or unable to pay for the construction. Upon project completion, the contractor would have to negotiate with the owner regarding real or imagined deviations between the work and the specifications. Similarly, the owner would object to paying for the entire construction prior to commencement, because the owner would have no assurance that the work would be done properly or within the time periods specified by the contract. Progress payments provide the contractor with payments in stages based on predetermined criteria and incentives for making sure that the work is done properly. They also enable the owner to pay for work as it is completed.

To obtain payment, the contractor usually submits to the owner or engineer a request for payment, with documentation evidencing the right to receive payment. The documentation might include bills of sale for material acquired, evidence that the subcontractors and suppliers have been paid, and an indication of the amount of work left to be completed.

The architect or engineer then inspects the construction to confirm that the work has been properly completed and complies with the progress payment schedule and the plans and specifications. In addition to progress payments, the amount requested in payment for the completed work should be subject to retainage, which is a certain percentage (usually 10 to 20 percent) of the amount due to be paid on each progress payment that is retained by the owner until the final completion of all the work (see Example). Without retainage, there might not be a sufficient amount of money withheld to enable the owner to hire a replacement contractor to finish the job if the original contractor stops working or does not perform properly. If the contractor fails to finish the job, the retainage is used to pay for the final work.

Another problem occurs if the contractor fails to pay its subcontractors when it receives the progress payments, which is an issue of paramount importance to the owner. To protect itself from being required to pay the subcontractors, because the contractor has failed to do so with the payment it has received, the owner should insist that checks for progress payments be made payable to both the contractor and the subcontractors. One of the biggest problems in construction jobs is that the contractor does not pay the subcontractor, and the developer or the lender then has to pay to remove liens from the property.

Although the contract may provide that if the payments are not made on time, they will then bear interest either at the prime lending rate or at the current market rate of interest, the contractor's reaction to the

EXAMPLE

Assuming a retainage of 10%, the typical construction contract might require the following progress payments:

Item	Cost	Retainage	Payment
Replace roof	$76,189	$7,619	$68,570
Replace windows	41,678	4,168	37,510
Replace lintels	72,190	7,219	64,971
Rebuild parapet	23,150	2,315	20,835
Replace bricks	19,350	1,935	17,415
Repair terraces	18,980	1,898	17,082
Waterproofing	22,350	2,235	20,115
Scaffolding	9,850	985	8,865
Security services	5,750	575	5,175
Repair entryway	6,500	650	5,850

owner's refusal to pay can range from an attempt to negotiate a resolution of the problem to the termination of work on the project. The least difficult alternative with which to deal is if the contract precludes termination unless adequate advance notice is given to the owner. Alternatively, the contractor can also suspend providing services until the owner becomes more reasonable. The contractor could contend that the nonpayment of the progress payment is a material breach of the contract, thereby permitting the contractor to terminate the contract. Moreover, the contractor cannot accidentally waive the breach by continuing to work on the improvements. If the contractor is justified in terminating the contract, then he or she would be able to obtain damages for the breach of contract.

Upon completion of construction, the contractor requests final payment, and the architect or engineer has to determine whether all the work has been properly completed. Because the final payment by the owner could be considered a waiver by the owner of any claim against the contractor, except as to those issues that have previously been raised, the owner must be very careful in reviewing the project before authorizing the payment. If the owner refuses to make the final payment because the job has not been completely performed, the contractor may attempt to receive the contract price for substantially completing the work, with an offset for the reasonable cost of getting someone else to complete the work. The contractor's getting payment on substantial completion rather than complete adherence to the terms of the contract prevents the contractor from being adversely affected by minor defaults in performing the contract. Although such payment permits a contractor that has substantially completed a contract to be substantially compensated, the owner should carefully consider making such payment because it creates completion problems for the owner. It can be very difficult for the owner to locate another contractor who can expeditiously complete the project for the small amount of money that remains to be paid. Undoubtedly, the owner will have to pay a substantial premium to get the work done.

Finally, the construction contract provides the framework for the owner and the contractor to preserve their rights and to protect their interests if the other party fails to adequately adhere to the terms of the contract. It should also contain whatever warranties or guaranties are being provided by the contractor.

ANNUAL REVIEW OF LEASES

The property owner must have a clear understanding of all attributes of his or her property in order to be aware of changes that may affect the property's value and to take advantage of favorable situations that develop. One way of staying ahead of circumstances is to periodically review the leases on the property to be aware of, and concerned about, the rights and obligations of both the landlord and the tenant under each lease. A lease may contain something as obvious as rent increases at certain periods of time or adjustments to the rent level based upon fluctuations in the consumer price index, or the lease may provide the landlord with the right to pass along to the tenant various expenses that the landlord is forced to pay. Additionally, in operating the property, the landlord may have forgotten other benefits that were part of the original lease negotiation.

Another thing to consider in reviewing the lease is whether the tenant has unintentionally violated one or more of the lease provisions. This error may enable the landlord to terminate the lease and obtain a tenant willing to pay a higher rent, or may provide the owner with a framework to at least negotiate with the existing tenant for a higher rent or other concessions. These concessions may include additional rent or percentage rent, or the tenant's agreeing to pay for a larger portion of the common area maintenance costs or other property-related charges. A tenant's violation of the terms of the lease could provide the landlord reason to renegotiate some or all of the lease terms as a condition for waiving the default.

Another reason to periodically review the lease is to make certain that none of the tenants are violating the use provisions contained in their leases, which could expose the landlord to liability from other tenants whose exclusives are being violated or from local zoning or building code provisions. The landlord should also ascertain that the lease has been properly executed and that, if a mortgagee has the right to approve the terms of the lease or any changes in the lease documents, the mortgagee's approval has been properly obtained. The annual lease review should also include the landlord's confirming receipt of any sales reports required from the tenant under the lease. The tenant of a retail facility may have an obligation to pay additional rent to the landlord based upon sales at the property and, because the threshold for making such payments was not reached during the early years of the lease, either the landlord or the tenant has forgotten about or chosen to ignore the existence of these provisions.

Another significant portion of the lease to consider is the tenant's obligation to pay a pro rata share of increases in real estate taxes or other operating expenses. The annual lease review provides the owner with an opportunity to ascertain whether the tenant is paying the correct percentage of the current real estate tax or operating expense. Finally, the periodic lease review provides the landlord with the opportunity to be refamiliarized with the tenants and the terms and conditions of their leases and could result in the landlord's deciding to make valuable alterations to the property or the tenants.

REPLACING TENANTS

One of the most important considerations for the property owner is finding ways to maximize the cash flow from the property. Cash flow can be improved by either increasing income or reducing expenses. One method of increasing income is to add improvements; however, this may not be cost-effective and may not generate sufficient income due to limited additional space available, building law requirements, and needs of the existing tenants. Another way of increasing the income generated by the property would be to replace existing tenants with tenants willing to pay a higher rent due to the more profitable nature of their businesses or the fact that they are willing to pay a premium for location.

If space is available, that space can be leased to a new, more profitable tenant. However, the landlord should not be constrained by the absence of additional space. If the property is fully leased, the landlord may feel limited to current tenants for the balance of their lease terms. However, if the landlord has determined that the disparity between the amount of rent these tenants are paying and the current market rent for the property is so great as to provide the landlord with an opportunity for substantially increasing the income for the particular parcel, the landlord should seriously consider replacing the tenants. This can be done by either identifying lease defaults by a tenant or buying out an existing tenant's lease to make the space available to a replacement tenant.

The lease purchase price would be based upon the discounted amortized value of the higher rent the landlord believes he or she could receive for the space from another tenant. Conversely, if the existing tenant is having a difficult time operating economically in the space, the landlord can examine the lease and the tenant's operation carefully to determine if the tenant is abiding by all the terms and provisions of the lease and, if not, proceed to terminate the lease and evict the tenant. If this is not an available course, however, the landlord could consider the buy-out option. Meanwhile, negotiations with the replacement tenant should be occurring so that when the landlord pays the existing tenant to leave, the lease with the new tenant is ready. Otherwise, the landlord may be left with a vacancy. To maximize the profit, the landlord must orchestrate the change in tenants very carefully and make certain not to wind up with a net cash loss for the transaction.

PREINSURANCE INSPECTION

Until relatively recently, obtaining and retaining insurance at a reasonable cost was not a herculean task. However, in the last few years, increasing rewards against insurers have caused insurance companies to become much more cautious regarding accepted clients, the limits of the coverage, and the condition of the property. Insurance carriers now regularly inspect every property that they insure. If the properties do not measure up to the insurer's requirements or if the insurer believes that the owner's actions are exposing the owner to extraordinary liability, then the insurer adjusts the rates and eliminates the coverage or increases the deductible provisions. This section not only discusses the physical structure of the property, but identifies the conditions that could expose the carrier to great liability.

The owner should be prepared for periodic inspections by the insurance carrier, as well as by inspectors sent to properties by the lenders who hold the mortgages. Lenders, like insurers, have become very concerned about their potential liability exposure if they should be required to take title to the property in lieu of their mortgage. The owner should inspect the entire property, including those portions leased to third parties. The insurers' and lenders' concern is that the property owner will be held responsible and liable as the property owner even if someone is injured in a leased portion of the property and the lease provides indemnification of the owner. The owner must protect his or her interest by having a preinspection of the property to correct any problems prior to an insurer's or lender's inspection. Because these inspections are unannounced and can occur at any time, the owner must be constantly vigilant.

POSSIBLE CHANGES TO THE PROPERTY

Regardless of the rate of absorption of empty property into a glutted real estate market, there may come a time when the owner will determine that it will take too long for the real estate market to strengthen sufficiently to cure the property's problems. In those instances, the owner could consider changing the use of, or market for, the property as a means of increasing the likelihood of its success. It would only take time and capital to redevelop a shopping center into an office park, or an office building into a mixed-use apartment building with several floors of shopping, or a department store into a school, a warehouse, a factory, or even office space. Of course, this modification presumes that there is a use for the space that is not already glutted in other parts of the community.

Probably the easiest change is to retain the same basic use, but to change the marketing to attract a different economic group. Apartment buildings can be made more attractive by adding amenities and combining smaller apartments to form fewer, more valuable larger apartments. The addition of medical offices or boutiques on the first floor could also improve the property's marketability. Likewise, dividing apartments into smaller, less expensive units, may increase a property's marketability if there is a shortage of smaller apartments. However, no attempt should be made to change the use of the property until the owner has received (1) a current, detailed demographic study of the area to make certain that there is a market for the renovated facility and (2) detailed cost estimates as to the actual cost of reconfiguring the space. The owner must also consider the time it might take to obtain the required municipal approvals and to reconstruct the space, and the likelihood that during that period of time either the market for the current use will change or the market for the alternative use will become glutted. In either case, it would be better for the owner to leave the property in its current state, maintain it, and be prepared for the change in the market.

The owner could also consider changing the form of ownership of the property by converting the building, regardless of its use, into a cooperative or a condominium and selling the units (e.g., as stores, offices, apartments) rather than leasing the units or selling the entire project to a single purchaser. The sum of the parts could be worth significantly more than the current value of the whole. Although most cooperatives and condominiums are residential housing units or, to a small degree, office space, there is no reason why large and small office buildings, shopping centers, industrial parks, and commercial properties of all varieties could not be commonly owned by tenants.

To the tenant/purchaser, the economic benefit of purchasing rather than leasing could be phenomenal, especially if the monthly payments toward debt service on the acquisition loan and the owner's share of common expenses are not significantly greater than the rent would have been. This is especially true since the purchaser would also be building equity in the property instead of simply paying rent. Moreover, the purchaser would share directly in the ultimate success of the property, the refinancing proceeds, and the decisions regarding the property's operation and maintenance. With all the problems that the savings and loan associations, banks, and insurance companies are presently having with their real estate loans, common ownership may very well provide a significant portion of future financing or property development and ownership.

The owner might also consider the most frequently utilized method of increasing a property's popularity: leaving the property in its current condition, but providing incentives for purchasers or tenants. The incentives could include rent abatements, construction of additional amenities, reimbursement for tenant improvements, payment to a new tenant for breaking a preexisting lease, or providing a new tenant with the opportunity to share in the ultimate success of the property. The latter option would reward the tenant with a share of the proceeds that are ultimately received on the sale of the property.

It might seem rudimentary to lower the rent and increase the incentives or amenities to attract tenants or purchasers. However, an owner sometimes becomes so enamored of a property or project that he or she is unable to make objective business decisions regarding the property, including thinking of seemingly simple solutions. Under those circumstances, the problem can sometimes be resolved by bringing in a third party to examine the situation and make simple recommendations.

REFINANCING

Refinancing is the borrowing of funds from one lender and using all or a portion of those funds to pay off a lender who already holds a mortgage on the property. This can result in increasing the owner's cash flow and return on investment if the refinancing occurs at a time when the interest rates are lower than those of the existing mortgage or the existing loan has been amortized down to the point where the majority of each debt service payment is being used to pay principal on the loan rather than interest. Refinancing in such an environment will result in the owner's paying less debt service, thereby increasing cash flow. The debt service will be reduced because the interest will be accruing on a smaller principal balance.

The best way to determine whether it is an opportune time to refinance the mortgage depends on general economic conditions. The refinancing decision is based upon the amount that would have to be borrowed, the existing and proposed interest rates, the size of any prepayment premiums that have to be paid to the existing lenders, and the points, commitment fees, and closing costs that would have to be paid on the new loan. Generally, if the debt service on the new loan is more than 10 percent less than the original mortgage, and the various closing costs and related expenses can be capitalized into the purchase price, the owner should seriously consider refinancing.

Another time to consider refinancing is when the owner needs to obtain access to the equity in the property. The owner then has the option of taking a second mortgage, which would have a higher interest rate than the first mortgage because a second mortgage entails a higher degree of risk.

An alternative would be to refinance the entire first mortgage for a higher amount of money, and thereby obtain a portion of the owner's equity in the property and use the balance of the new loan to pay the original loan.

There is a time, however, when refinancing becomes essential for the owner. Regardless of the activity in the market for loans, the fluctuations in interest rates, and the cost of refinancing, the owner must begin considering refinancing a loan three years prior to the maturity of an existing loan. Although the process of refinancing should not take longer than three months, it is important to begin watching the rates and making assumptions three years prior to loan maturity. This provides the owner with ample time to react to lower rates when it appears that the rates will go up and facilitates the owner's waiting for rates to recede, if it appears that rates are unreasonably high. The last thing the owner would want is to be forced to refinance when interest rates are at a high or mortgage money is not available.

It should be apparent to any owner that, because debt service is probably the owner's largest single expense, refinancing into a significantly higher interest rate will cause the property's expenses to increase and the owner's cash flow to decrease. The difference between the debt service on a self-liquidating 25-year loan of $5 million at 9 percent and 13 percent interest is the difference between $503,517.82 and $676,701.18 per year. That is a difference of $173,183.36 per year, or 34 percent! An owner who ignores an interest rate fluctuation and loses $173,183.36 per year in cash flow is going to have a very difficult time surviving in a downturn.

3

Warning Signs
of Problems

THE ROLE OF THE PROPERTY MANAGER

Real estate has been considered an excellent investment since the Middle Ages, when the concept of an individual's right to own property first evolved. Unfortunately, although fortunes have been made by acquiring or disposing of real estate at the correct time, real estate ownership is so labor intensive that it is not always a good passive investment. Fortunes have been lost by relying on the wrong person to manage or operate a property. If a property is subject to a triple net lease (i.e., the tenant pays rent and all operating expenses) to a creditworthy tenant, there should be a limited amount of risk to the owners. However, creditworthiness recently has become a questionable concept due to the onslaught of corporate acquisitions, overleveraging of subsidiaries, and junk bond–induced takeovers of successful operations, which have caused successful tenants and the landlords who lease to them to quickly become insolvent. Moreover, a profitable property can easily fall victim to the economy, a casualty, deferred maintenance, or competition, and can lose its tenants and the owner's profit almost overnight. Therefore, even if the owner owns one of the most attractive properties in an area and it is fully leased to a Fortune 500 company, the successful owner must maintain a vigilant watch over the property at all times.

Vigilance is easy when an investor is the sole owner of a single property and it is located near his or her home. However, this is rarely the case.

Although an investor's first property will usually be close to his or her home, with each subsequent investment, the distance expands between the owner and the properties being acquired. Moreover, as the number of properties grows arithmetically, the amount of supervision required to protect the investment in each property increases geometrically. Even if all the owner's interests will be in the same vicinity, one person can deal successfully with only a finite number of problems. Furthermore, most neophyte investors and many investors with multiple interests invest in someone else's properties through an entity such as a limited or general partnership, trust, corporation, or joint venture rather than operate or control the property alone. This leads to the need to have a property manager.

The property manager could be an independent managing agent, or a general partner of a partnership, or the trustees or officers of a trust or corporation in which the owner has invested. In any of these situations, the owner relies on the integrity and capability of a property manager, who could be his salvation or his nemesis.

Regardless of whether an investor is the owner of a property being managed by a professional manager or a partner in a partnership that owns property being managed by a general partner or an owner of multiple properties who must rely on the expertise and professionalism of a staff, the investor is at risk if the property manager is overextended, incompetent, dishonest, or negligent. The right manager can ensure the success of a property and transform a lackluster property into a jewel, whereas the wrong manager can ruin a property much faster than it took to build its reputation. This chapter describes the warning signs that problems are developing, examines the property manager's role, and reviews how the property owner can properly supervise the manager's performance and act immediately to protect the investment in the property if that performance turns out to be less than expected.

Depending on the circumstances, the property manager is required to perform some or all of the following functions:

- Accurately calculate, bill, and collect the rent
- Arrange for the property to be kept fully leased, properly maintained, and repaired
- Keep the property fully insured against all risks
- Keep the property properly staffed
- Maintain compliance with all leases, mortgages, and other agreements affecting the property.

This role is all the more difficult because the manager must also perform these tasks in as efficient and cost-competitive manner as possible, while making certain that he or she is properly compensated for performing this herculean task.

Because the success or failure of the investment depends on the manager, it is critical that the owner has a way of determining whether the job is being done properly. This means that the owner must be able to interpret the warning signs that the job is not being properly handled, prior to the property's failure. However, although the owner may recognize one or more of the warning signs, there is no certainty that the investment will fail or that the property is being mismanaged. A warning sign merely provides the owner with an indication that closer attention should be paid to the property to determine whether a serious problem does exist. Notwithstanding the existence of a warning sign, it is possible that the property is being properly managed and changing managers could have a catastrophic effect on the property's long-term viability. Suffice it to say that a warning sign is like a blinking yellow light; it indicates caution and a need to slow down, but it does not necessarily require a full stop.

FINANCIAL REPORTS

The most obvious place for the owner to examine whether the property is properly managed is the financial reports that the owner should receive regularly from the manager. Moreover, the cautious owner should follow up the examination of the periodic financial reports by having the owner's own accountant review the property's books and records. The review could provide a great deal of insight into the manner in which the manager does business and the potential for large, catastrophic problems in the future.

The owner should be concerned if the financial statements do not arrive or are not sent on a timely basis. How frequently they should arrive and how much detail they should contain will differ based on the size of the property and the owner's investment, and whether the property's operation is passive (i.e., net leased to a single tenant) or requires a great deal of on-sight management and constant supervision and decision making. The more involved the operation, the more detailed and frequent the reports should be.

The kind of financial reports that can be distributed to the owner range from simple income and expense statements and balance sheets, to copies of the checkbooks and check registers, to elaborate reports describing the income and expenses and comparing them on a monthly, weekly, or daily basis to the budget of the prior year or another period of time. In reviewing these reports, the owner should be concerned with such matters as:

- The inability of the manager to reconcile the bank statements with the checkbooks or the manager's need to force the reconciliation in order to balance the accounts
- The commingling of accounts of all the properties or partnerships managed by the manager instead of separate accounts for each property or investment entity, demonstrating the possibility that one property's funds are being used for another property
- The manager's inability to account for income that the owner knows should have been generated by the property
- Income from the property that is seriously below the level of income that should have been produced by the property
- The receipt of dunning notices from suppliers of goods and services to the property
- Requests by vendors for deposits prior to supplying goods or services and the requirement by vendors of payments in cash on delivery of supplies or services, demonstrating a problem with the creditworthiness of the property or the manager
- A sudden and unexplained increase in the property's expenditures, which can indicate serious problems with the property or the manager
- The need for the manager to pay interest or late payment penalties due to the manager's delay in paying the property's bills
- The inclusion in the statements of inaccurate information or mistakes in mathematical calculations, indicating that the numbers on the statement may have been backed into rather than that they reflect what was actually on the property's books and records
- Payment of the property's expenses in cash, which makes it more difficult to supervise and reconcile the payments
- The payment of bills that have inadequate supporting documentation as to what goods, labor, or services were covered
- A significantly higher price for goods, labor, or services than what the owner believes comparable expenditures would cost, which could indicate the manager's taking kickbacks or not doing competitive bidding, or at least not obtaining competitive prices

- Expenses that are significantly higher (i.e., more than the consumer price index plus 10 percent) than those of the previous year or than what was budgeted

- The payment of bills for goods or services rendered quite some time ago with no intervening bills, which may indicate that the bill is over-stated and the supplier is counting on the manager's not remembering the exact amount of work that was done

- A significant number of insurance claims or a high deductible, which may indicate that the insurance underwriters are uncomfortable with the risk of insuring the property.

These examples of warning signs should alert the owner to the possibility that the property has, or is about to have, significant and damaging problems. However, the warning sign could also be an aberration or something totally irrelevant to the property's success. Accordingly, the existence of a warning sign is not indicative of a problem, but, as the name implies, it is an indication that the owner needs to further review the situation.

MORTGAGE MATURITY

An additional financial concern for the owner must be the interest rate and maturity of any mortgage on the property. The owner should begin seeking refinancing at least six months prior to the mortgage's maturity date to have sufficient time to identify the lenders who are still in the market (for both the kind of security that the property represents and the size of loan required by the owner) and take the actions necessary to close the loan. It is a mistake to leave the refinancing to just before the date when the existing loan matures. The owner should keep constantly aware of the mortgage market and make certain that the manager is also aware of market conditions to take advantage of any reductions in interest rates and avoid being forced to refinance at a time when interest rates are high.

Accordingly, warning signs of the need to refinance are changes in interest rates offered by institutional lenders, as well as the maturity of the mortgage on the owner's property at least three years prior to the actual maturity date of the mortgage. By watching for these signs, the owner can avoid the trap of being forced to refinance on the maturity of the mortgage when interest rates are high. In this same regard, if interest rates fall significantly during the term of the loan, the manager should advise the owner that it may be time to refinance the mortgage on the property. Refinancing may be in order even if the mortgage does not mature for a number of years, if interest rates are lower and the costs of refinancing (i.e., the pre-payment penalty on the existing mortgage, commitment fees on the new mortgage, and the other costs of closing the new loan) are not so excessive as to eliminate the benefit of the lower interest rates.

The reason that the mortgage is considered an important warning sign regarding the manager's performance is that the mortgage debt service is usually the property's largest operating expense, and a fluctu-ation in the interest rate could eliminate the owner's entire cash flow or cause a profitable property to have a negative cash flow. The manager should, therefore, maintain a watchful eye on the property's mortgage and the mortgage market in general to benefit from positive fluctuations in the rates and avoid the disastrous results of not acting at the right time. If a manager fails to take advantage of lower interest rates without a reason, the owner should examine many of the manager's actions.

COMPLAINTS ABOUT THE MANAGER

The most obvious time that the owner should be concerned about the manager's actions and potential effect on the property is if the owner re-ceives complaints from third parties regarding the manager. It is unlikely that anyone would complain about the manager to the owner unless the situation was intolerable, particularly since the complainant would proba-bly have to go to some trouble to determine who owned the property. The owner could simplify this process by identifying himself or herself to the mortgagee and the most important tenants and suppliers and requesting copies of some or all correspondence relating to the property.

Although this procedure is appropriate if the owner is the sole owner of a property being managed by a professional manager, it is dangerous and inappropriate for one limited partner of a limited partnership to take actions with regard to the property. The reason is that the language in the partnership agreement provides the general partner with all the power to act with regard to the property. The limited partner's actions could result in the loss of his or her limited liability and becoming a de facto general partner, if the limited partner becomes involved in the management of the property or the partnership. The problem is further compounded by the fact that a limited partner could become the subject of a lawsuit by the other limited partners or the general partner for interfering in the operation of the property, if it turns out that the limited partner's involvement adversely affected the property or the partnership. The limited partner could also be sued by the general partner if the limited partner's actions were such that they defamed the general partner, even if it was unintentional. Accordingly, a limited partner should be very careful in acting with regard to a partnership investment and should first seek the required information from the general partner and then follow the prescripts identified in the partnership agreement for dealing with a general partner's intransigence.

The complaints about the manager can vary from the insignificant to the catastrophic. Although a complaint may seem insignificant to the owner, it could indicate either a far more serious problem with the manager or the property or, perhaps, a difficult tenant. Nevertheless, any complaint that finds its way to the owner should be thoroughly examined to avoid far more serious consequences.

The complaints regarding the manager could range from the manager's unresponsiveness in taking care of problems raised by the mortgagee, tenants, neighboring property owners, or local government officials to complaints by vendors that bills are not being paid on time or at all. However, because an owner receives a complaint about the manager does not necessarily mean that the manager is inadequate or at fault. If the manager is acting in the owner's best interest, at times, third parties will complain about the manager's actions. A tenant may complain if the manager refuses to spend money that the manager believes to be unnecessary or not within the landlord's obligations under the lease. The manager will also refuse to pay bills on occasion, if he or she believes the work was not properly done or the vendor has not acted in good faith. The manager also has the right to challenge municipal violations, if the manager believes that the regulation is inappropriate or the inspector overlooked a particularly relevant fact. It therefore behooves the owner to investigate the facts surrounding the complaint and not simply assume that the manager has acted improperly.

Conversely, if the tenant has complained continuously about the manager's failure to comply with provisions in the lease, and a review of the facts indicates that the tenant is not mistaken in the complaint, then the owner should be concerned about the manager's actions. If the tenant has made a request and the manager believes it is inappropriate, then the manager should respond to the tenant in writing with an explanation. Such a letter may appear to be self-serving, but it will indicate the manager's rationale at a later date if the tenant attempts to claim that the landlord defaulted in fulfilling the lease terms. Nevertheless, the warning sign is the existence of tenant or other third-party complaints that the manager has failed to address, either by complying with the request or responding to the inquiry in writing.

Other warning signs of potential problems with the manager are complaints from the professionals retained by either the owner or the manager to service the property's needs. Such professionals might include the attorney, accountant, engineers, contractors, or on-sight managers. These complaints require a careful analysis because professionals do not usually complain about other professionals or the people who retain them, unless the situation has gotten out of hand.

The biggest warning signs are problems with the property's finances about which the manager has not warned the owner. These include expenditures that are higher than past years' expenses or the current year's budget, if there are no facts that would explain a sudden increase in costs or a sudden decrease in income. Such a change could be explained by a sudden increase in energy costs, a recession, a war, or the need to replace a major piece of equipment at the property. However, as discussed later, there are financial warning signs for large expenses to maintain the property. Prior to the furnace's needing replacement, the energy costs will escalate, just as prior to replacing the roof, the cost of repairing leaks will increase dramatically.

Another indication that the manager may not be performing his or her job is if the building begins to fail inspections or if the insurance rates suddenly escalate or if any of the concerns raised in the earlier section on financial reports begin to occur. In each instance, a closer examination of the manager's actions must be undertaken as quickly as possible.

The other thing the owner should consider is seeking information about the manager. If the manager responds to every tenant's complaint by resolving the problem regardless of the cost, the actual necessity of doing the work, or an obligation to do the work, then the owner has a problem even though no one would be complaining about the manager. In such circumstances, the owner might not even realize that the cash flow from the property could be higher if the manager were more careful with spending the owner's money. This kind of problem can be determined only by a careful review by the owner of the manager. In a strange way, the warning sign would be the absence of complaints about the manager. However, as indicated earlier, a warning sign is usually the equivalent to a blinking yellow light—a method of advising caution, but certainly not an absolute method of predicting an imminent collapse.

PHYSICAL CONDITIONS

The warning signs of physical problems with the property become more obvious as the property deteriorates and the defects become more expensive to repair. Every owner understands that this kind of problem will happen to every property, and, although the warning sign indicates that it is time to attend to the problem, neither the owner nor the manager should wait until the warning sign appears to prepare for this eventuality. The manager and the owner should prepare a capital budget for every major component of the property, containing an indication as to the remaining useful life of that component, the cost of replacing it, and the most cost-efficient manner of replacement. The manager's failure to prepare for this eventuality is one of the most obvious signs that the manager is not doing the job adequately. One benefit of preparing a capital budget and doing long-term planning is that it is the most cost-efficient manner of handling the problem. It is a matter that should not be neglected by the owner or the manager.

Although it is less costly to patch leaks in the roof than to replace the roof, a time will come when the roof is so aged that fixing the roof is no longer a viable option and replacement becomes essential. This occurs when the repairs become so costly and the occupants so annoyed at the constant leaks that the roof must be replaced to properly maintain the property. The warning sign, the repetitive leaks, should cause the owner to consider the preparation of a capital budget with the object of replacing the roof by a certain point in time. In fact, anytime there are similar, repetitive problems with the property, the owner must consider a major investment in the property as a likely result, and the manager should include the replacement as part of the alternative solutions to the problem.

Nevertheless, higher repair bills alone are not indicative of a structure that is in immediate need of a complete replacement. The need for repairs could also be a sign of the manager's caution, a difficult tenant, or dishonesty by the manager or a contractor or employee. Sometimes the manager will be overly cautious and want to replace the roof as soon as a leak occurs or repave the parking lot at the first sign of cracks. However, making such major capital improvements at the first sign of trouble can eventually bankrupt the owner. There is a difference between preventive maintenance and prematurely rebuilding the property. Accordingly, the owner has to consider a warning sign to be sudden excessive amounts spent on maintenance, repairs, alterations, or improvements. Like most of the other warning signs, the need for repairs is not tantamount to the existence of a major problem, but it should require the owner to consider the possibility that something is amiss, and to investigate further.

Conversely, the absence of repair costs may be a warning sign that the property manager is not paying close enough attention to the property and its condition. In the first few years of ownership of a newly constructed property, the costs of repairs and maintenance should be fairly low, but as the property ages, the repair costs should escalate. This is truer with residential property than with commercial property; however, it is a fact with which the owner must deal. If the manager is skipping necessary or desirable repairs to increase the apparent profitability of the property, the manager is placing the owner's investment in the property at risk for a short-term benefit of a higher return on investment.

A history of small problems is an obvious example of a warning sign of a potentially serious physical problem. It is the less obvious signs that the owner must consider. For example, if the costs of heating the property are significantly (i.e., more than 10 percent) higher than the prior year, the cause could be one or more of the following factors:

1. Higher energy costs for the same amount of heat

2. A colder winter this year or a warmer winter last year

3. A problem with the heating system that is causing higher consumption

4. The manager's charging your project a higher cost per gallon for oil, to offset the lower cost per gallon for the projects that the manager owns rather than manages

5. The oil company's delivering oil to another project and adding the cost to the bill for your project

6. A combination of these factors.

The way to determine which reasons are causing the higher heating costs is through investigation. If this winter is significantly different from the prior year, or if local, national, or international events are causing oil shortages that result in higher prices, the reason for higher costs is easy to find. It is also easy to prove problems with the heating system, which is potentially the most expensive to resolve because it requires a capital investment. This problem may be detected or resolved through an examination of the equipment by a heating engineer. Nevertheless, if the owner intends to retain a heating engineer or any other professional to do an inspection, the owner must make certain that the professional is not affiliated with any company that sells a product relating to that specialty or the owner will most likely be paying for a new system, even if the property does not yet require it. The fourth and fifth reasons for the higher costs can be determined by keeping better controls on the actual amount of fuel being used and the cost per gallon charged by other oil companies in the area. The heating engineer also can advise the owner on the approximate number of gallons the building's systems should be utilizing during a typical season.

Another sign of potential trouble is when the property fails its building inspections or is not regularly inspected by the local municipal officials. The concern here is that the property is not being properly maintained by the manager or that the manager, to hide the condition of the property, is circumventing the usual inspection procedure. This could result in higher repair costs at a later date plus fines and penalties. Worse, the manager's failure to properly maintain the property could cause the insurance to be canceled or the insurance carrier to disclaim liability for a casualty to the property or the injury or death of someone utilizing the property, thereby exposing the owner to a huge potential liability.

Building code violations also could indicate far more serious problems for the property that have to be dealt with by the owner. These may include problems with the heating, ventilation, and air conditioning (commonly known as the HVAC) system; plumbing; electrical; structural components (roof, exterior walls, and foundation); or other aspects of the building. Each of these portions of the property, as well as the interior of the property, can have a problem that results in a violation being placed against the property based on the municipality's building code, fire code, sanitation code, and health code. Such a violation merely indicates that the building does not comply with local requirements and must be corrected as quickly as possible or the owner will be at risk for more severe penalties.

The warning signs of physical problems can be the most expensive to resolve because, unlike the other warning signs, they usually indicate work that has to be done rather than incompetence or dishonesty by the manager. Physical problems must be resolved to prevent the property from deteriorating and cannot be resolved by changing the manager, unless there actually were no physical problems or the replacement manager is capable of correcting the physical problems. Certainly, physical problems should never be ignored because they only get worse.

VACANCIES

One of the most obvious signs of a problem at a property is sudden vacancies in space that had previously been rented or used. However, there could be other reasons for the vacancies that should not be discounted. If the property was not leased or is property that would not ordinarily be leased in the first place, then vacancies would not make a difference. Moreover, if the owner or manager has made a business judgment to upgrade the property or improve the tenancies, then vacancies should not cause concern for the owner. Vacancies become an issue only if they are unintended and relatively sudden. When the owner learns that the property has become unexpectedly vacant, it is time to examine the situation further.

The owner may find that the vacancies are a natural condition, which occurs regularly and is affected by certain events over which neither the owner nor the manager has control. For example, property located near a college will undoubtedly have vacancies during the summer; one would expect this and make plans for either an alternative use of the property during that time or for maintenance and repairs. Nevertheless, concern must be raised if the vacancies are sudden and unexpected.

The problem with vacancies is that the property's income is reduced while the expenses that relate directly to the number of tenants or occupants at the property may or may not be reduced and the fixed expenses are unaffected. The owner then must identify other sources of income or capital to meet the property's operating expenses. Therefore, if a vacancy is an intentional action by the manager to upgrade the income from the property, the owner should make certain that the manager has made arrangements for paying the operating expenses until the property is fully leased. If the manager has planned vacancies without arranging for funding the shortfall, the owner should be concerned about the manager's ability or integrity. The reason for being concerned about the manager's integrity occurs if the manager's actions are motivated by the desire to generate leasing commissions rather than concern about the needs of the owner or the property.

SUBLEASES AND ASSIGNMENTS

Another telling sign of problems is a sudden desire by tenants or occupants to vacate their space. This problem becomes apparent when the owner is advised that more than one tenant is suddenly interested in either subletting their space or assigning their lease to a third party. Of course, this could also indicate that the property is increasing in value and the tenants want to benefit from this increase by conveying their leasehold interest in the property to someone willing to pay the tenant for the privilege of obtaining the space. However, the purpose of the warning signs is to provide the absentee owner with notice of potential problems so the owner can take the appropriate steps to rectify or prepare for the situation. As indicated earlier, warning signs are not necessarily crystal balls foretelling doom.

A sublease occurs when a tenant gives another the right to use all or a portion of a leased space for all or a portion of the lease term, while the tenant retains its interest under the lease. Regardless of the sublease term, the relationship is a sublease if the tenant reacquires the space prior to the expiration of the lease term. In an assignment, the tenant conveys its entire right, title, and interest in the lease to another person or entity and retains no interest in the lease or the space. In neither a sublease nor an assignment is the tenant's liability under the lease eliminated unless the lease so provides or the landlord agrees to release the tenant and look primarily to the assignee or the subtenant as the tenant.

The problem for the property owner from a change in tenancies through a sublease or assignment is threefold. Such an action indicates a certain instability in the property, denies the landlord the opportunity of choosing the tenants for the property, and could introduce the wrong tenants into the property and upset the delicate balance of the property's mix. The landlord's concern is that a subtenant that caters to a clientele different from the other tenants' customers, could adversely affect the reputation of the property or the business of the other tenants. This could be particularly important to the landlord if the landlord shares in the prosperity of the property through percentage rentals or other revenue-sharing arrangements. Furthermore, if the subtenant's business requires excessive use of the building's utilities, common areas, or parking facilities, the wrong subtenant or assignee could unreasonably tax the property's amenities without increasing the landlord's return on the investment. The subtenant's or assignee's business may also require the landlord to make far more frequent and expensive repairs to the property to maintain the value of the asset. The difference between the tenant's and the landlord's needs and desires is that the landlord is concerned about the long-term viability and profitability of the property, whereas the tenant entering into a sublease or an assignment is concerned only about the short-term effect of transferring the risk of the lease to someone else or obtaining an immediate profit on the transfer of the lease.

Although the subletting or assignment of the space could also have the opposite effect and enhance the property's reputation, the owner cannot ignore the potential problems. Ignoring the situation could deny the owner the ability to resolve the problems at the early stage. A sublease or assignment also could have a beneficial effect if the tenant's reputation or financial strength is not as strong as it was when the lease was originally executed. The appearance of a new, stronger, better operated subtenant or assignee could breathe new life into the property and increase the revenue generated by the property by making it more attractive for other tenants and customers.

MUNICIPAL VIOLATIONS

The proper maintenance of the property is extremely important to long-term success and profitability, although it may reduce the short-term cash flow from the property. If the manager is deferring repairs or maintenance to bolster the cash flow from the property, it could cause huge long-term expenditures for the owner and lead to a genuine and permanent decline in the property.

Only through preventive maintenance and taking care of the property's physical problems as they arise can the owner be certain of the property's long-term viability. A small leak, left unrepaired, could cause severe internal damage to a property or could indicate larger problems beneath the surface of the property. A physical problem, once apparent, does not disappear; it only grows worse.

Although a tenant may complain about a problem that may come to the attention of the owner or the owner may retain an engineer to identify areas of potential concern, it is more likely that the local municipality will periodically inspect the property and, if there are any dangerous conditions, will place a violation against the property. Although the fine associated with the violation is usually small, the existence of the violation is particularly telling. Not only does it indicate that the manager may not have been properly maintaining the property, but the violation is usually something apparent to the municipal inspector on a visual inspection. It could also be a harbinger of far more serious problems beneath the surface.

The most difficult thing for the owner to understand is why the manager did not identify the problem prior to the violation's being posted against the property. Naturally, although one violation is troubling, multiple violations indicate a far more serious deficiency on the part of the manager. Even if the property is subject to a net lease to one or more tenants, the manager should periodically visit the property and point out deficiencies to the tenant. The existence of a long-term, triple net lease does not relieve the property owner from responsibility for the property if someone is killed or injured, and the owner must be concerned about the long-term value of the property in anticipation of the day when the owner will regain possession of the property from the tenant. Even if the lease has a 75-year term, the owner may obtain possession sooner than expected if the tenant defaults. Moreover, if someone is killed or injured and the tenant is uninsured, underinsured, or insolvent, the owner may be held liable for the incident. Accordingly, the owner must be concerned about the condition of the property regardless of who has possession and for how long.

If the manager is able to disguise the property's condition from the owner, how can the owner learn about the existence of the violation?

The owner may learn of the problem by seeing the payment of the fine on the property's cash flow statements, or the owner could periodically order a municipal violation search through one of the servicing firms that handle such problems.

Nevertheless, the existence of the violation alone is not reason enough for the owner to change managers or to assume that the property is not being properly managed. Violations vary and have different consequences. A violation due to the basement's being painted the wrong color or having the wrong wattage lightbulb is important, but far less serious than one due to the building's structural integrity. Also, tenants in apartment buildings tend to complain to the municipality of inadequate conditions or services as a method of fighting for increased services or lower rent increases, or to alleviate their own frustrations with everyday life. Additionally, the number of violations is not necessarily damning, if the violations are minor and are being corrected by the manager. Frequently, the reason for multiple violations is that, once municipal inspectors enter a building, they do not look for only a single violation, but for whatever violations they can find. Moreover, each time they return to the building to inspect the work that was done before removing a violation, they tend to look around to identify additional violations. Nonetheless, violations are a warning sign to the owner to pay greater attention to the situation at the property and avoid a far more serious problem.

CONCLUSION

There are both positive and negative aspects to having property managed by a third party. The positive is that the owner obtains the benefit of utilizing an expert, a professional who can devote the necessary amount of attention to the property, enabling the owner to do more productive work. The negative is that the manager may not have the same incentive that the owner has to maximize the owner's return on an investment. Maximizing the return does not necessarily mean getting the most money as quickly as possible; it means obtaining the highest return possible for the longest period, which in the long run will provide the owner with a far greater return. This also means that the manager must devote the same attention to each property he or she manages as the manager would devote to a property he or she owns.

It is imperative for the passive owner to be able to identify the warning signs and act expeditiously to eliminate the problem at the first sign of trouble. The alternative to fast action could be the loss of the entire investment.

4

Commercial Property

Regardless of whether the real estate investor is considering acquiring a distressed property or attempting to resuscitate an existing property that he or she already owns or is troubleshooting to avoid potential problems, the cautious investor must be able to analyze the assets and liabilities of a particular property. This analysis should be done more frequently than immediately prior to acquiring the property. To be certain that the investment is being protected, the owner should periodically review the property, including the physical components of the property, as well as the business relationships which the owner has inherited with the property or into which he or she enters.

Accordingly, no agreement should be executed unless and until the owner fully understands its terms and the manner in which it will inter-relate with the other agreements pursuant to which the property is subject. The wrong agreement or the wrong provision in an otherwise ideal agreement, can create a nightmare for the owner and ruin the safest investment. Nevertheless, the owner should remember that the attitudes of the parties to the agreement are as important as the terms of the agreement. That is not to say that the owner should be careless about negotiating the terms of the agreement, but that regardless of how well drawn the agreement is, if the parties fail to act in good faith, the terms of the agreement are irrelevant.

This chapter examines the various agreements the commercial property owner will probably execute and discusses the salient and problematic provisions that may be contained in each kind of agreement. Only with an understanding of an agreement and the effect of different provisions contained within the agreement can the owner be protected from making a mistake. This knowledge will also facilitate the owner's working with professionals in negotiating an agreement that makes business, legal, and economic sense. The bulk of this chapter discusses leases, because that is the agreement that will have the largest effect on a commercial property's success or failure.

GROUND LEASES

The ownership of real property consists of many rights and obligations, which are neither mutually inclusive nor mutually exclusive. To say one owns real estate, one could mean many things. The owner could own the land and/or the buildings and improvements constructed on the land and/ or the right to develop buildings and improvements on the land and/or an easement across the land and/or the air rights above the land. It is not usual for the owner of the buildings and improvements not to own the land upon which the buildings and improvements are constructed, but merely have a leasehold interest in the land. That means that the owner of the leasehold interest in the land has either leased the land directly from the land owner pursuant to a land lease or ground lease, or received an assignment of the land lease or ground lease from the tenant. For example, for decades, the land under Rockefeller Center in Manhattan was owned by Columbia University and leased to the Rockefeller family. There are both advantages and disadvantages to being a tenant under the ground lease. The biggest disadvantage is that at the end of the lease term, the tenant loses its entire interest in the property, unless it buys the land from the land owner or is able to convince the land owner to extend the term of the ground lease.

The basis of the relationship between the land owner and the tenant is the ground lease, which must be carefully examined to establish the rights, remedies, and obligations of the landlord and the tenant. Unlike a situation in which the real estate is owned rather than leased by the occupant, the alternative courses of action relating to the land owner's and the tenant's uses of the property are limited by the terms of the ground lease. Although the tenant has the exclusive use of the property for an extended period of time, no action can be taken by the tenant relating to the property that is contrary to the terms of the ground lease. In a ground lease situation, the improvements are owned or will be constructed by the tenant; however, even if the improvements are constructed by the tenant, they revert to the land owner either upon the completion of their construction or the termination of the lease, unless the tenant removes them from the property.

A ground lease permits the tenant to acquire possession of (but not legal title to) the property for an extended period of time without being required to pay a downpayment, closing costs, transfer taxes, financing costs, debt service, or other expenses associated with the actual acquisition of legal title. The tenant's only obligation is to make monthly rental payments to the land owner and to construct improvements on the land if desired. Similarly, the ground lease enables the owner of the land to have someone develop the property without being required to pay the construction costs, financing costs, or debt service, or deal with the aggravation of development or redevelopment of the property. The land owner is able to structure the rental payments to provide itself with an interest in the success of the property and, if the tenant fails to make a payment at anytime during the lease, the land owner can reacquire the property regardless of the amount of money the tenant has spent on the property and the amount of time remaining on the lease term.

An additional advantage of the ground lease is that it avoids the complications and negative tax ramifications involved in selling the property. A ground lease is also an effective method of limiting estate tax problems because the long-term ground lease establishes the valuation of the property based upon the income rather than a hypothetical sale price, and the ground lease avoids transfer taxes and other expenses that are incidental to a sale. Nevertheless, the ground lease also provides the land owner with disadvantages, including the fact that the land owner's equity in the land remains tied to the future success of the real estate, unless the land owner is able to finance its position. To a large extent, however, the land owner's ability to obtain financing is limited by the economics of the lending marketplace at the time when the land owner attempts to finance or refinance the property. Moreover, the amount of financing available is based upon the land owner's income from the property rather than the fair market value of the land unencumbered by the ground lease. Additionally, unless there are increases built into the lease, the ground rent is determined at the beginning of the lease, thereby locking the land owner into a rent that, in future years, could be significantly below the market rent for similar properties. (See Example.)

A ground lease also has advantages and disadvantages for the tenant. One primary benefit of the ground lease to the tenant is that it enables the tenant to virtually own the property during the lease term without being required to pay the purchase price. The ground lease also preserves the tenant's capital and credit for use in developing rather than purchasing the property. Additionally, the tenant's leasehold interest in the property can be mortgaged or sold, and the tenant's rental payments are fully deductible for tax purposes. Moreover, a ground lease may be

EXAMPLE

The incentives for the land owner and the developer to enter into a
ground lease rather than to purchase the land can be observed from
the following chart, which demonstrates that leasing the land can be
financially more favorable for both the landlord and the tenant.

	Ground Lease Tenant	Land Purchaser
Purchase Price	$ 0	$1,000,000
Cost of improvements	5,000,000	5,000,000
Annual interest on loan to purchase land or lost opportunity	0	100,000
Annual depreciation	158,730	158,730
Ground rent	100,000	0

	Ground Lease Landlord	Land Seller
Gross sales price	$ 0	$1,000,000
Income tax on sale	0	300,000
Net sales price	0	700,000
Ground rent	100,000	0
Return on cash (10%)	0	70,000
Value of land on expiration of lease	6,000,000	0

an expeditious resolution to a zoning or other land use problem. Zoning
restrictions may preclude subdividing the land into separate parcels,
whereas a ground lease and subsequent subleases may enable the property to be effectively divided without local approval. The disadvantage
of the ground lease to the tenant is that the tenant's interest in the
property is an asset, whose value is reduced as the lease term draws to a
close. Furthermore, the tenant is unable to benefit from the long-term
appreciation it has created in the property because its ability to sell or
refinance the property is based upon the remaining term of the ground
lease rather than the fair market value of the improved real estate.

A ground lease is usually a triple net lease (in which the tenant pays
all operating expenses) containing an extended term of 50 to 99 years.
In a ground lease, the tenant retains a great deal of discretion in developing the land to maximize the return on its rent and its investment in

the property. Because most ground leases contain a broad use clause and an extended term, the tenant is in effect the equitable owner of the property during the lease term and has the ability to finance the development of the property through leasehold mortgage financing. Usually, the tenant, after developing the property, subleases it to one or more operating subtenants.

An inverse relationship exists between the remaining term of the ground lease and the economic value of the leasehold interest. The value of the tenant's interest in the ground lease does not decrease by a fixed amount each year; it decreases insignificantly during the initial years, is reduced dramatically by the middle of the lease term, and becomes minimal long before the termination of the lease. This accelerated reduction in value is because during the last 20 years of the lease, the tenant will probably be unable to sell or refinance the property without a large discount in the price because the purchaser will have a relatively brief period of time to recapture the investment.

The tenant's inability to finance the leasehold interest in the property is directly attributable to the reduced value of the lease as the term progresses. The remaining term of the ground lease is probably one of the single most important elements of the lease, which is due, in part, to the tenant's need to recoup expenses from constructing the improvements or otherwise preparing or purchasing the property from the rents or profits generated by the property. For this reason, if the ground lease does not have an extended original term (i.e., at least 35 years), the tenant will, at least, have the option to extend the term of the ground lease.

If the lease term is for less than 35 years, the lease probably would not be financeable. However, the lender may consider the loan even if there is a short lease term if the location is so valuable or the rent is so low that the tenant has an opportunity to obtain a substantial return on investment without receiving an extended ground lease term. No tenant considering financing the acquisition or development of a leasehold interest in property should proceed with the acquisition without first checking with its lenders to determine the lenders' requirements with regard to leasehold financing. Moreover, for additional protection, the tenant should require that the ground lease provide that it could be reasonably modified or extended to facilitate financing.

Due to the importance of the lease term, the tenant must be certain at all times that it has neither taken any action nor failed to take any action that could accelerate termination of the lease. If the lease term is not long enough to finance the improvements to the property, the tenant should attempt to obtain a longer lease term from the land owner. Although this may seem an unlikely alternative, it is not as unrealistic as may appear.

The land owner would probably not agree to extending the term as a charitable act; however, if the tenant agreed to increase the rent to the current market rent for similar land, the land owner might agree to the extension. Moreover, if the land owner has subordinated its interest in the land to the tenant's leasehold financing, it would be in the owner's best interest to grant the extension in lieu of being required to repay the outstanding balance of the loan.

Lenders frequently object to lending against a leasehold interest and require subordination prior to making the loan. Subordination does not mean that the land owner is personally liable for the indebtedness; however, if the land owner fails to make the payments or fails to ensure that the mortgage terms are satisfied, then, although the owner cannot be sued personally for the loan, the owner can lose the property. If the tenant is considering seeking development financing to improve leased land, the land owner may be required to subordinate its interest in the land to the tenant's leasehold financing. The result of subordinating the land to the tenant's leasehold financing is that the leasehold mortgage would also be a lien against the land. Therefore, if the tenant defaults in paying the debt service on the mortgage, or does not complete construction of the improvements, or otherwise fails to comply with the terms of the mortgage, the land owner would be required to pay the debt service, take the required action, or otherwise cure the tenant's default, or risk losing the property in a foreclosure proceeding.

Many land owners are reluctant to subordinate their interest in the land to the tenant's mortgage, unless the land owner's share of the increased value is quite large or some other incentive is contained in the ground lease or the relationship with the tenant. Unless the ground lease provides to the contrary, the land owner is usually under no obligation to agree to the subordination provision, and the land owner may very well refuse to risk the interest in the land to help the tenant obtain financing. Nevertheless, there are times when the land owner would agree to subordinate its interest in the land to the tenant's leasehold financing. The land owner might agree to subordination to enable the tenant to obtain financing, thereby facilitating the development of the property.

If the land owner agrees to subordinate its interest in the land to the tenant's leasehold financing, the additional security for the loan would add a great deal of value to the tenant's interest in the property. The added security could also allow the lender to more readily agree to a lower interest rate on the loan or otherwise improve the loan terms. Traditionally, a borrower whose loan is secured by a leasehold interest in the land would be charged a slightly higher interest rate than a borrower whose loan is secured by an interest in the land, in order to compensate the lender for the increased risk entailed in financing a leasehold interest in the land.

It is important for the tenant to make certain that the ground lease contains a broad use clause. A narrowly drawn use clause, which limits the use to which the property may be put, will preclude the tenant from being able to develop or use the property in such a way as to maximize its return on the investment in the property. Additionally, the tenant will want the ground lease to contain a provision permitting the tenant to have an almost unrestricted right to develop, redevelop, and use the property, and to take whatever action is necessary to obtain local approval for the development and use of the property.

Nevertheless, the ground lease should also provide the land owner with the right to review the tenant's plans for the property and require that all work be done in a first-class manner in order to not jeopardize the owner's interest in the property. In reviewing a ground lease, the tenant should consider whether limitations on the use of the property will adversely affect the likelihood that the property will be profitable. If the use clause is narrowly drawn, the tenant is limited from being able to maximize its return. In such an event, the tenant should consider attempting to renegotiate the use provisions of the ground lease, even if it means offering the lessor a participation in the profit from the property's success or a cash payment.

Other major concerns for the tenant in reviewing a ground lease are the provisions relating to the use of insurance and condemnation proceeds after a casualty to, or condemnation of, the property. It is beneficial for the tenant to be able to use the proceeds to restore the property in the event of a casualty or a partial condemnation. Although a leasehold mortgagee will want the ability to use the proceeds to prepay its mortgage, the land owner will want the right to terminate the ground lease and receive a share of the proceeds. However, because the tenant owns the improvements during the term of the ground lease, the bulk of the casualty insurance should belong to the tenant. Conversely, ground leases frequently provide that a condemnation award be shared by the landlord and tenant based on the portion of the award attributable to the land, the leasehold estate, or the improvements. Under those circumstances, the ground lease may provide that the land owner is to receive the portion of the award equal to the residual value of the owner's interest in the land together with the present value of the land rent the owner would receive under the lease, whereas the tenant would receive an amount equal to the unamortized value of the improvements and the difference between the land rent and the rent the tenant would receive from subtenants for the balance of the lease term, which would then be discounted to its current value.

Ground leases also frequently require that the tenant restore the improvements after a casualty or condemnation. However, a problem can occur if this provision is contradicted by the terms of the mortgage on the land, which might allow the mortgagee to determine whether to permit the insurance or condemnation proceeds to be used to restore the improvements. Alternatively, the ground lease may provide different provisions, depending on whether the casualty or condemnation occurs during the early part of the lease term or toward its conclusion. During the earlier years of the lease, the tenant will undoubtedly be required to restore the property, whereas during the final years, the tenant may have the option of not restoring improvements if the ground lease is terminated after a condemnation.

Usually, the lender will want the tenant to have the option as to the use of the insurance and condemnation proceeds and to take such action as will ensure the likelihood that the loan will be repaid. If the ground lease allows the tenant to terminate the lease and retain the casualty or condemnation proceeds, then a lender would not want the tenant to exercise such an option.

The ground lease should also provide the tenant with the right to obtain leasehold financing and to be able to refinance any existing financing throughout the ground lease term. If the ground lease does not contain such a provision, the tenant will not be able to finance the development or redevelopment of the property and, even if the tenant is able to develop the property without financing, a prohibition against leasehold financing will preclude the tenant from being able to obtain any portion of its equity in the property.

Due to the magnitude of the tenant's investment in the property and the tenant's loss of its entire investment at the end of the lease term, the ground lease should provide either a right of first refusal enabling the tenant to purchase the land on the same terms as a bona fide third-party purchaser or an option for the tenant to purchase the land at certain times during the lease term for either a fixed price or a price based upon a formula. Due to (1) the inverse relationship that exists between the length of the remaining term of the lease and the value of the tenant's leasehold interest in the property and (2) the fact that upon termination of the lease, the improvements revert to the landlord unless the tenant is prepared to remove them, the tenant's ability to acquire the land provides the tenant with a tremendous incentive to improve and maintain the property. The tenant's ability to acquire the land also increases the financeability of the tenant's position and the likelihood that the tenant can survive financial difficulties.

In many instances, the ground lease will include rent adjustments. The ground rent may increase by a fixed amount at regular intervals or may fluctuate during the lease term to reflect either increases in the consumer price index or the increased value of the property as it is being developed or redeveloped. Accordingly, the tenant should separately confirm that the current rent is accurate and also determine how frequently and under what circumstances the rent can be adjusted. If the rent is based upon a formula, the tenant must understand the formula. As a precaution against surprises, the tenant should also attempt to project the likely rent into the future. This exercise is necessary to determine whether the property will be able to carry itself or whether the rent payable to the land owner may escalate faster than the income produced from the property.

The tenant should also determine whether the ground lease requires the tenant to construct new or additional improvements at the request of the land owner, which could require the tenant to obtain funds for the construction in future years. If the tenant is required to construct additional improvements, the tenant must also determine whether the ground lease provides a method for the financing of the improvements or whether the leasehold estate can be financed to pay for the improvements. Alternatively, the potential tenant must determine whether it has another source of financing.

The tenant must carefully analyze the subletting and assignment provisions of the ground lease. If the tenant cannot sublease portions of the property, the tenant may not be able to pay the ground rent or to develop or use the property. Because the land owner would be concerned with the tenant's ability to obtain a windfall and assign the property to a successor with whom the land owner has not had dealings in the past, the ground lease usually contains detailed limitations on the tenant's ability to assign the ground lease. The lender's ability to find a substitute tenant, by way of either a sublease of the property or an assignment of the lease, is an important means for the lender to replace a tenant having financial difficulties.

OPERATING LEASES

Commercial property is usually constructed for use by the owner or lease by the user. If the owner does not intend to use the property, then regardless of whether the property is a shopping center, office building, apartment complex, industrial facility, or mixed-use facility, the owner's main concern is that as much of the space as possible is subject to leases to creditworthy tenants. The existence of executed leases for a significant portion of the property increases the likelihood that the property will be successful and will produce sufficient revenue to pay the property's operating expenses and debt service. However, the lease itself is not sufficient if the terms are adverse to the landlord's interests or require large expenditures by the landlord to satisfy its provisions.

The key consideration in reviewing a lease is the financial strength of the tenant. If the tenant is leasing a substantial portion of the property and has a high credit rating, then the lease will be significant because (1) it provides the landlord with a great deal of security, (2) it provides cash flow to the landlord, and (3) it draws other tenants to the property. Alternatively, if the tenant does not have a strong operating history or the actual tenant is a subsidiary of a stronger corporation, but the landlord is not receiving a guaranty by the parent corporation, then the tenant and the lease will have less importance to the landlord. Accordingly, a property's success depends not so much on the existence of a lease or its specific terms, but on the strength of the tenant and the likelihood that the tenant can and will fulfill its lease obligations.

Important considerations in analyzing the terms of the lease are the relative obligations of the landlord and the tenant. The landlord's ability to collect a higher rent will be meaningless if the landlord has numerous, expensive obligations under the lease. The extent of the landlord's obligations is what differentiates leases. Leases usually fall within one of three categories:

1. *Gross leases*—The landlord pays all building expenses, and the tenant pays only rent.
2. *Semigross leases*—The landlord pays some, but not all, of the building's operating expenses, and the tenant has an obligation to pay its rent and certain expenses (frequently real estate taxes and some nonstructural repairs).
3. *Net leases*—The tenant pays rent and all operating expenses, and the landlord's only obligation is to pay its mortgage debt service, if any.

A net lease provides the landlord with the safety of a fixed return during the term of the lease, although the rent will probably not be excessive, whereas a gross or semigross lease requires that the landlord provide certain services, but may also contain certain escalations in the rent to compensate the landlord for the increasing expenses (see Example).

There is one word of caution regarding net leases. Sellers and brokers frequently use the terms *net lease* and *triple net lease* interchangeably or incorrectly, which can be a very expensive mistake for the owner. Occasionally, a purchaser will be told that the property is encumbered by a net lease, which should mean that the landlord has no expenses; however,

EXAMPLE

The difference between success or failure for a landlord could depend on whether the leases are net or gross. The following chart indicates who pays each kind of expense.

Expense	Net Lease	Semigross Lease	Gross Lease
Utilities	Tenant	Tenant	Landlord
Fuel	Tenant	Landlord	Landlord
Repairs	Tenant	Landlord	Landlord
Maintenance	Tenant	Tenant	Landlord
Ground rent (if applicable)	Tenant	Tenant	Tenant
Debt service			
(on land mortgage)	Landlord	Landlord	Landlord
(on leasehold)	Tenant	Tenant	Tenant
Fire insurance	Tenant	Tenant	Landlord
Liability insurance	Tenant	Tenant	Landlord

when reviewed, the lease actually provides that the tenant has to pay all operating expenses, and the landlord has to pay for structural repairs. For this reason, brokers and sellers began to use the term *triple net leases* to refer to leases in which the landlord has absolutely no obligations. However, not infrequently, in reviewing a supposed triple net lease, one will find that the landlord has obligations to pay certain expenses. It is therefore imperative that the purchaser or owner carefully review the portions of the lease describing the landlord's obligations.

A lease is similar to the conveyance of all or a portion of the property, but is only for a limited time period. During the lease term, the tenant has possession of the property, while the landlord retains the legal ownership of the property. The other differences between a lease and a conveyance of the property include the tenant's obligation to pay rent, the limitations on the tenant's use of the property, and the landlord's obligation to comply with the terms and conditions of the lease and the requirements of local law. However, if the lease contains sufficient limitations on the landlord's actions during the lease term, then as long as the tenant pays the rent and complies with the other lease provisions, the landlord cannot regain possession of, or exercise any control over, the property during the lease term.

One of the most important provisions of the lease is the remaining term of the lease. The landlord's concern in reviewing the lease term will be its effect on the long-term viability of the property. If the lease is relatively short term (i.e., 1 to 3 years), the landlord should be less concerned with having the right to obtain rent adjustments than with precluding the tenant from attempting to make major property renovations. Moreover, the tenant of a short-term lease should not be given rent concessions or contributions for its alterations unless it is paying above-market rent. A tenant who has signed a long-term lease (i.e., 10 to 20 years) for a significant amount of space provides the landlord with far greater concerns. The landlord wants to be certain that a long-term lease protects the landlord's ability to profit from the lease, and must therefore take into account the effect of inflation, a substantial increase in the value of the property, or an increase in the property's operating expenses. Although a landlord should be in favor of a long-term lease, one problem with a long-term, fixed-rent lease is that the tenant is able to obtain a tremendous bargaining advantage during the original lease negotiation and is frequently able to obtain substantial concessions that it believes are merited through its "investment" in the property. Accordingly, a long-term lease with a financially secure tenant may be particularly one sided in favor of the tenant, and should be carefully reviewed by the landlord. It is therefore important to note that a long-term lease is not enough to make a property successful. If the lease terms are disadvantageous to the landlord, the long term can only hurt the landlord and the property's viability.

The relevance of the lease term includes such peripheral issues as the need for the lease to identify the specific commencement and termination dates of the lease. If the commencement of the lease is conditioned upon an event over which the landlord has little or no control, the tenant could obtain a tremendous amount of leverage over the landlord. If the lease term and the tenant's obligation to pay rent do not commence until the tenant obtains certain approvals or finishes construction or until the tenant is satisfied with the construction of the property, the tenant is in the position of determining when the lease will commence. The tenant's ability to decide when it will pay rent based upon a subjective determination, places the landlord at a great risk in the event that the tenant never believes the condition is satisfied. Accordingly, the lease should contain an objective standard for determining when the conditions have been satisfied. Of course, a lease that has no preconditions to commencement or continuation would be preferred.

The most important issue relating to the term of the lease is its length. To avoid any confusion at a crucial time, the lease should specify the date the lease term commences and the date it terminates. A problem can arise if the lease provides for commencement and termination dates in an obscure fashion or if one is tied to an event over which the landlord has no control. The landlord should also be concerned with any renewal options contained in the lease, especially if the lease or the options are at a below-market rent. The lease should specify the renewal options, if any, and indicate the preconditions for their being exercised. It should also provide that, if the options are not exercised in writing by a certain date, they will be considered waived. The renewal options should also provide that they will be invalidated if the tenant defaults during the lease term. The lease should also indicate the amount of rent payable during the renewal term.

The landlord should recognize when negotiating the terms of the lease that renewal options at a fixed rent will be exercised only if the fair market rent is higher than the renewal rent contained in the lease or the tenant's moving costs are excessive. If the fair market rent is lower than the renewal rent contained in the lease, the tenant will either choose not to exercise the option or attempt to negotiate a lower renewal rent. The landlord should also be aware that if the renewal option does not specify the rent during the renewal term or does not indicate a formula for arriving at the new rent, and the option indicates that the tenant can renew the lease on all the same terms and conditions, then the tenant will be able to exercise the option and continue paying the same rent during the renewal term.

Important concerns for the landlord in reviewing the lease are the rent and additional rent that the tenant will be obligated to pay during the lease term. The tenant's financial obligations under the lease could include the following obligations:

- Fixed rent
- Percentage rent
- Rent escalations
- Cost-of-living adjustments
- Porter wage escalations
- Increases in real estate taxes
- Increases in other operating expenses during the lease term.

The landlord must also be prepared to offset these obligations against any rent concessions or abatements the tenant has received from the landlord. It is in the landlord's best interest for the lease to contain rent escalations, as well as the tenant's obligation to pay a proportionate share of any increase in the property's operating expenses. The amount the tenant is obligated to pay can be increased further if the landlord can increase the calculation of square footage leased by the tenant that is contained in the lease. It is important for the landlord entering into a long-term lease to protect its cash flow by including in the lease rent escalations and adjustment provisions; otherwise, the landlord's return on the lease would reduce in terms of real dollars due to inflationary conditions in the economy or increased expenses in the property.

In leases having terms longer than five years, the landlord should arrange for the fixed rent to increase every two or three years, thus protecting the landlord's interest in the appreciation of the property. Moreover, during the term of a 10- to 20-year lease, as the property becomes more valuable, the landlord should receive a higher return on its investment due to the increasing value of the property. The landlord should also ascertain that the mathematical calculations of the monthly and annual rent are accurate to avoid a claim by the tenant that it was overcharged. Such a problem could arise if the landlord and tenant negotiate a certain rent per square foot and there is a difference of opinion as to the number of square feet contained in the property. It is therefore beneficial for the lease to contain the precise amount of the actual rent.

In addition to specifying the amount of rent, the lease should describe when, where, and to whom the rent is payable. Also, to avoid problems caused by mathematical mistakes, the lease should indicate the monthly rent as well as the aggregate annual rent payable by the tenant during the lease term. If the tenant defaults, the lease will support a claim by the landlord for all the rent coming due during the remainder of the lease term, not only the rent due at the time of the default.

To adjust fixed rent for increasing expenses caused by inflation during the lease term, commercial leases frequently contain rent escalation clauses. The forms of rent escalation clauses used in leases include those that are based upon fluctuations in the consumer price index, the Porter Wage Scale, or other similar formulas that are utilized to determine increased costs in the area in which the property is located. If a large-credit tenant negotiates a cap on rent escalations, then, regardless of the amount of inflation that occurs in the economy, the landlord is limited in the increase in expenses that can be passed along to the tenant. The stronger tenants might also attempt to negotiate to have the rent adjusted only periodically (i.e., every five years) rather than annually. The effect of such limitations is that the landlord's return in current dollars will be reduced.

The concept of additional rent is that the tenant is obligated to reimburse the landlord either for all expenses relating to the property expended by the landlord or for any increase in operating expenses after the tenant executed the lease. The purpose of additional rent is to protect the landlord's cash flow that is being generated from the property and to maintain the landlord's profit. The idea is that the landlord's profit should not be placed at risk if expenses increase substantially during the lease term. Indirectly, the additional rent provisions will also protect the tenant from the effect of the landlord's cutting costs and not properly maintaining the property when expenses increase significantly. The operating costs that are usually part of the additional rent calculations include:

- Real estate taxes and assessments
- Water and sewer charges
- Common area maintenance
- Insurance premiums
- Repairs and maintenance.

An issue that frequently arises in additional rent provisions is determining whether the allocation of a particular tenant's share of the expenses is accurate. The lease might provide that each tenant will pay its pro rata share of particular costs or that a tenant will pay any increases in particular costs, unless the cost is directly attributable to the activities of a single tenant, in which event that tenant would pay the entire cost. The lease should also specify the meaning of the term *pro rata*. If pro rata is defined to be the ratio of the square footage of the tenant's floor space to all the floor space in the property, then the tenant will pay the same amount regardless of how much of the property has been leased to other tenants. However, if the lease provides that the tenant will pay the ratio between the square footage area leased to that tenant and the square footage leased to all other tenants, then the tenant will pay a proportionately larger amount if there are vacancies in the property. The landlord would certainly prefer the latter formulation rather than the former. Nevertheless, the lease should provide that if a particular tenant is the cause of the increase, then that tenant would be responsible for the entire increase rather than merely a pro rata share of it.

Although the additional rent provisions usually include all or a portion of the property's real estate taxes and assessments, if the tenant is leasing a substantial portion of the property, the tenant may have negotiated to have its own tax lot designated and pay its real estate taxes directly to the municipality. Likewise, the tenant may have the right to pay its own water and sewer charges and/or insurance costs. If the tenant has the right to pay those expenses directly, the landlord should make certain that the tenant is actually making the payments so they do not become a lien on the property and ultimately become the landlord's obligation. The landlord should also limit the tenant's ability to challenge the property's tax assessment without the landlord's being involved. Although, the tenant will probably take all actions that are required to see that the taxes are minimized, the landlord must be certain of the tenant's actions. If the tenant fails in an attempt to challenge the assessment, it could result in the landlord's being required to pay higher taxes in the future.

The landlord would prefer the lease to contain a provision requiring the tenant to pay its pro rata share of the real estate taxes and water and sewer charges arising from the property or, as an alternative, any increase in the real estate taxes. Regardless, the tenant should be obligated to pay any increase in taxes that is caused directly by its use or improvement of the property. Nevertheless, even the existence of such a clause will not eliminate all problems for the owner. A tenant who is accused of causing a tax increase and is therefore obligated to pay the cost of it, will certainly argue that the increase was not its fault. Water and sewer charges can be more confusing than taxes, since water and sewer charges can be based on a number of factors, including a fixed charge based upon the size of the property or the actual amount of water utilized by the property. Certainly, a tenant who uses a substantial amount of water in a business should be required to install a separate water meter to avoid disputes over the portion of the water bill attributable to the tenant.

The landlord should also be concerned about being able to pass along the cost of property insurance to tenants. Although insurance used to be easily obtained at a minimal expense, it has now become a significant portion of the landlord's operating budget. Accordingly, the lease should provide that the tenant is obligated to pay its pro rata share of the cost of casualty, liability, rent loss, elevator, boiler, glass, and worker's compensation insurance, as well as other risks incurred by the landlord. To be further protected, the landlord should make certain that the lease requires the tenant to comply with one of the following provisions:

- Provide insurance for the entire property with the landlord named on the policy as an insured and supply a copy of the policy to the landlord
- Reimburse the landlord for the tenant's pro rata share of the landlord's cost of insurance for the property
- Maintain part of the insurance, and the landlord maintains the balance, with the landlord passing on the cost of its portion of the insurance to the tenant.

The lease should also provide that if the increased cost of insurance is due to a particular tenant's use of the property, that tenant will be required to pay the entire cost of any insurance increase.

The lease should also require that any insurance provided by the tenant conform to the requirements of any mortgage on the property. This means not only that the insurance must be for a certain amount, but that the carrier must have a high rating. The requirement that the tenant maintain the insurance may cause a problem for a tenant who wants to self-insure or to include this property on its blanket coverage of all properties it leases. The risk to the landlord from a tenant's self-insuring or having a property included in a blanket coverage is that, if the tenant has financial difficulties or a great number of disasters affecting its leasehold properties during a relatively short time period, the tenant may not have the wherewithal to rebuild the property after a casualty or be able to pay a liability judgment.

Percentage rent is another form of additional rent that is frequently included in retail leases and is based upon the tenant's sales from the property above a certain threshold. Percentage rent is an attempt by the landlord to share in the success of property that it owns. The premise is that the fixed rent is calculated based upon a certain minimum sales figure by the tenant and, if the property is so successful as to exceed that minimum sales figure, the landlord should share in the benefit to the tenant. If the lease contains a percentage rent provision, it should describe the percentage to be used; the threshold of sales before the percentage is calculated; the tenant's expenses, if any, that are deducted from either gross sales or the percentage rent; and the frequency with which the tenant is required to provide sales information or payments to the landlord. The landlord should retain the right to audit the tenant's books and records, and, if the tenant's reports are inaccurate, the tenant should be obligated to reimburse the landlord for the cost of the audit (see Example).

Occasionally, the lease may provide the landlord with the right to terminate the lease unless the tenant reimburses the landlord for the percentage rent the landlord expected to receive. Such termination occurs if the landlord leased the space expecting the location to generate a substantial amount of percentage rent, which does not occur. Conversely, the lease could provide the tenant with the right to terminate the lease if sales do not reach a certain level. In this way, both the landlord and the tenant can protect their expectations from a property they considered to be valuable. Under such circumstances, if the tenant decides that the store is not sufficiently profitable, the landlord could induce the tenant into staying at the location by offering more attractive lease terms for a limited period of time.

The percentage rent clause could provide that the tenant will provide sales figures to the landlord and a payment of the landlord's share of

EXAMPLE

In a typical shopping center lease, the tenant may pay a base rent of $175,000 per year and a percentage rent of 1 percent of annual gross sales above $17,500,000. Therefore, if the gross sales are $18,350,000, the total rent would be $183,500, which includes $175,000 of base rent and $8,500 of percentage rent. The $17,500,000 threshold for the percentage rent is $175,000 divided by 1 percent, so the base rent is 1 percent of the first $17,500,000 in annual gross sales.

percentage rent annually. However, landlords who either require the cash flow to operate the property or are concerned about the tenant's owing a large sum, may require in the lease that the tenant will supply the sales figures and pay the percentage rent monthly based upon the portion of the annual amount of sales achieved for the month in issue. However, requiring that the percentage rent be paid monthly places the tenant in a difficult position because it will be paying a substantial amount of percentage rent after busy months, whereas that rent might be needed to get through the slower months of the year, when sales not only fail to produce percentage rent, but also fail to provide cash flow to pay the minimum rent.

A cautionary note for purchasers is that, in purchasing property, the purchaser should not place a heavy emphasis on the property's percentage rent. There is no certainty that the tenant's gross sales will exceed the threshold or be higher than the previous year's sales volume. Percentage rent, unlike fixed rent, can stop or be reduced if the tenant closes the store, the business becomes less successful, the tenant changes the business, the store is subleased, the offsets against the sales figures increase, or business at the property decreases. The construction of a competing business on an adjacent property could abruptly stop a percentage rent that has been paid annually for many years. Moreover, a tenant who regularly achieves increasing percentage rents is prone to open newer, larger stores in the vicinity of a successful store.

The landlord should also determine if the tenant has the right to avoid paying rent due to a rent concession that has not been used. Landlords frequently provide tenants with rent concessions in order to lease vacant space as quickly as possible. A rent concession is a period of time in which the tenant pays no rent or a reduced amount of rent. The purpose of the rent concession is to subsidize the tenant for either the costs associated with moving a business or the start-up costs of opening a new facility.

Occasionally, the rent concession is payable over several years. For the tenant, spreading the rent concessions over several years serves to improve the tenant's operating statement. If the rent concession occurred in only the first year of the lease, then the reduced rent will be offset by the increased costs of opening the facility. However, if part of the rent concession is taken in the second or third year of the lease, the higher operating costs in the first year will be anticipated by the tenant's lenders and investors, due to the costs associated with opening a facility. Thereafter, the reduced operating expense during the second or third year will make it appear as if the location is more successful and less expensive to operate. This provides the tenant with additional time to improve the performance of the new facility; however, it can provide the landlord or a purchaser with a deceptive understanding of the property's cash flow.

Typically, rent concessions include free rent for periods that can range from several months to over a year, and are usually based upon the creditworthiness of the tenant and the softness of the market. Another form of rent concession is that the rent does not commence to accrue until the space is turned over to the tenant, the fixturing of the space is completed, the tenant opens and operates its business from the facility, or a certain number of other tenants open for business.

The landlord should also be concerned with whether the lease provides the tenant with the right to stop paying rent or to offset the rent for any reason. The landlord should identify any circumstance under which the tenant can withhold rent, regardless of how short a period of time is involved. The following provisions occasionally provide such a right:

- The original rent concession
- A casualty or condemnation
- The failure of the property's utilities or HVAC systems
- The leasehold or the property becomes inaccessible
- Failure of the landlord to perform under the lease
- An action or inaction of a third person.

Dealing with the abatement of rent due to the action of a third party is difficult, because it involves matters that might be out of the landlord's control. Moreover, actions by third parties are not usually covered by rental insurance. In this regard, the landlord should be concerned about any lease provision that refers to actions that have to be taken, or may not be taken, by anyone unrelated to the landlord. The landlord should be particularly concerned when one tenant's rent is dependent upon the continuation in business of another tenant. In such a circumstance, there is little the landlord can do to prevent a tenant from ceasing operation even if the possibility is precluded by that tenant's lease.

The landlord's desire to maximize the return from the property requires just as much concern about reducing its obligation to pay expenses as about collecting the rent. Expenses include both ordinary operating expenses, which are susceptible to projections contained in a budget, and the property's required repairs and maintenance. Repairs to a property frequently comprise a landlord's single largest expense; however, unlike the property's other operating expenses, repairs cannot usually be predicted or budgeted, and they can be made more expensive by the tenant's use of the property and the activities of the tenant's employees or customers. Although the commercial landlord is not usually obligated to maintain or repair the property except as provided in the lease, the landlord will certainly want the property to be maintained in first-class condition at all times due to the investment in the property.

Commercial leases usually require that interior repairs are the tenant's obligation, whereas exterior and structural repairs remain the landlord's obligation, the cost of which may be passed onto the tenant through additional rent obligations. Therefore, it is important that the landlord review the repair clause contained in the lease to determine the repair and maintenance obligations of each party to the lease. Simply because a clause indicates that one party is not required to make certain repairs, does not necessarily mean that the other party is obligated to make the repair. The landlord must be certain who has the responsibility for repairs and maintenance because the landlord's asset will deteriorate and become unleasable if no one is obligated to make the repairs.

Additionally, regardless of which party is required to make ordinary and necessary repairs to the property, the tenant should be obligated to repair any damage to the property caused by its use of the property in an unauthorized or unsafe manner, or caused by its negligence, or due to the actions of its employees, agents, or customers. Moreover, because the lease provides the tenant with the obligation to maintain the property during the term of the lease, the tenant is not necessarily obligated to make structural repairs to the property. The term *structural repairs* refers to repairs to the exterior walls, roof, foundation, and plumbing, electrical, and HVAC systems. The tenant is obligated to make specific repairs only if the lease identifies the obligation of each party and specifies whether such repairs include exterior and interior repairs, structural and nonstructural repairs, ordinary and extraordinary repairs.

The lease should also identify which party must prepare the property on the commencement and termination of the lease. This issue is important because it goes to the heart of when the rent obligation of the current and future tenant will commence. If the lease provides that the landlord is obligated to renovate the property at the beginning of the lease term, an issue could arise as to whether the work has been done to the tenant's satisfaction. If the landlord is reviewing the lease prior to its execution, the issue is whether the landlord will be responsible for the initial improvements to the property. If the renovation is the landlord's obligation, the lease or a work letter executed simultaneously with the lease should specify the work that the landlord will be required to do. This will avoid a later claim by the tenant that the landlord was required to do more work than was done and claim the landlord's failure as a breach of the lease and a reason to avoid paying the rent. If the tenant is permitted to do the work at the landlord's expense, the landlord should have the right to approve the work being done by the tenant to avoid a situation in which the tenant's actions reduce the value of the property or increase the cost to the landlord. Thus, the description of the work to be done should be as specific as possible. The specificity in either the lease or the work letter of the landlord's obligations will avoid disputes as to the nature of the modifications and whether a certain item is within the obligation of the party doing the renovations.

The issue of the work letter sometimes leads to a dispute between the landlord and the tenant over whether the landlord will do the work or will reimburse the tenant for doing the work. The tenant's concern is that the landlord will do the work as inexpensively as possible, whereas the landlord will want to avoid paying an unnecessarily high price for the work. One solution is for the landlord to do the work subject to the approval of the tenant's architect, who will confirm that the work has been done pursuant to the specifications. The landlord should be able to have the work done as inexpensively as possible, while the tenant's only interest should be protecting its interest in having the work done to a certain standard of quality.

Alternatively, the lease may require that the tenant return the property to its original condition on the termination of the lease. Under such circumstances, the return of the tenant's security deposit may be tied to the tenant's satisfaction of its obligation to restore the property at the termination of the lease. If the tenant is obligated to maintain the property during the lease term, the landlord must be certain that the tenant does not defer repairs during the final years of the lease or do the repairs as cheaply as possible, in order to minimize the cost of maintaining the property. If the tenant defers maintenance, the landlord could be required to pay a substantial amount to prepare the property for the next tenant or accept a lower rent or offer a larger rent concession to release the property. Accordingly, by making certain that the tenant restores the property at the end of the lease term, the landlord is protecting the long-term investment in the property.

The cost of repairing and maintaining the property is not easily subject to budgeting, can be the landlord's largest expense, and is frequently tied to the tenant's use of the property. Frequently, commercial property requires fewer repairs than residential property and, while commercial tenants can be required to restore the property on the termination of the lease term, residential tenants do not usually make repairs even if the landlord is holding a security deposit. It is not uncommon for residential tenants to fail to pay rent during the last month or two of the lease in order to use up the security deposit. Residential tenants believe that landlords will not return security deposits and know that it would take several months for a landlord to evict a residential tenant for failing to pay rent. Conversely, commercial tenants, concerned over their reputation and the possibility of needless litigation, are unlikely to avoid paying rent at the end of the lease term.

The lease should also specify whether the landlord will be obligated to modify the space to satisfy any new building codes related to the property that arise during the lease term and, if so, at whose expense. Changes in building codes can involve requirements of habitability, compliance with environmental protection laws, removal of asbestos, installation of sprinkler systems, and so forth. Because these changes could result in a substantial expense, the landlord would want the lease to provide for reimbursement of the cost by the tenant. The lease should also preclude the tenant from making any improvements or alterations to the property without the landlord's prior written consent. Such a provision protects the landlord's investment in the property by precluding the tenant from altering the property in ways that the tenant believes will facilitate its use, but could reduce the value of the property, which is adverse to the landlord's interest. The lease will frequently allow the tenant to make nonstructural alterations without obtaining the landlord's consent. Alternatively, the landlord will not be allowed to unreasonably withhold its consent to nonstructural alterations by the tenant. However, structural alterations should be kept within the exclusive province of the landlord. If the tenant is allowed to do whatever it wishes to the property, it could seriously diminish the value of the property because the tenant's primary concern is the short-term facilitation of business and not the long-term value of the property.

In reviewing the lease, the landlord should be concerned by a requirement that the landlord provide the tenant with a larger leasehold at the tenant's request, which can have serious financial consequences for the landlord. Such a provision could require the landlord to obtain additional land, if the existing land is inadequate for a larger building, or to obtain financing for the construction. Regardless of whether the tenant is obligated to reimburse the landlord, the tenant could exercise the option at a time when financing is impossible to obtain or extraordinarily expensive. Particularly troublesome for the landlord would be the tenant's having the right to terminate the lease if the landlord is unable to expand the tenant's leasehold. If the landlord cannot avoid being required to provide expansion space for the tenant, the lease should specify the size and location of the proposed expansion space, as well as the method of acquiring and constructing the new space, and the manner in which the new space will be integrated with the remainder of the property. This specificity will enable the landlord to accurately determine the cost of complying with the lease. The landlord must also determine whether the space is available or whether it is already subject to a lease to a third party. The landlord should make certain that the lease provides for the rent to be adjusted after the space has been completed and that the increased rent will cover the cost of the expansion and provide a profit for the landlord's time, expense, and aggravation involved in constructing additional space. Nevertheless, the most acceptable expansion provision is one in which the tenant is required to construct, at its own expense, the additional facility, which becomes the landlord's property upon completion. Alternatively, the lease could provide that the landlord has the option to build the additional facility and, if the landlord fails to act expeditiously, the tenant can build the addition without any loss in rent to the landlord.

An issue that must be clearly explored and provided for in the lease has to do with the rights and obligations of the landlord and the tenant after a fire or other casualty to the property. The lease should provide for the critical issues relating to a casualty, including the following:

- Which party is obligated to restore the property after a fire or other casualty?
- Does the landlord have the right to terminate the lease if it does not restore the property or if the insurance proceeds are inadequate, or can the tenant demand restoration?
- Does the tenant have the right to void the landlord's attempt to terminate the lease after a casualty by agreeing to pay for the cost of restoring the property?
- Does the landlord have the right to precondition its restoration of the property to the tenant's exercising its renewal options?

- In what manner are the insurance proceeds to be applied if the property is not restored?
- Does the tenant have the right to terminate the lease after a casualty, or can the tenant terminate the lease if the property is not restored quickly enough?
- Do the lease provisions relating to a casualty comply with the requirements contained in the mortgage?
- Does the landlord have the ability to reconfigure the property after a casualty, or must it be restored exactly as it was before the casualty?
- Does the tenant have the right to abate its rent after a casualty, and, if so, how much of the property must be affected before the abatement goes into effect?
- If rent does abate, what criteria is used to determine when the rent recommences?

Although a fire or other casualty to the property does not automatically relieve the tenant from its obligation to pay rent and otherwise perform its obligations under the lease, many states have adopted statutes that provide that, unless the lease contains contrary provisions, the tenant has the right to terminate the lease after a casualty as long as the casualty was not caused by the tenant's negligence. Because the word *casualty* can refer to the complete destruction of the property or a minor condition that can be readily resolved, the lease provision that is too broad or too narrow can adversely affect both the landlord and tenant. Therefore, the best result will be achieved if the lease provides that, in the event of a complete destruction of the property or one exceeding a certain portion of the property or costing more than a certain amount to repair, the lease would terminate and the landlord would have the right to utilize the insurance proceeds at its discretion.

The landlord should also be concerned if the tenant has the right to terminate the lease if it is unable to utilize the property for more than a specific limited period (i.e., three to six months). However, the landlord should have the right to terminate the lease after a casualty, because the landlord is protected by not being required to restore the property if it chooses not to rebuild. Frequently, the landlord will retain the right not to restore the property after a casualty, if the casualty occurs during the last five years of the lease term unless the tenant exercises its renewal options under the lease.

The landlord should also be concerned about a lease provision that requires it to restore the property after a casualty at its own expense. The landlord would then be obligated to utilize the insurance proceeds arising from the casualty to restore the property and to fund any additional amount from its own sources. For this reason, the landlord should be certain that the insurance it maintains on the property conforms to its obligations under the lease and that the insurance and restoration provisions of the lease conform to the landlord's obligations under the mortgage. If the landlord ignores the terms of relationship between the lease and the mortgage when purchasing insurance, it could find itself being obligated under the lease to restore the property while the mortgage requires that the insurance proceeds be used to reduce the principal indebtedness. The landlord should be concerned about the insurance even if the tenant is obligated to maintain the insurance or restore the property or if the casualty is caused by the tenant's negligence. The landlord will want the lease to obligate the tenant to pay for the restoration if the casualty is attributable to the tenant's negligence.

A problem can also develop for the landlord if the tenant is obligated under the lease to restore the property. If the lease contains such a provision, the landlord should receive a copy of the tenant's insurance policy, so the landlord can satisfy itself that the tenant's insurance is adequate and that the provisions of the policy will insure that the casualty will be restored. If a casualty were to occur to the property, the landlord would not want the tenant's insurer to disclaim liability. In such an event, the landlord would have to finance the cost of the improvements and seek redress against a possibly insolvent tenant. The landlord and any mortgagee should be named as an additional insured under the tenant's policy, and the policy must provide that it is noncancellable without advance notice to the landlord. If the tenant is obligated to restore the property, the tenant may attempt to negotiate for the right to terminate the lease if the casualty occurs during the last few years of the lease. This will avoid the expense and time involved in restoring a property that will not be used for any extensive period of time.

The lease should also provide whether the rent will continue to be paid after the casualty. The lease should contain a requirement that the tenant maintain rent insurance to insure that the income continues while the landlord or the tenant rebuilds the property. Whether the rent abates depends, to a great degree, upon the issues involved in the particular situation. If the lease is for a retail establishment and the tenant is still able to operate its store although its business is reduced, the landlord may agree to accept a rent equal to a percentage of the tenant's sales rather than the fixed rent provided in the lease. Conversely, the lease may provide that the rent will continue unless the casualty exceeds a certain percentage of the property or the tenant loses access to its leasehold for more than a certain period of time (i.e., several months). Alternatively, the landlord may be able to have the tenant accept a partial abatement equal to the portion of the premises affected by the casualty.

The lease should also specify the kind of casualty insurance that must be obtained. The four kinds of casualty insurance are the following:

1. Fire insurance, which insures against fire and lightning
2. Fire and extended coverage insurance, which includes fire and lightning, as well as any damage caused by windstorms, hail, explosion, riot, and damage by aircraft or vehicles
3. Extended coverage insurance, which can also be endorsed to insure against loss from vandalism, malicious mischief, snow, sleet, ice, water damage, glass, and sprinkler damage
4. An "all risk" policy, which provides insurance coverage in the event a loss occurs, regardless of the cause of the loss, although it does exclude losses due to floods, earthquakes, and nuclear reactions, unless additional insurance against such losses is obtained.

The lease should also deal with the issue of coinsurance, which protects the insurance carrier from a property that is insured for less than its insurable value based upon the assumption that any loss would not totally destroy the property. Without a coinsurance clause, a property owner could insure a $5 million property for $4 million, assuming that in the event of a complete casualty, it would not be required to expend $5 million to restore the property, but only $4 million. The owner would therefore be able to purchase less insurance than the actual full value of the property. A coinsurance provision provides that, if the property is not insured for a substantial portion of its value (i.e., 80 to 90 percent), in the event of a casualty loss, the insurance company will pay only for the percentage of the loss that the amount of insurance carried bears to the overall loss. Accordingly, if a property valued at $5 million is insured for $3 million and has a $1 million loss, the insurance company would pay for only three-fifths of the $1 million loss, or $600,000, because the property is insured for only three-fifths of its value. For this reason, the landlord should be concerned that if the lease contains a coinsurance clause, the landlord will become a self-insurer for any loss in excess of the amount covered by the insurance company.

The landlord should review the casualty insurance policy being carried by the tenant, to satisfy itself as to the financial strength of the carrier, the amount of insurance being carried, and the deductible on the policy. The deductible amount is the portion of the loss that the insurer does not cover. For example, if a $5 million policy contains a $250,000 deductible, the party carrying the insurance must pay the first $250,000 of the claim and the insurer is obligated to pay only the cost of restoration in excess of the deductible. Frequently, insurance with a higher deductible is requested because it costs significantly less. However, the issue of a policy's deductibility can be critical if the tenant is maintaining the insurance and the landlord is obligated to restore the property, or if the landlord is maintaining the insurance and the tenant is obligated to restore the property, or if the tenant is obligated to maintain and restore the property and the landlord is concerned about the tenant's creditworthiness.

The landlord should also consider the effect of the lease provisions relating to the condemnation or taking of the property for public use by the government's exercising its right of eminent domain. The lease should deal with two fundamental issues: whether the condemnation will have an effect on the lease and, if so, the manner in which each party will be compensated for the taking of all or a portion of the property. Basically, there are three kinds of condemnation: a total taking, a partial taking, and a temporary taking. In each form of condemnation, the landlord and the tenant have each lost a portion of its interest in the property.

In a total taking, the landlord loses its right to possession of the property and the improvements on the property after the termination of the lease term. The landlord also loses its income from the property during the lease term. Additionally, the tenant loses the difference between the fair market rental value of the property in excess of the amount the tenant is obligated to pay to the landlord, as well as the loss of its improvements during the remainder of the lease term. Neither the landlord nor the tenant can recover the value of its lost profit on the property, its goodwill, or the cost of removing its personal property or business from the property. This is because, in theory, the business is separate from the property, and the only compensation from the government is for the loss of the property.

In a partial taking of the property, the tenant will receive an award for the diminished value of its leasehold, and the landlord will be awarded for the loss of its right to receive the property at the end of the lease term, together with the value of the improvements on the property on the date the lease was supposed to terminate. If there is no provision in the lease for a rent abatement or reduction, the landlord would have no claim for the reduced income from the property.

In a temporary taking of all or a portion of the property, the tenant is frequently entitled to receive the entire award. This is because the tenant will be liable for the rent, and the landlord will not be affected by the taking unless the temporary taking extends beyond the end of the lease term, in which event the landlord would be entitled to the fair rental value for the period after the lease terminates. In the event of a permanent taking, the tenant can claim compensation for its nonremovable fixtures, together with the value of any right to renew the lease. However, the tenant would not be compensated for the loss of an option to purchase the property.

The lease should provide the landlord with the right to terminate the lease in the event of a taking of all or a substantial portion of the property. It should also preclude the tenant from making a claim for any portion of the condemnation award. The reason for such a requirement in the lease is that the condemning authority will make an aggregate award for the property and then allocate it between the landlord and the tenant. Therefore, if the tenant does not have the right to a portion of the award for the unexpired term of its lease, then the landlord's portion of the award would increase dramatically. A clause that provides the landlord with the right to terminate the lease also provides the landlord with the ability to determine whether there is an economic reason to restore the remaining portion of the property after the condemnation without interference from the tenant.

A taking of all of the property, resulting in a termination of the lease and an award to the landlord, would limit the tenant's ability to make a claim for anything other than the value of its nonremovable fixtures. Moreover, the lease should provide the landlord with the ability to terminate the lease in the event of a sale of the property to the condemning authority in lieu of condemnation, to enable the landlord to negotiate without interference from the tenant. In this way, the landlord will be able to negotiate a maximum price without having to pay the costs of a condemnation. However, this also precludes the tenant from claiming a portion of the condemnation award to reimburse it for the value of its interest in the property. If the lease provides that the tenant's fixtures and improvements become the landlord's property upon completion of their installation, then the tenant would have no right to compensation for the loss of such fixtures, regardless of whether there was a condemnation or a sale in lieu of condemnation. Not only would the tenant lose the value of its improvements under these circumstances, but the existence of the improvements would benefit the landlord further by increasing the property value.

A partial condemnation presents more complicated problems, because the parties will have to determine whether (1) the lease will continue, (2) the property will be restored, and (3) the condemnation will affect the rent. The landlord would prefer that the tenant not have the right to terminate the lease in the event of a partial termination that reduces the size of the tenant's leasehold or the property's common elements. Alternatively, the tenant may have the right to terminate the lease, which can be voided by the landlord if it can replace the portion taken within a reasonable period of time. It is also possible that the condemnation could make the property more desirable for the tenant and more valuable for the landlord. A condemnation of a portion of the parking area to widen the highway in front of the property or to upgrade the surrounding area, will have a positive effect on the property and the interests of both the landlord and the tenant in the property.

The landlord must also seriously consider the uses to which the property can be subject. Unless the lease provides to the contrary, a tenant may use leased property for any lawful purpose. However, if a lease merely provides that the property is to be used for a certain purpose, that does not limit the tenant from using the property for other purposes. A landlord who wishes to limit a tenant's use must be certain that the lease specifies that the property can be used for no other purpose. Moreover, if the particular use to which the tenant is to put the property is important to the landlord, then the lease should provide for such use and restrict other uses. Additionally, the landlord should be certain that the projected use does not violate the building's certificate of occupancy or the exclusive rights granted to any other tenant, or any easement or restriction of the landlord's title to the property. The landlord should also be certain that the particular use to which the tenant intends to put the property is not in excess of the building's capacity to handle the use.

If the use to which the property is to be put requires an alteration to the building or the property's certificate of occupancy or the approval of another tenant or a government agency, the lease should indicate whether it is the obligation of the tenant or the landlord to make the alteration or to obtain the approval. The landlord should be certain that the tenant does not have the ability to terminate the lease if the intended use subsequently becomes impossible to achieve. The landlord should also be certain that the lease does not contain a representation that the particular use is permissible. Moreover, the lease should not provide that, if at any time in the future, the use becomes illegal or impossible, the tenant would have the right to challenge the change at its own expense before it can terminate the lease. The landlord will also need to know if the tenant's use entails a substantial increase in utilities, parking facilities, or employees, or will impose a hardship on other tenants.

A problem can occur if the anticipated use is contrary to the interests of existing tenants. This happens if the landlord of a shopping center leases space for a recreational facility (e.g., a movie theater, a game room, a bowling alley) where the common areas will be used exclusively by the patrons of the recreational facility who are unlikely to shop in the stores. Moreover, the existing tenants may object to the people attracted to the recreational facility. Tenants of office buildings also become concerned about other tenants who have an excessive number of people coming through the building, thereby reducing security and taxing the facilities. The landlord will be concerned about each of these problems and their effect on the viability of the property.

The landlord should also be concerned about exclusive use provisions contained in leases. The landlord would not have the right to grant an exclusive to a tenant for a particular type of merchandise if the landlord has already signed leases permitting other tenants to use the stores for "any lawful purpose." Moreover, once the landlord grants an exclusive use to one tenant, it runs the risk that another tenant having a better operation or willing to pay a higher rent will refuse to lease a portion of the property. Additionally, some stores (supermarkets, discount stores, drug stores, and department stores) carry such a wide variety of merchandise that it is virtually impossible for them not to violate another tenant's exclusive right to sell a certain item. By executing different leases, the landlord could be creating a problem for itself. Alternatively, the lease could provide that the landlord will not grant an exclusive for the same product to any other tenant, while excluding from the provisions of the exclusive any merchandise carried in department stores, drug or discount stores, and supermarkets.

The landlord should also be concerned about the sublease and assignment provisions of the leases. The landlord should prefer that the lease contain a restriction on the tenant's ability to sublease the property or assign the lease without receiving the landlord's prior written consent, in order to protect the tenant mix at the property. However, a tenant may argue that such a limitation restricts the tenant's ability to reduce the amount of space it has leased, or precludes it from selling a valuable lease to a third party if its circumstances change. Moreover, if the tenant has managed to negotiate a financially attractive lease from which it intends to obtain a benefit through a sublease or assignment, the landlord should have the right to share in the benefit accruing to the tenant from that lease, since it is based upon the property's appreciating value.

The landlord's concern over subletting or assignment goes to the very nature of the landlord–tenant relationship and the control that the landlord should have over who is operating at its property. Although the same rent would still be payable to the landlord regardless of the sublease or assignment, the landlord's concern has to do with allowing the tenant to have the ability to change the property's tenant mix or the use of the property in a way that is contrary to the property's (and the landlord's) best interest. The landlord may also be concerned that the tenant could circumvent the lease's percentage rent provisions. This could be accomplished by the tenant's moving to another location that does not require it to pay percentage rent and recovering the cost of having two leaseholds in the same general area by subletting the unused space to a subtenant who does not generate enough sales to pay percentage rent.

The landlord must be concerned that a change in the use or occupancy of its space will change the tenant mix or appearance of its property, and could result in the substitution by the tenant of a prestigious and creditworthy tenant for a less creditworthy tenant to whom the landlord might not have leased the property in the first place. The conveyance of an interest of the landlord's property by the tenant could trigger a general decline in the property due to the appearance that the landlord is leasing space to less attractive tenants. The landlord may also be concerned because the rent and other terms of the lease were set based upon the financial strength and reputation of a particular tenant. It is also possible that leases executed with other tenants are conditioned upon a particular tenant's operating a store at the property. Thus, the effect of the sublease or assignment could result in a violation of another tenant's lease, a situation over which the landlord would have no control.

Unless the lease specifically precludes both an assignment or sublease, the tenant would have the right to assign the lease or sublet all or part of the property without the landlord's consent. Moreover, the lease must specifically preclude both a sublease and an assignment, or the one that is not referred to would be permitted. There is a significant difference between an assignment and a sublease. An assignment of a lease is the conveyance by the tenant of its entire interest in the lease and the property. A sublease is a transfer by the tenant of less than its entire interest in the property because it is either for a term that is shorter than the lease term or for less than all the space leased to the tenant. In an assignment, the tenant is replaced by the assignee, and the tenant no longer has any interest in the lease or the property. In a sublease, the tenant remains primarily liable on the lease, and the subtenant has no direct relationship with the landlord. In neither a sublease nor an assignment is the original tenant released from its obligations under the lease unless and until the landlord specifically agrees to release the original tenant. Similarly, neither the landlord nor the tenant has an obligation to the subtenant, and the subtenant has no obligation to the landlord.

If the subtenant defaults in performing its obligations under the sublease, it could trigger a default in the lease. This could cause a termination of the tenant's interest in the property regardless of the tenant's involvement. Additionally, if the subtenant is paying a substantial rent to the tenant and the tenant is failing to pay its rent to the landlord, the landlord cannot sue the tenant for failing to pass the rent along to the landlord. Subtenants frequently require that the tenant obtain the landlord's execution of a nondisturbance agreement, which protects the subtenant from a default by the tenant. The landlord may want to recognize the subtenant so that the landlord can require, as a condition of its permitting the sublease, that the subtenant recognize the rights of the landlord in the event that the lease between the landlord and the tenant is terminated.

The landlord will also want to be certain that the lease requires the tenant to indemnify the landlord against any loss, liability, or expense arising from the tenant's use of the property or the use of the property by the tenant's customers, employees, and invitees. Indemnification makes the tenant liable for any expense incurred by the landlord in defending itself or paying any costs or expenses of settlement regardless of whether the tenant is actually at fault for the expense. The indemnification provisions should specify the tenant's obligation to indemnify the landlord. The landlord should be indemnified by the tenant due to the tenant's exclusive control over the property during the term of the lease, so that the tenant should be responsible for anything that occurs on the property during the lease term.

If the tenant has limited its indemnification only to claims arising during the term of the lease and only to the extent of the insurance that is being carried against such risks, the landlord should determine that the lease requires the tenant to maintain comprehensive general liability insurance against any accidents in the tenant's portion or in the public areas of the property. The lease usually requires that the tenant either will pay for the cost of the insurance or will include the cost as part of the landlord's reimbursable expenses. Liability insurance insures against death or injury to persons or property to a maximum fixed amount per accident. The landlord should be certain that the lease requires a reasonable minimum amount of such insurance. Insurance against bodily injury insures only against physical injury to a person, whereas personal injury insurance includes such torts as false arrest and malicious prosecution.

MANAGEMENT AGREEMENT

Many properties are managed by professional managing agents, who receive a fee for managing the property for the owner. Many, but not all, managing agents are quite adept at their jobs. As indicated in Chapter 3, the property owner must frequently manage the managing agent to be certain that the interest in the property is being properly protected.

The basis of the relationship is a fiduciary one, and the manager owes the owner a high duty of care in handling the property. Many managing agents are hired for extended periods of time and are subject to detailed management agreements.

The most important aspect of the management agreement is that the funds received from the owner's property should not be commingled with the managing agent's other funds, including funds received by the managing agent for other properties. In this way, the owner can easily check on the status of the funds. Similarly, expenditures for the property should be paid out of the owner's funds and not a general disbursement account. The managing agent should also be required to bond employees, to protect the owner from any funds being stolen.

Among the managing agent's obligations, which should be stated in the agreement, are the hiring and firing of employees; the paying of the property's expenses, mortgage debt service, and real estate and other taxes; and the maintaining of certain minimum levels of insurance. Whether the owner wants to rely on the agent to perform other tasks depends on the needs of the owner and the property and the expertise and trustworthiness of the managing agent.

The agreement should require the managing agent to deliver monthly reports to the owner not later than the middle of the following month. The reports should contain detailed descriptions of all the property's income and expenses. This allows the owner the opportunity to carefully monitor the property. The owner may also want to sign every check, or checks over a certain amount (e.g., $500), or only checks for unusual expenses. The managing agent can also be utilized as a leasing agent, if he or she has the capacity to perform this function.

5

Residential Property

Residential real estate can be a rental apartment building, garden apartments, townhouses, a cooperatively owned building, or a condominium building. The property may contain a handful of units or thousands of units in a single building or may be a complex containing dozens of buildings. Regardless of the property, all residential real estate has one thing in common: Because the property is being used as a residence, it will require a high degree of maintenance and the owner will be forced to deal with tenants who will not approach problems from a business perspective.

Basically, residential property falls within four categories:

1. Property that is tenant owned (e.g., cooperatives and condominiums)
2. Property that is subject to governmental rental laws
3. Property that is rented based upon the free market rent without governmental intervention
4. Housing that is financed or otherwise provided by the government.

Of the four categories, the most problematic for the owner is property that is subject to government-imposed limitations on rent increases and obligations to renew leases to tenants.

The reason for the problems involved in housing that is subject to rent laws is directly related to the housing scarcity that results from the limitations placed on the laws of supply and demand. Whether or not rental laws are necessary is a political decision, however, the effect of the laws is obvious and all manner of housing is affected. The arbitrary limitations imposed on rent increases prevent developers and owners from increasing the supply of housing, because their return will be limited. Such laws also turn landlords into cooperative and condominium converters to enable them to maximize their return on the property, and preclude many landlords from being able to, or wanting to, maintain property in the highest possible standard.

Herein lies the problem in discussing residential real estate—identifying and solving the problems of residential real estate are far more difficult than doing so for commercial, industrial, or recreational real estate. Moreover, the problems of residential real estate are more directly related to the local laws, regulations, customs, and environment than any other form of real estate investment. The problems of residential real estate are also tied to the emotional attachments of tenants to their homes. Regardless of the reason, the landlord is frequently considered the enemy, which leads tenants to do and say inappropriate things. Because some landlords treat their tenants despicably and provide minimum services or upkeep of their property, these tenants become frustrated with the conditions in which they live. Someone working in a commercial building with a leaking roof or a broken toilet will fix the problem, whereas someone living with the same condition will find it unbearable. The tenant is unhappy about the situation, blames the landlord, and does not want to know that the landlord is being tightfisted because of economics. Similarly, the landlord resents the tenant for objecting to pay what the landlord believes is the higher market rent while wanting an increase in services, which the landlord cannot afford.

The benefit of leasing property to commercial tenants is that most understand the factors that influence the landlord's actions, do not require the high level of service that residential tenants require, and, except in unusual circumstances, maintain the property themselves. Moreover, in many instances, commercial leases are net and triple net leases, in which the landlord is not required to perform any services. The ownership of residential property requires the owner's full-time attention, because of the numerous factors that require the owner to act immediately and the possibility that a successful property can deteriorate quickly. This chapter explores the factors that can adversely affect residential property and describes actions the owner can take to protect his or her investment in the property.

RENTAL PROPERTY

The ownership of residential rental real estate with its concomitant short-term leases has both advantages and disadvantages over commercial real estate. The short-term residential lease means that the property's owner has the ability to project rents that appreciate faster in an inflationary market; however, this also means that the income can fall faster if newer and better equipped properties open in the vicinity of the owner's property. In markets that have enacted residential rent controls, which place an artificial impediment to the laws of supply and demand, the rent control laws reduce the likelihood that tenants will give up their low rents and move. There is also no motivation for older tenants to surrender larger low-rent apartments for smaller high-rent apartments. This limitation on movement precludes the landlord from being able to increase rents in order to maintain a return on investment in direct relation to the cost of living.

Another issue in residential property that causes the landlord difficulty is competition. Residential properties are constantly being constructed and upgraded, thus competing for tenants with existing properties. Each time a property is constructed or renovated, the tenants in an existing property consider moving out of their existing homes. Sometimes they are precluded from acting expeditiously by the terms of their leases, the significantly higher rents in the new location, the arbitrarily lower rents that are affected by government intervention, and the inconvenience of moving. However, the tenants' failure to move is rarely caused by a loyalty to the existing landlord. The relevant factors are ones over which the landlord has little or no control. Under such circumstances, the landlord must then spend significant sums of money to compete to retain its existing tenants. Also, if the tenants remain, they will probably refuse to pay renewal rents that are as high as they would pay at the new location.

The problems are not limited only to the properties that have controlled rents. The problem with properties that are subject to short-term residential leases is that short leases force the landlord to deal with changes affecting the property much faster than for similarly situated commercial properties. The rental income derived from the property can be adversely affected by something as broad based as a general economic recession or a deteriorating neighborhood or something as localized as a single tenant who is a nuisance and who causes other tenants to move. Unfortunately, short-term leases permit tenants to react to problems by moving or negotiating for a lower rent regardless of the landlord's operating costs. Moreover, all residential leases are short term (i.e., six months to three years), so there is no continuing base of support for the property as in a shopping center, where an anchor tenant may be committed to the property for 20 or 25 years. However, the anchor tenant's long-term lease protects it from increasing rents in an inflationary economy, whereas a residential tenant (where property is not subject to rent control laws) can face rent increases each time the lease comes up for renewal.

Residential properties frequently develop vacancies quickly due to the tendency of tenants to leave when problems begin to develop. This forces the landlord to lease the space to less desirable tenants or for lower rents to maintain its occupancy rates. If the owner is unable to continue paying its operating expenses and debt service, it is forced to keep the property leased. This places the landlord in the unfortunate position of being required to generate cash in whatever method is available, including accepting the first prospective tenants who want to lease an apartment. This could further accelerate the property's decline.

Another problem with residential rental property is that the industry is highly regulated, regardless of whether the locality imposes any controls on the rent that the landlord can charge. Because tenants and their children live and sleep at the property, the local government is very concerned as to the health, safety, and general well-being of the residents and, therefore, the physical condition of the property. This concern results in numerous laws, rules, and regulations with which the owner must comply at all times.

Moreover, developing rental residential property is one of the riskiest projects that can be undertaken. Although the lead time can be the same three to five years as in developing any other kind of property, unlike commercial property, the landlord cannot have leases executed until the project is completed and ready to open. This problem is exacerbated by the fact that few tenants are able to project their space needs over lengthy periods of time and are less likely to be able to deal with an economic downturn than are businesses.

An additional problem is that residential rental real estate requires extraordinary amounts of repairs to maintain the property in its current condition. There is an inverse relationship between the amount of money that will have to be expended to maintain the property and the income level of the inhabitants. The least expensive housing requires the highest degree of repair and maintenance, while the owner is the least able to afford to have it done properly. Leasing property to higher income individuals does not necessarily resolve the problem, because they have a higher demand for services and expect the property to be maintained in a new condition. However, there is a steady flow of a much higher level of income with which to maintain the property.

Financing rental property also creates problems for the owner due to the absence of long-term leases. Lenders are extremely cautious in lending against residential property, especially newly constructed projects. The lender's concern is that the landlord will not be able to quickly lease enough space to creditworthy tenants to cover the property's debt service and operating expenses. However, the lender must be able to project the property's income and expenses before it issues its construction and permanent financing commitment, which in some instances occurs years before the property is due to open. The lender is therefore forced to gamble on the owner's ability to attract a sufficient number of quality and qualified tenants to enable the owner to profitably operate the property. The difficulty is that the lender must make this determination before the owner can approach any tenant and, even if it can, a potential tenant is unlikely to commit to the project significantly in advance of its being available. Individuals are not commercial enterprises that can anticipate their space needs years in advance.

Notwithstanding all the problems that have been discussed, residential property is still probably the most popular form of real estate investment, particularly for small investors. To the small investor who is prepared to use his or her savings to acquire the property and then upgrade it through "sweat equity," residential property can be the perfect investment, particularly if the investor intends to reside in or near the property. Sweat equity means that the owners actually maintain and manage the property themselves.

The ownership of residential real estate is a labor- and management-intensive business, in which a substantial portion of the operating income is utilized for three items: real estate taxes, debt service, and operating costs. The success of a property therefore requires the owner to maintain and increase the rental income, while maintaining control over the three major expense items. Very little can be done about escalating real estate taxes, other than for the owner to file a tax certiorari petition every year to protest the municipality's assessment of the fair market value of the property for real estate tax purposes. The amount of debt service is directly related to the amount of debt on the property, the interest rate, and the other loan terms. Therefore, the property's success depends upon the owner's ability to control the operating expenses, which is not usually easy to accomplish.

The other thing owners have attempted to do to improve the return on their investment in a property is to increase the income the property generates. To accomplish this daunting task, the owner probably has to make a capital investment in the property by improving the condition of the property, providing additional amenities or services, or attempting to increase the rent without losing all the tenants. Although rent can be increased gradually over time, as leases come up from renewal, the increased rent will probably not do much more than cover increases in operating expenses since the last increase in rent. If, however, the rent is increased by something more than a marginal amount, the owner should attempt to avoid the tendency of retaining it and, instead, should invest the money back into the property to be able to obtain rent increases from other tenants.

The landlord can also increase cash flow and improve the property's reputation by adding amenities. This could require a capital expenditure by the landlord to pay the cost of any of the following:

- New windows
- New kitchen or bathroom fixtures
- Painting
- Repaving the parking lot
- Redecorating the lobby or hallways
- Installing a swimming pool
- Installing a health club
- Landscaping
- Automating portions of the building
- Building indoor garages
- Combining apartments to make larger units, to satisfy demand
- Subdividing apartments into smaller units, to satisfy demand
- Utilizing available space for a playroom or a storage facility
- New carpeting.

Although each of these additions will cost additional sums, if the market for the apartments exists, it can be money well spent.

If, however, the area is in an economic recession and the likely tenants cannot afford to pay higher rents or to move into the project, then the cost of adding amenities will further erode the landlord's diminishing cash flow. Under such circumstances, the landlord should find ways of reducing its overhead without diminishing the services performed for its tenants. There is no reason to act in such a way as to create additional problems, by unnecessarily antagonizing the existing tenants.

Another method some rental landlords have found to increase their profit on rental real estate is to convert the property from a rental to a cooperative or condominium form of ownership. In such an event, the landlord sells portions of the property to the tenants and receives in return far more than it could have received by selling the entire property to another rental landlord. Where another landlord would pay only seven to ten times the annual rent for the property, individual purchasers

EXAMPLE

A building contains 75 apartments and has an aggregate rent roll of
$675,000 per year and net operating income after expenses of
$275,000. A typical sales prices as a rental building would be between
eight and ten times the building's net operating income, or a sales
price of between $2,200,000 and $2,750,000. If the building was
converted to cooperative or condominium ownership, the apartments
would sell for their market value as residences, which would be based
only indirectly on the rent roll. Accordingly, the sales price might be
as much as $5,625,000, if the 75 apartments were two-bedroom
apartments and would sell for $75,000 cash. There would, therefore,
be a significant premium in converting the building to common
ownership, provided that a market for such housing exists.

would pay their estimation of the fair market value of the individual
apartments, virtually without regard for the rent the former tenants
were paying (see Example).

COOPERATIVE CORPORATIONS

A cooperative corporation is an ordinary business corporation that owns a
property. However, the corporation's stockholders have a right, because
of their ownership of stock in the corporation, to the exclusive use of an
apartment or a specified portion of the buildings constructed on the property. The right of the stockholders to the exclusive use of an apartment or
other portion of the property is contained within a proprietary lease for
the apartment in which the shareholder resides. Therefore, each shareholder receives a stock certificate, which indicates his or her interest in
the corporation, and a proprietary lease, which describes the right of the
stockholder to the apartment and the rights and obligations of the stockholder and the corporation with regard to the apartment.

The cooperative corporation is governed by its certificate of incorporation and the bylaws of the corporation, and is subject to the corporate law
of the state in which it was formed. The bylaws establish the rules by
which the corporation will operate, describe the procedures to be used to
elect officers and directors, identify when shareholder meetings and di-
rector meetings can and should be held, specify the manner in which
stock certificates should be issued, and describe the rights and remedies

of the shareholders. The bylaws also describe the manner in which the apartments or other portions of the property are to be distributed among the shareholders and the shares allocated to the lessee of each apartment or other unit. The bylaws describe the procedure to be followed in transferring and financing the shares of the corporation and the method of adopting rules and regulations for the operation of the corporation. The bylaws also provide the board of directors with the ability to set the maintenance payments (i.e., the monthly charges paid by the tenants/shareholders for the use of their apartments or units), the right to allocate the shares among the units, the exclusive right for the owner of certain shares to use a specific apartment or office, and the board of directors' right to approve or disapprove of the purchaser of the corporation's shares and any shareholder's right to finance its shares. The bylaws also provide the board of directors with the right to regroup space. Most importantly, the bylaws provide that, notwithstanding any shareholder's financing, the corporation has a first lien on each shareholder's shares as security for any indebtedness or obligation owed by the shareholder to the corporation. This provision protects all the shareholders by requiring a particular shareholder's lender to make certain that the maintenance is paid by that shareholder to preclude the lender from losing its lien on the shares.

The proprietary lease distinguishes a cooperative corporation from any other kind of corporation. This lease provides the shareholders with the exclusive use of a portion of the corporation's property (i.e., an apartment or other defined portion of the building), notwithstanding the fact that the property is owned by the corporation, which is owned by all the shareholders. The proprietary lease requires that the shareholder/lessee pay its pro rata share of the corporation's expenses through monthly maintenance payments, which are similar to rent payments. Unlike an ordinary residential lease, the amount of the maintenance charges is not fixed in advance when the lease is executed, but is subject to the continuous examination and determination by the board of directors based upon the costs of operating the corporation and the real estate it owns. Each shareholder's share of the maintenance charges and assessment is based upon that shareholder's percentage of shares in the corporation.

The holder of a proprietary lease has the right to the exclusive use of a specific apartment as long as the shareholder continues to own the shares allocated to that apartment or unit and is in good standing with regard to its obligations to the corporation. The proprietary lease is not irrevocable and provides the corporation with the right to terminate the lease if a shareholder/lessee fails to pay his or her maintenance charges or assessments; or fails to maintain the unit; or attempts to sell, encumber, or sublease the unit; or makes structural changes to the unit without the board of directors' consent.

The maintenance payments are used to pay the corporation's expenses in operating the real estate, including the real estate taxes on the entire property and debt service on any mortgage the corporation has on the real estate. If a shareholder fails to make his or her maintenance payments, the other shareholders would be required to pay the difference, because the property's operating expenses, real estate taxes, and debt service still have to be paid. Unlike virtually any other kind of corporation, the shareholders of a residential cooperative corporation can deduct on their income tax the portion of the monthly maintenance payments attributable to the real estate taxes and interest paid by the corporation, providing that the corporation satisfies the conditions contained in the Internal Revenue Code.

CONDOMINIUMS

Property can also be commonly owned through a condominium association. A condominium more closely resembles the actual ownership of a real property than a cooperative. A condominium usually refers to a multiunit property, each unit of which is owned exclusively by a separate individual or entity, with the property's common elements owned by all the unit owners. In this way, a single building or a group of buildings can be divided into a group of condominium units, or a part of a building can be turned into a condominium with smaller portions of the building or buildings becoming the units. The basis of the concept of a condominium is that the individual owners actually receive deeds and own undivided portions of the building.

The unit owner has the exclusive right to the use of the unit, together with the right to sell, mortgage, lease, or otherwise convey the unit, except as limited by the association's declaration of condominium or bylaws. Each unit owner has the right to use the common elements, but such use is limited to the use for which each common element was intended. Nevertheless, no unit owner can do anything to his or her unit or the common elements that would adversely affect the use, enjoyment, or safety of the other unit owners with regard to their units or the common elements. The basic elements of a condominium are (1) the individual ownership of each of the units, (2) an undivided interest in the common elements, and

(3) an agreement among the owners relating to the use, maintenance, and operation of the common elements. The common elements in a condominium include the building's foundation, walls, roof, lobbies, stairs, elevators, entrances and exits, basement, recreational facilities, parking areas, land upon which the building is constructed, and heating, electrical, plumbing, and air conditioning systems.

A condominium is formed at such time as the declaration of condominium is filed, providing the local requirements for the filing are satisfied. The declaration is recorded in the same manner as a deed. The declaration states that the property is being converted to condominium ownership, contains a legal description of the property, describes all the units and their share of the common elements, states the voting rights of each unit owner, and provides for the enactment of the bylaws. Declarations of condominium frequently describe the use to which the units and the common elements can be put and can also include any other details relating to the condominium or its operation, unless it is specifically precluded by the local condominium law. The declaration of condominium is similar to a subdivision map in that it separates the building or buildings into subunits and it describes the condominium use, and the relation of the unit owners to each other and to their relative interests in the common areas. The declaration describes the common areas, the percentage interest that each unit owner has in the common areas, and the method of allocating shared expenses.

The declaration usually provides the condominium association with a right of first refusal, allowing the association to purchase the unit of any unit owner wishing to sell to an outsider whom the board of managers finds objectionable. This is as close as a condominium board gets to the right of a cooperative's board of directors to reject a purchaser. Because a condominium involves an interest in real estate rather than stock, the condominium board does not have the right to reject a purchaser, but can only purchase the unit that the owner is attempting to sell. Therefore, the selling unit owner is not placed in jeopardy by the board's refusal to permit a transfer or financing.

Like a cooperative, a condominium operates pursuant to the terms, conditions, and provisions contained within its bylaws. The condominium's bylaws provide for the operation of the condominium, establish procedures for the election and operation of the condominium's board of managers, and provide for the use and regulation of the common areas. The bylaws also provide for the formation, purpose, and powers of the condominium's board, and establish the board's power to create a budget, collect common charges, and authorize expenditures for the condominium (see Example).

EXAMPLE

The following chart indicates the differences between a cooperative and a condominium.

	Cooperative	Condominium
Monthly payment	Maintenance	Common charge
Ownership document	Stock certificate and proprietary lease	Deed for unit
Board rights on sale	Can reject buyer	Right of first refusal
Mortgage on building	Yes	No
Financing unit	Security agreement	Mortgage
Board approval of financing	Yes	No
Decision maker	Board of directors	Board of managers

COOPERATIVE OR CONDOMINIUM FINANCING

Two levels of financing are possible in a cooperative or condominium: (1) financing by the ownership entity (i.e., the cooperative or the condominium) secured by the entity's property (i.e., the building) in order to acquire or refinance the property or to finance improvements, and (2) financing by a cooperative shareholder or a condominium unit owner of his or her interest in his or her unit. A condominium unit owner in any state can finance his or her condominium unit the same as any other form of real estate; however, only seventeen states (Alabama, Alaska, California, Connecticut, Georgia, Illinois, Maine, Missouri, Minnesota, Nebraska, North Carolina, New Hampshire, New Mexico, Pennsylvania, Rhode Island, Virginia, and Wisconsin) and the District of Columbia permit financing of an operating condominium building. The reason for the difficulty in financing a condominium building is that the condominium association owns nothing other than the common elements, and financing would require the approval of each unit owner, each of whom would be required to execute the loan documents.

There is no difficulty, however, financing a cooperatively owned building, which can have a mortgage placed on the cooperative corporation's real property as with any other kind of real estate owned by a business corporation. Authorization for the loan can be made by either the affirmative vote of the majority of the directors or, if required by its bylaws or certificate of incorporation, by a majority vote of the corporation's shareholders. Regardless of whether the shareholders vote for financing, the corporation and all the shareholders are bound by the terms of the financing, and the mortgage becomes a first lien on the corporation's real estate. Accordingly, even though the shareholders are not personally obligated to repay the indebtedness, the corporation's failure to comply with the terms of the mortgage could result in the loss of its interest in the property and the shareholder's loss of their equity in the corporation and their homes.

Except in those instances where condominium financing is allowed, the situation is different for a condominium. Each unit owner has the right to arrange for his or her own financing. A mortgage cannot be placed against the entire building unless every unit owner agrees to subordinate his or her interest in the condominium building to the lien of the mortgage. Therefore, if an individual unit owner fails to pay his or her mortgage, it will not create a financial problem for the other condominium owners. However, this limitation on financing does not preclude financing to be placed on the building or the unsold units by the sponsor or developer of the condominium, whose construction loan is secured by the unsold portions of the property. Although the sponsor's default in paying the debt service on such financing will not directly jeopardize the unit owners, if neither the sponsor nor the lender pays the common charges on the sponsor's unsold units and the condominium does not have the income to pay its operating expenses, the other unit owners' interests will be placed at risk because there will not be sufficient income to operate the property.

Moreover, notwithstanding the mortgages that exist on cooperatively owned buildings, there are inherent risks in such financing for the shareholders. The risk arises from the fact that even though the mortgage is a lien on the corporation's real estate and no shareholder is personally obligated to repay all or any part of the indebtedness, because the payment of the mortgage's debt service comes from the shareholder's monthly maintenance payments, no shareholder can pay that shareholder's pro rata share of the indebtedness. Accordingly, even if there are shareholders whose maintenance payments are current, if a number of shareholders fail to pay their maintenance and the mortgage goes into default, the entire building could be taken and sold at the subsequent foreclosure. Moreover, the mortgage can be foreclosed and the ownership of the real estate can be lost even if the mortgage default is caused by a nonmonetary default or a highly technical reason or is caused by something over which the shareholders have no control, such as casualty or condemnation to the building or the embezzlement of the corporation's funds.

To prevent this from happening, the proprietary lease and bylaws of the cooperative corporation should provide the cooperative corporation with the ability to act quickly after a shareholder fails to pay his or her maintenance. This includes the right to terminate the proprietary lease and cancel the stock certificate of a defaulting shareholder. In this way, the corporation can sell the stock (and concomitant right to the unit) at auction, repay itself for the unpaid maintenance charges, and pay the debt service on the building's mortgage and the other operating expenses. The balance of the auction proceeds, after the costs are paid, go to the defaulting shareholder or its lender. The alternative would be for the shareholders to pay the maintenance costs of those who are in default or otherwise make up the shortfall.

This problem is avoided in a condominium, where each unit owner arranges for his or her own financing. The nondefaulting shareholders or nondefaulting unit owners have no obligation to satisfy the indebtedness if the individual shareholder or unit owner fails to repay the loan. The difference between the condominium share loan or unit mortgage and the mortgage on the cooperative building is that, in the former, the lien is against the assets of the particular borrower rather than the interests of the group. However, the problem in a condominium occurs if the condominium building requires a major repair or a substantial sum of money is otherwise required. In such an event, the condominium association assesses the unit owners because a condominium does not have the wherewithal to obtain a mortgage on the jointly owned property. The condominium association must then hope that the unit owners pay the assessment expeditiously or the condominium's board could be forced to declare a default.

Both the owners of interests in cooperative shares and the owners of condominium units are able to finance the acquisition of their interests or to use the stock or unit as security for a loan at a later date. In a condominium, the unit owner owns his or her unit, which is an interest in real estate, and the owner can borrow against the interest and give the lender a first (or subsequent) mortgage on the borrower's unit without involvement by the condominium board. A cooperative shareholder, however, is unable to provide the lender with a mortgage on real estate because the shareholder does not own an interest in the real estate; the shareholder only owns stock in a corporation that owns the real estate. Therefore, the lender's lien will be on the borrower's stock in the corporation, and the loan document will be a security agreement, rather than an actual mortgage. Furthermore, the borrower is unable to provide his or her lender with a first lien on the stock, because the corporation has the first lien on the shares as security for the shareholder's obligation to pay his or her maintenance. To complicate matters further, the shareholder cannot complete the loan without the approval of the cooperative's board of directors, which can unreasonably withhold or delay approval. Because the lender obtains a lien against the stock, which is subject to the corporation's lien, the lender must also obtain the corporation's agreement to notify the lender in the event of a default by the borrower in his or her obligations to the corporation and provide the lender with the opportunity to cure the default. This is usually done with the execution of a recognition agreement by the borrower, the lender, and the corporation.

What complicates matters further is that the cooperative's board of directors has the right to approve any purchaser at a foreclosure sale or any purchaser to whom the lender attempts to sell the shares. If a condominium unit owner defaults in making his or her mortgage payments, however, the lender can simply foreclose upon the mortgage and sell the apartment without any difficulty.

The other problem for lenders is actually acquiring the property if a default does occur. It is difficult to declare a default on, and possibly foreclose, a lien against a commonly owned piece of real estate, whether it is a cooperative or a condominium. The problem is an emotional and political one for the courts, faced with depriving a large group of people of their homes and investments. The mechanics of the foreclosure depend on the laws of the state in which the property is located, and these frequently protect the borrower, particularly a residential borrower. If the cooperative corporation fails to pay the debt service on a mortgage encumbering its property, then the mortgagee has the right to accelerate the indebtedness and declare the mortgage note due and payable. Therefore, if a cooperative corporation or condominium association fails to obtain the property prior to or at the foreclosure sale, the shareholders or unit owners would lose the right to own their units and the building would revert to rental status.

Moreover, those shareholders who had previously pledged their shares or gave mortgages on their units in order to borrow funds (regardless of whether it was to finance their acquisition or an improvement or to obtain their equity), would find that those share loans have become immediately due and payable because of the foreclosure. Unlike the mortgage on the building, the share loans would be with full recourse against the borrowers. The former shareholders or unit owners would then have to deal with both the loss of equity in their units and having their personal loans becoming payable.

SPONSOR/DEVELOPER DEFAULTS

In most instances, the biggest risk to the cooperative corporation or the condominium association is a default by the developer or the sponsor of the conversion to cooperative or condominium ownership, due to the number of units he or she owns. The sponsor of the conversion of an existing building to cooperative or condominium ownership or the developer of a new building to be owned in common would attempt to sell as many units to occupants or nonresidents as the market would allow and then would have to retain ownership of the units that were not sold. This would force the sponsor to pay the maintenance or common charges on the unsold units, although the sponsor could retain whatever rent was received from the rental tenant of each unit that was not sold. If the rent was greater than the maintenance or common charges and real estate taxes for the sponsor's unit and the sponsor's debt service on the unit, if any, the sponsor would have a positive cash flow and would continue to pay its obligations and the cooperative or condominium would not be adversely affected by the sponsor's default.

However, if the proceeds from the sale of units and the rents the remaining units could produce were lower than the sponsor's carrying charges for those units, the owners would be at risk that the sponsor would stop paying the maintenance or common charges. The sponsor's default would not initially be obvious to the shareholders who purchased shares or units in the cooperative or condominium buildings. The sponsor, as the majority shareholder and manager of the corporation and the building, would collect the maintenance or common charges, pay the expenses, and provide the minority shareholders with no information regarding the corporation's or condominium's deteriorating financial condition, which would be due to the sponsor's failure to pay its maintenance or common charges. The problems would accelerate because of the absence of sales and the sponsor's being required to continue paying high interest rates. The sponsor would soon run out of capital or refuse to use its remaining capital and would begin to default in meeting its obligations.

In theory, sponsors could default in one of the following ways:

- Simply stop paying the maintenance or common charges on the unsold units
- Not only stop paying the maintenance or common charges on the unsold units, but fail to pay some or all of the operating expenses, especially the mortgage or the real estate taxes on the building, in

order to hide the fact that they are not paying the maintenance on the unsold units

- Take back a wraparound mortgage as part of the purchase price for the building and are paid debt service on the wraparound mortgage by the cooperative corporation, but do not pay the debt service on the underlying mortgage.

There would be an inverse relationship between the seriousness of the problem and the percentage of interests owned by the sponsor. Sponsors who owned few units would be at a small risk to the building and would have more of an incentive to avoid default. In most instances, the sponsor's default would not be obvious because the sponsor's failure to pay its maintenance or common charges would be hidden by the operating expenses or debt service that the sponsor failed to pay. Unfortunately, the problem would not become obvious until the deficiency became so large that the sponsor, the shareholders, and the unit owners could not readily resolve the problem. Eventually it could be resolved only if the shareholders or unit owners were willing and able to pay large assessments or tremendous increases in maintenance or common charges to avoid a calamity. However, they could not afford this alternative, especially while the sponsor, usually the owner of the largest number of shares or units, was in default.

The first step in analyzing the strength and weakness of a cooperative or condominium building would be to determine the portion of the building that is owned by resident shareholders or unit owners and the portion that is owned by the sponsor. If the building is substantially owned by individual resident shareholders or by a sponsor who is not in default, there is less reason to worry that the property will not survive as a cooperative or condominium. However, if the property is in default and is substantially owned by resident shareholders, or if the sponsor is current in paying its maintenance but the resident shareholders are in default, then it is unlikely that the building will be able to carry itself unless another source of income can be identified.

If a cooperative or condominium building requires additional income, that income may come from renting or selling either professional spaces for significant up-front payment or space in the building that is not currently being used or is being used inefficiently. In such an event, the corporation will have significant additional income, thereby permitting the maintenance charges to be reduced, which should increase the number of shareholders who pay their maintenance or unit owners who pay their common charges. Conversely, if the building is unable to meet its obligations due to reasons other than the sponsor's default, then either the unit owners are unable to meet their financial obligations or the building itself has such serious problems that the expenses are significantly in excess of the amount that the owners can afford to pay. Under such circumstances, the maintenance or common charges will have to be increased and the shareholders or unit owners may be forced to sell their units to those who are better able to make the higher monthly payments. The units can be sold; however, the sales prices will be affected by the monthly maintenance or common charge obligation. A default caused by the sponsor's failure to pay maintenance can be cured either by selling the remaining shares at the current market value or reducing the price of the shares to the point where they become an economic investment.

Another alternative would be for the cooperative or condominium to obtain and then give away the sponsor's units for free. This is possible because the other owners' concern is merely finding replacement owners who are willing and able to pay the monthly maintenance or common charges and not the actual fair market value of the shares. As long as the existing shareholders or unit owners use the appropriate means of obtaining the sponsor's units, they may have the wherewithal of resolving the problem by reselling the units, unless the units are occupied by tenants who are paying a below-market rent. Under those circumstances, the owners will be required to subsidize the difference between the tenants' rents and those units' shares of the building's operating expenses until the occupying tenants either purchase or vacate the units. An additional solution for this problem is to offer the occupants money to abandon the unit and terminate their leases or to offer the occupants an attractive discounted price to purchase the units. In either event, the cooperative or condominium will no longer be forced to subsidize the rent.

Each tenant's response will depend on the length of time the tenant is likely to remain in the unit, the age and business of the occupant, the financial condition of the building, and the market value of the unit, taking into account the number of unsold units available and the market for this size unit. If several adjacent units are available, regardless of whether they are next to each other or on top of each other, the other owners may consider combining the units to make a single, more valuable unit. Conversely, if the market exists for smaller units and the cooperative has a lien against a larger unit, then it may consider dividing the larger unit into two or more smaller units.

Another problem that may occur is if the maintenance is too high due to the existence of a large mortgage or a mortgage with a high interest rate. Because debt service is the largest component of maintenance, a reduction in the mortgage or the interest rate would result in a lower maintenance cost and a more saleable unit. Under these circumstances and assuming the lender has a significant number of unsold apartments in the building, and there are a number of units available in the building for sale, it might be worth the board's time to consider funding the reduction of the mortgage and refinancing the indebtedness to reduce the interest rate.

In deciding the best manner of proceeding, anyone considering acquiring units in the building should obtain copies of and review the following:

- The building's financial statements for the last few years to determine whether the operating expenses have been consistent or are subject to fluctuations, and whether capital improvements are necessary or desirable to improve the value of the property

- The financial statements to determine whether a low interest rate mortgage is due to mature in the near future or whether a tax abatement is about to end

- The minutes of the board of directors or board of managers and the minutes of the annual meetings to determine whether the property has long-term problems that have been discussed by the board or the unit owners and need to be considered by the lender as a potential risk

- Any recent engineering report of all or portions of the building to determine whether there has been significant deferred maintenance that will have to be addressed in the near future

- The title report for the property and a local, municipal violation search to determine whether there are liens, encumbrances, or other limitations on the title to the property or work that must be done to resolve the property's problems

- Insurance reports to see if portions of the property concern the insurance carriers as having potential risks to the owner, and therefore the possibility of future expenses, thereby causing an assessment or a maintenance increase.

In each default scenario, it is in everyone's best interests for each participant to remain as flexible as possible. Flexibility does not mean allowing the unit owners to ignore the problem and take whatever steps the building's lender deems appropriate. Flexibility means that the parties must consider the problems of the individual unit owners, who are really innocent victims of a softening real estate market, and the sponsor's and lender's optimism. It is important to note that there are different levels of problems with which the parties must deal.

Most members of the cooperative's board of directors or the condominium's board of managers are unsophisticated in real estate matters and are busy with their full-time occupations. Thus, to protect everyone's investment, the building's lender may be forced to take the lead in resolving the problems. This is a particularly thankless job because the shareholders and unit owners will not trust the building's lender and may believe, in some instances rightfully, that the building's lender is interested only in protecting its own interests in the property. However, it is readily apparent that both the lender and the resident owners have a common interest of protecting their investments in the property and making certain that the property does not deteriorate in value. Nevertheless, the building's lender will believe that is has the greater interest because it has far more money invested in the building than any other owner, whereas the residents will feel they have the greater interest because they live in the building.

The most significant problem arising from the sponsor's default is the sudden shortfall in the building's cash flow, which would require the nondefaulting owners to make up the difference in maintenance or common charges until the default ends. If the sponsor owns 75 percent of the units, each nondefaulting unit owner would have to pay four times as much in maintenance or common charges as before the default to have sufficient funds to operate the building; this situation would be unacceptable, if not impossible, for the unit owners.

Therefore, the only course available to the corporation or the condominium is to obtain and resell the sponsor's unsold units or shares as quickly as possible or, if the sponsor has financed the unsold units or shares, require the sponsor's lender to begin paying the maintenance or the common charges as quickly as possible. The failure of the cooperative or the condominium board to act can have a catastrophic result for the unit owners or the shareholders. If the corporation does not act and the underlying mortgage goes into default, the corporation's only recourse would be to either delay the foreclosure or file for bankruptcy protection. Foreclosure is a horrendous consequence for the shareholders for the following reasons:

- The bank takes the building.
- The shareholders lose their equity in their units and become rental tenants at the current market rent.
- The loans the shareholders obtained to secure the purchase of their stock in the corporation (i.e., the purchase of their apartments) would be immediately due and payable because the security for the loan has been lost.

- The shareholders would lose the tax deduction for any portion of their rent.
- Shareholders may have to pay recapture taxes if their loans exceeded their basis in the unit, which is possible for shareholders who borrowed against the equity in their units as the market rose.

Accordingly, in the event a judgment of foreclosure was imminent, there would be no alternative for the corporation and its shareholders but to seek the protection of the bankruptcy court. However, this also creates a problem for the holder of the underlying mortgage on the property. The ensuing reorganization could involve a cram down to alter the terms of the mortgage to assist the shareholders/tenants. More importantly, this may lead the local politicians to believe that the shareholders require legislative protection. This alternative should be anathema for the lenders.

A cooperative corporation or condominium association that finds itself in default in satisfying its mortgage obligations has a number of methods available to cure such a default, because the building is a valuable asset and the owners have the motivation to work together to resolve the problems. The following alternatives are available to the parties to help them work through the problems and avoid foreclosure:

- Seek a moratorium by the lender on payments of interest or principal while the building gets its financing in order
- Change the debt service payment schedule to reduce the required payments while the building uses the other approaches to generate additional cash flow
- Sell the corporation's other assets to reduce the indebtedness or increase the corporation's cash flow
- Sell the building, and lease back the units to the former owners at favorable rents
- Charge for, or increase the cost of, services being provided to the shareholders (i.e., laundry rooms, storage areas, recreational areas, meeting room, etc.)
- Impose assessments on the shareholders or unit owners
- Require a payment to the corporation to approve the sale or refinancing of shares or the renovation of units
- Increase the maintenance payments being charged to the shareholders

- Terminate the proprietary lease and cancel the stock certificates of those shareholders who are delinquent in the payment of their maintenance, and then sell the shares for their fair market price and reimburse the cooperative corporation for the maintenance charges and assessments that are delinquent
- Refinance the underlying indebtedness to improve the terms or obtain the benefits of a lower rate or better terms
- Sue the managing agent who may have failed to pay the debt service
- If the building was recently converted to cooperative or condominium ownership, sue the sponsor based on the failure to properly operate the building prior to, or immediately after, the conversion or the failure to disclose all the negative aspects of the acquisition or operation of the building
- Defer other payments or reduce services to the shareholders until the shortfall can be resolved
- Defend the foreclosure vigorously, especially if the mortgagee is in any way affiliated with the sponsor.

Notwithstanding the foregoing, if the sponsor financed its unsold units, the simplest solution is for the sponsor's lender to begin paying the maintenance or common charges on those units as quickly as possible. Unfortunately, the lender's instinct is to take time to consider its options, although the longer the lender waits to begin making the maintenance or common charge payments, the less valuable its collateral becomes. If the sponsor's lender fails to step in for the sponsor immediately upon learning of the default, and waits until the shareholders or unit owners have to reduce services or increase maintenance significantly, the units the sponsor's lender financed will have lost much of their original value. Alternatively, if the sponsor's lender acts quickly, such action will not increase the amount the lender pays to the corporation in maintenance because the lender is obligated for all the sponsor's past-due and current obligations; however, the units will not have deteriorated in value. Once the sponsor's units are acquired, the units can be offered for sale to either residents of the units or third parties for tremendously discounted prices. The lender or the cooperative or condominium can lower the prices for the sponsor's units below what the sponsor would have needed to charge because the sponsor had to achieve the release price set by the lender, but this is not necessary for either the cooperative or the lender.

Although initially the discounted prices would depress the market for all the units in the building, the values actually represent an increase over the nonexistent values of the units while the sponsor was in default. Remaining unsold units could then be held by the lender until the occupying tenant vacates the unit or the shares could be sold to an investor.

Alternatively, the lender or the board could offer to pay the occupying tenant to move, thereby allowing the unit to be sold at its full market value. The lender might also offer to sell its shares to the corporation, the condominium, or other investors and offer them purchase money financing. This would enable the lender to remove the loan from its books as a nonperforming loan and keep the lender out of the business of operating cooperative or condominium apartments. In any event, the first step is for the lender to recognize that, unlike other real estate collateral it might have obtained over the years, these units have significant value and, in time, the lender can be made whole.

If the units are not financed, then the nonsponsor unit owners must take control of the board of directors, terminate the sponsor's proprietary leases, and cancel its stock. The proprietary lease would also provide the corporation with the right to collect rent from the sponsor's subtenants, which the corporation should do as quickly as possible to provide the corporation with additional cash flow. In such an event, the corporation's shortfall is the difference between the maintenance that the sponsor should have paid and the rent that the rental tenants are paying. The corporation then has the same options with regard to the retention or sale of the shares as described above for the lender who financed the unsold shares.

The condominium default presents a particularly difficult situation with which to deal. The problem arises from the fact that the unit lender's lien is on the unsold units and not on the building. However, unlike with a cooperative, the lien for unpaid common charges by the condominium's board of managers is usually inferior to the lien of the first mortgage. Therefore, the holder of the mortgage on the unit is not required to pay the common charges for the unit to the condominium association. The problem that then arises is what the nondefaulting unit owners must do if the sponsor or another unit owner fails to pay its common charges, but the first mortgage lender fails to take any action.

The condominium association would then not have the money to meet its operating expenses, which could further reduce the value of the units on which the mortgagee has a lien. It therefore seems reasonable to expect that the lender should pay the common charges, just as it would pay the real estate taxes, to avoid a situation where the asset's value is reduced significantly, which would make it more difficult to sell the unit.

One option available for the condominium association would be to place a lien against the unsold condominium units to protect the association's interest in the units in case the mortgagee forecloses its mortgage. Thus, the association would be in the second position and would be reimbursed from the proceeds of the foreclosure sale after the mortgagee has been paid in full. Alternatively, if the condominium's liens were not in excess of the value of the property, the condominium's board of managers could foreclose its lien on the unit and sell the apartment subject to the mortgage.

6

Financing

One attribute of real estate ownership that makes it such a popular investment is the owner's ability to leverage an investment by being able to pay a small portion of the purchase price in cash and the balance by executing and delivering a mortgage on the property to the former owner or a lending institution or purchasing the property subject to an existing mortgage. Occasionally, properties can be purchased with a cash payment of as little as 5 to 10 percent of the purchase price, with the balance payable over an extended period of time by the purchaser's executing a purchase money mortgage and/or taking title to the property subject to a mortgage. Once the property is acquired, the owner is able to liquidate its entire investment in the property without surrendering the title to the property. This is possible because the owner is able to obtain financing for an amount that is based upon the property's current fair market value, rather than the original purchase price. Additionally, if the property's value increases further, the owner can still borrow 80 to 90 percent of the value of the property, which could be significantly in excess of the owner's cost of the property.

Thus, financing can be a more advantageous method for the owner to raise cash than selling the property, because financing does not require the owner to pay taxes on the amount received. Although the loan has to be repaid with interest, the money borrowed could be generating an equal or greater amount of money plus, in an appreciating rental market, the owner's ability to retain title to the property means that it will be able to benefit from the increased property value.

Being able to obtain financing for (and from) real estate is one of the biggest benefits available to an investor. However, excessive financing is also the greatest cause of the ruin of real estate investors and investments. Although overleveraging property or owning a property encumbered with excessive debt is one way of quickly generating a huge net worth in an appreciating real estate market, it is also the easiest way to be wiped out in periods of high interest rates or falling values or income. History is full of investors who made and lost fortunes by leveraging investments at the right time and then not being sufficiently liquid when the market turned downward (see Example).

As a matter of fact, between the late 1980s and early 1990s, real estate investors lost hundreds of millions and billions of dollars of equity when the real estate market stopped expanding and they were caught with excessive debt. The most well-known example was Donald Trump, who originally began to make money in the real estate slump of the mid 1970s, when a prior generation of investors were overleveraged, and he was able to begin accumulating property and making deals because he was not heavily financed. There is little doubt that the real estate recession of the 1990s will lead to another generation of investors who will reinvent real estate investment and then attempt to grow exponentially by leveraging investments to obtain financing for newer investments.

Basically, five levels of financing can encumber a property:

1. Purchase money financing
2. Construction and development financing

EXAMPLE

The problem inherent in overleveraging can be made apparent from the following analysis. A shopping center has a net operating income (gross income less operating expenses) of $275,000, including $50,000 in percentage rents. The property is encumbered by a $2 million mortgage bearing interest at 9 percent per annum and a 25-year amortization schedule, so the annual debt service is $201,407. The owner then refinances the mortgage to obtain an additional $250,000, so the mortgage is increased to $2,250,000 and the interest rate is increased to 10 percent, so the annual debt service payment becomes $245,349. This leaves the owner with almost $30,000 in cash flow until the real estate taxes increase by $25,000 per year and the property requires major structural repairs. The owner is then unable to pay the debt service. The problem is further compounded if the tenant paying the $50,000 in percentage rent decides to move to a larger or better equipped facility.

3. Permanent financing
4. Junior or second mortgage financing
5. Wraparound financing.

Each level of financing entails different risks to the lenders and, for that reason, the lenders have different requirements for each kind of loan. Of course, when problems arise, the lender's response to a defaulting borrower will differ based upon the kind of loan involved, the condition of the property, and the borrower's background. There are also distinct advantages and disadvantages to each kind of financing that must be carefully considered by the owner.

This chapter examines the various kinds of financing that might exist on the property and the matters that should concern the property owner in considering such financing for its property. Because the owner's biggest risks involve financing, it is important that the property owner understand the issues involving financing.

MORTGAGES

A mortgage or deed of trust is a written instrument creating a lien on real property or a leasehold interest in the real property pursuant to which the title to the real property is held as security for the repayment of a debt. (In this chapter, the word *mortgage* is used to describe any security interest on property, even though the terms used in various portions of the country may be *deed of trust, trust deed, mortgage deed,* or *deed to secure debt.*) The property owner borrows money from a lender, whose loan is evidenced by a promissory note and secured by a mortgage or other security interest, which is recorded as a lien against the property. The recording thereby provides notice to the world of the lender's interest in the property and precludes the owner from selling or further encumbering the property without the lender's involvement. This prevents the owner from circumventing the lender's ability to obtain the property in the event of a default. Usually, the loan documents include the promissory note, mortgage, an assignment of leases and rents, a security agreement, and financing statements. The last two documents provide the lender with a security interest in the personal property used with the real property. The lender may also receive a guaranty by the borrower or its principals.

The promissory note is the most important loan document, since it provides evidence of the loan, contains a promise by the borrower to repay the loan to the lender, and contains the terms of the loan's repayment. The promissory note must contain a written promise to pay a specific sum of money, be executed by the borrower to the order of the lender, and be payable either on demand or on a specific date. The promissory note may also contain more detailed payment terms, including the interest rate, a reference to the fact that the promissory note is secured by the mortgage, a description of the conditions that constitute a loan default, the existence of any grace periods, the late payment charges, and a statement as to whether the lender has an equity participation in the property. The promissory note must be executed by the borrower, but need not be recorded, although in some jurisdictions it is recorded with the mortgage.

A mortgage usually contains the following information:

- The name and address of the mortgagor (the borrower) and the mortgagee (the lender)
- The amount of the loan
- The obligation of the borrower to repay the loan and the borrower's obligation to properly operate and maintain the real estate
- A description of the property's boundaries
- A granting clause in which the borrower conveys to the lender a lien to the real estate
- Representations and warranties by the borrower as to its interest in the property and the fact that the property is free and clear of other liens except those elaborated in the mortgage
- A defeasance clause in which the lender agrees that upon payment in full of the principal debt and interest thereon, the mortgage shall be automatically void
- An elaboration of the events of default and the lender's rights in the event of a default by the borrower (traditional defaults include nonpayment of principal, interest, taxes, or ground rent; default in complying with the terms of a superior mortgage; waste of the property; structural alterations without the lender's consent; and failure to maintain insurance or to adhere to any of the conditions of the mortgage)
- An obligation of the borrower to perform all leases and to maintain the property in good repair and to maintain insurance
- An agreement by the borrower that the lender's failure to enforce any of its rights is not a waiver of such right of enforcement
- An agreement by the borrower not to sell, lease, or alter the property without the lender's consent
- An agreement by the borrower to adhere to all the loan documents.

The portions of the mortgage that require a full understanding because of the risk placed on the borrower are those provisions dealing with default, taxes and insurance, casualty and condemnation, and repairs and maintenance. It is important for the borrower to be able to understand these provisions from the lender's point of view, so that the borrower will be able to negotiate with the lender on terms that the lender will understand and can approve. This means that the lender will be more receptive to a borrower who is seeking assistance with a problem property if the borrower makes requests that do not increase the lender's risk or jeopardize its collateral for the loan. If the lender believes that the borrower wants to cooperate with the lender, the lender will be more willing to cooperate with the borrower.

The mortgage default provisions should be closely reviewed by the parties because the mortgage secures a promissory note and provides security to the lender for the payment of the indebtedness. The usual default provisions contained in the mortgage are the borrower's failure to pay the debt service on the mortgage; the borrower's failure to pay the real estate taxes, water and sewer charges, and assessments, or to maintain the insurance on the property in specified amounts, or to maintain the property; the borrower's bankruptcy or insolvency; the property's casualty or condemnation; or the borrower's taking certain actions without the lender's prior written consent. Another event of default is the sale of the property or the placement of another mortgage on the property if the mortgage contains a due on sale clause or a due on further encumbrance clause. These clauses provide the lender with an opportunity to review the loan to be certain that the interest rate is still current and that the borrower and the project are still creditworthy. It also provides the lender with an opportunity to charge the borrower a fee for consenting to the sale or refinancing.

The mortgage may provide that, to enable the lender to act quickly to protect its interest in the property, in the event of a default, the lender will have the right to accelerate the indebtedness, appoint a receiver, and commence a foreclosure proceeding as quickly after a default as possible. The lender may even refuse to provide the borrower with notice of and an opportunity to cure the performance defaults, because this could preclude the lender from acting expeditiously after a default. The borrower should attempt to negotiate an obligation on the lender to provide it with written notice of a performance default and a reasonable period of time to cure a default, unless the default is not one that can be cured quickly. In the latter event, the borrower should attempt to obtain as much time as it takes to cure the default, providing the borrower commences curing the default immediately and continues diligently to cure the default.

Lenders also are concerned that the real property taxes assessed against mortgaged property are paid on time because a tax lien is usually superior to the mortgage lien, regardless of when the taxes are due or the lien filed. Mortgages usually contain a clause either requiring the borrower to escrow the taxes in advance with the lender or providing that it is an event of default if the borrower does not make the tax payment prior to a lien's being placed on the property. If the borrower is having financial difficulties, the lender will not agree to the traditional provisions allowing the borrower to avoid being required to escrow taxes with the lender. The borrower will also be obligated to maintain a certain amount of insurance on the property. The insurance will include loss from a fire or other casualty with a highly rated insurance company. The lender will retain the right to approve the type and amount of insurance, as well as the carrier, and the borrower will be required to either provide annual proof that the premium has been paid or escrow the cost of the premium with the lender in monthly increments. This is caused by the lender's concern that, in the event of a casualty, the insurance proceeds are sufficient to restore the improvements or satisfy the loan and all superior loans.

The casualty and condemnation provisions of the mortgage may also provide the borrower with certain problems. In the event of a fire or other casualty, the lender will want to have the right to accelerate the loan and apply the insurance proceeds to reduce the unpaid indebtedness. However, this leaves the borrower with equity in a damaged building but no money to restore the property. The borrower should attempt to negotiate to have the right to use the insurance proceeds to restore the property regardless of the extent of the damage. In addition, the parties must deal with the manner in which the funds are applied. If the proceeds are applied to prepay the last payments due on the mortgage note rather than the current payments on the mortgage note or if such payments are not applied to reduce the principal indebtedness, the borrower will remain obligated to pay its regular installments of debt service, even though the casualty will preclude the property from producing cash flow to pay the debt service. Accordingly, the borrower should attempt to have the lender agree to provide for the borrower's right to apply the insurance proceeds to restore the property, provided the loan is not in default. If the insurance proceeds are to be applied as a prepayment, the prepayment either should reduce the indebtedness and modify the debt service on the mortgage note or should be applied in payment of the next debt service payments due to be made. In either event, the borrower would receive an immediate benefit from the insurance proceeds, even if the borrower must arrange for other sources for the restoration.

The parties must also deal with what to do in the event of a casualty to the property if the insurance proceeds are insufficient to pay the cost of restoration or if the insurance is in excess of the cost of restoration. The lender will want to provide that those funds should be applied to reduce the outstanding indebtedness, to reduce the lender's concern that if the borrower is to receive the excess funds, the borrower may restore the property as inexpensively as possible. A problem will occur if the mortgage does not permit prepayment or allow secondary financing and the casualty requires funds in excess of the available insurance proceeds to restore the premises, or if the lender will apply the insurance proceeds to the restoration only after it is completed. The issue then is the borrower's need for cash during the restoration. One solution is for the mortgage to preclude the borrower from receiving the insurance proceeds until it can demonstrate ability to obtain sufficient funds to complete the restoration and pay the usual cost overruns.

The lender will also be concerned about the coinsurance and loss payable clauses. A coinsurance clause provides that the property owner will be a coinsurer with the actual insurer in the event of a partial loss if the property is underinsured. The lender's concern is that the property owner will insure only 80 or 90 percent of the property's value, considering that some part of the proceeds would be attributable to the value of the land. However, in the event of a partial casualty, the owner will attempt to have the insurer pay 100 percent of the cost of a partial casualty, whereas the insurer will want to pay for only 80 or 90 percent of a partial casualty. The lender, however, will want to be certain that 100 percent of the costs are available to restore the property in the event of a casualty. A mortgage loss payable clause provides that the lender is to receive the insurance proceeds pursuant to its interest in the property. For this reason, the mortgage will require that the lender be named as an additional insured and that, even if the borrower defaults in the mortgage and the property is acquired by the lender, the lender is still covered under the insurance provisions.

A condemnation—the taking of all or part of the property by a government or quasi-government agency—usually results in an award being paid to the owner of the property in an amount equal to the fair market value of the interest being taken. A condemnation proceeding has a direct effect on the continued use of the property and its value as security for the indebtedness. The mortgage clause describing the effect of a condemnation and the use of the condemnation award will depend upon whether the condemnation involves all or part of the improvements, or an unimproved portion of the property. If the entire property is taken, the mortgage will provide that the indebtedness will be accelerated and the condemnation award will be used to satisfy the mortgage on the property and that the balance, if any, will be paid to the owner of the property. However, a partial condemnation can cause a problem between the borrower and the lender as to the application of the condemnation award. A lender may have agreed to apply the proceeds of a partial condemnation to restore the premises, if the tenants agree to remain in occupancy. However, in those instances where the award is to be used for restoration, the lender may insist upon receiving the condemnation award in escrow and applying it to the payment of the cost of restoration in the same manner as if the condemnation award were a construction loan.

Another issue to be considered in the mortgage is the borrower's ability to prepay the loan. The lender will want to restrict the borrower's ability to prepay the indebtedness to retain the benefit of a loan with a good interest rate or a secured loan, or to recoup its costs for making the loan. Therefore, the lender will attempt to restrict prepayment or, as a condition for permitting prepayment, may require that the lender be paid a prepayment premium prior to permitting a prepayment. However, the borrower's ability to prepay the loan can have dramatic consequences for the profitability of the property. If the property is encumbered by a $1 million mortgage with a 13 percent interest rate and the mortgage can be refinanced at a current rate of 9.5 percent, the borrower can reduce its payments from $135,000 to $95,000 per year, a $40,000 savings. Lenders limit prepayment because they do not want to lose the high interest rate loans, which are more profitable for them when rates fall.

Because the lender will be concerned about the property's physical condition, every mortgage requires that the property be properly maintained and repaired at all times. However, this language must be limited because it allows the lender to make a subjective determination as to when the repair is required. The lender will not want to be restricted as to when it can request repairs, and the borrower will not want the lender seeking to use the repair clause to require unnecessary improvements. Therefore, the borrower will want the mortgage to provide a standard as to what is considered a necessary repair or maintenance item. This results in the question as to who is to set the standard of what is a reasonable repair and maintenance to the property. The lender has the right to be concerned if the property is being run down because, if the borrower defaults, the lender will have to satisfy the tenants' demands in order to be certain that their leases remain in effect. If the local municipality places violations against the property because the property does not meet the various municipal codes or if the insurance carrier inspects the property and objects to its condition, then the lender certainly would have the right to demand immediate improvements. The lender should have the right to send inspectors to periodically look at the property to make sure it is being properly maintained and, if it is not being properly maintained, to require that the borrower immediately respond to its concerns.

Frequently, in commercial properties, the most valuable parts of the property are the operating leases, without which the property would not produce the income to pay the debt service on the mortgage. Accordingly, to fully protect its interest in the property and to enable it to operate the property after a default, the lender will receive from the borrower an unconditional assignment of the leases and rents. Notwithstanding the assignment, the borrower will be permitted to continue collecting the rents and profits from the property until the borrower defaults in satisfying the terms of the note and mortgage. Lenders insist on unconditional assignments to preclude a bankruptcy court from voiding a conditional assignment. The lenders are desirous of receiving the rent to prevent the borrower from being able to delay the mortgage foreclosure for several years after a default and continue collecting the rent without paying debt service on the mortgage. If the borrower is able to continue collecting rent from the property and is not obligated to apply the rent to the lender's debt service or the property's operating expenses, the lender's interest in the property will be placed at risk because the lender will eventually acquire title to the property and will then be required to repair the property and pay the unpaid real estate taxes and insurance. The assignment of the leases and rents enables the lender to immediately apply the rental income against the debt service and operating expenses.

In addition to obtaining a security interest in the buildings and improvements, lenders usually want the security for their loan to include any of the borrower's personal property that is used in conjunction with the mortgaged real property. A lender can obtain a security interest in personal property by executing a security agreement and executing and recording a financing statement in the office of the Secretary of State and/or the County Clerk in the locale of the property. A financing statement provides notice to the world of the creditor's interest in personal property. The security agreement, which can be a separate document or can be included as part of the mortgage, should describe the personal property, its locale, and the debtor and creditor. The security agreement and financing statement preclude the borrower from conveying the personal property and require that the property be maintained and insured, but, unlike mortgages, which remain in effect until terminated, the financing statements must be refiled every five years or are void.

As additional security for a loan, the lender may seek the personal guaranty from the principals of the borrower. The guaranty will stipulate that it is unconditional and, in the event of a default by the borrower, that the lender can proceed against either the guarantor or the borrower regardless of the guarantor's interest in the property. Notwithstanding the existence of the guaranty, the lender may be faced with a dilemma if the local jurisdiction requires an election of remedies in which the lender loses its right to foreclose the mortgage if it elects to sue the borrower on the guaranty. Additionally, a court could determine that the guarantor's obligation is not to pay the difference between what is obtained at the foreclosure sale in the amount of its guaranty, but rather the difference between the fair market value of the property and the amount of the loan, which could be considerably less.

Additionally, a lender could be concerned that the guaranty may not be permanent. If, when making the loan, the lender agrees to limit the guaranty to a certain period of time or a certain portion of the loan proceeds, the guarantor may be protected if the property is initially successful and then subsequently has problems. Another form of guaranty is one in which the borrower or a third party agrees to execute a lease for any unleased portions of the property in order to provide the lender with the rent that is required to support the mortgage being obtained. The guarantor then pays rent on the property, and if it is able to sublease portions of the property at a higher rent, it can even make a profit.

Regardless of whether the guaranty is or can be used, its existence tremendously increases the lender's control over the situation and reduces the borrower's flexibility. Without the guaranty and assuming that the loan is nonrecourse (which means that the lender will proceed against the property in the event of a default and not personally against the borrower), the borrower could merely walk away from the property when the value of the property depreciates to less than the outstanding balance of the mortgage. The guaranty forces the borrower to continue to use its best efforts to resolve the property's problems. For the borrower, the execution of the guaranty means that nothing can force the lender to cooperate in the event the property develops problems and the borrower needs assistance from the lender.

With that in mind, one must ask why anyone would execute a guaranty and place his or her personal wealth at risk for his or her or someone else's real estate investment. The reason is simple. Previously, lenders would not make many kinds of loans, especially relating to undeveloped property, without a guaranty. The banking and real estate crises have made the problem even worse, because now the lenders will make virtually no loan without personal recourse against the borrower. It is possible that, based on the competitive nature of banking, this will ultimately change, but not for many years.

PURCHASE MONEY FINANCING

It is not uncommon in real estate investments for a significant portion of the real estate's purchase price to be financed by the purchaser's executing a promissory note and the seller's taking back a junior mortgage on the property to secure the indebtedness. The seller's motivation in accepting a purchase money mortgage as part of the purchase price is not so much receiving interest on its debt as on increasing the likelihood that the seller will be able to sell the real estate for as high a price as possible. Because the seller's motivation is encouraging the sale, the terms of the purchase money financing will not necessarily bear a true relationship to the then-current market for financing (see Example).

The disadvantage of purchase money financing for the seller arises from the risk to the seller of a default by the purchaser and the fact that the seller must then be concerned with the continued viability of property that it no longer owns. There is also a concern as to what the seller should do if financing that has a superior position to the purchase money mortgage goes into default, which would eliminate the seller's lien on (and equity in) the property. The purchase money financing could be an inferior lien, either because it is placed as a lien on the property after the institutional financing is placed on the property or because a subsequent institutional lender refuses to provide financing without receiving the superior position and the seller agrees to give it the superior position.

Purchase money financing is particularly common in the acquisition of unimproved land, which institutional lenders rarely finance due to their concern over:

- The difficulty in establishing the real value of the property
- The absence of any significant cash flow from the property from which the debt services can be paid

EXAMPLE

Purchase money financing works in the following way. Jones sells a property to Smith for $2,500,000, payable $100,000 on execution of the agreement of sale, $400,000 on closing of title, $1,600,000 by Smith's taking title to the property subject to an institutionally held first mortgage, and $400,000 plus 10 percent interest payable to the seller over the following four years in equal installments of principal of $100,000 each year. The purchaser is then able to purchase a $2,5000,000 property with only $500,000 in cash (20 percent of the purchase price.)

- The uncertainty that the purchaser has any significant equity in the property
- The legal restrictions and limitations on financing the purchase of unimproved land
- The risk that the approvals for development or redevelopment will not be granted in a timely manner for an economically cost-effective project
- The risk that the construction will not be efficiently carried through to completion
- The risk that the property cannot be profitably owned or developed
- The increasing cost of complying with an ever increasing number of federal, state, and local environmental laws, regulations, cases, and rules
- The possibility that an abrupt change in the area's demographics or economy or competition may reduce the property's profitability or preclude a profitable development.

If an institutional lender is willing to make a land acquisition loan, it is usually based upon the creditworthiness of the borrower, rather than the loan-to-value ratio of the property being acquired. The loan will also be for a relatively small portion of the purchase price. It will be even more difficult to obtain institutional acquisition financing in the future due to the recent plethora of bank losses on such financing. Due to the limited availability of institutional financing, the usual source of acquisition financing of unimproved land is for the seller to finance the acquisition of the land by taking back a purchase money mortgage from the purchaser.

As its name suggests, a purchase money mortgage is a mortgage that secures the indebtedness from the buyer to the seller, although it could include a loan from a third party that enables the buyer to purchase property. A purchase money mortgage is similar to any mortgage that secures a loan, except that it secures the deferred portion of the purchase price for a piece of property. For this reason, in a number of states, a purchase money mortgage is granted priority over any other lien and is considered a prior lien to previously executed, but unrecorded mortgages, even if the previously executed mortgage is recorded after the purchase money mortgage is recorded.

One particularly significant benefit of purchase money financing is the flexibility that it provides the parties in structuring their deal. By fluctuating the terms, the purchaser and seller are able to increase the apparent return on investment from the transaction (see Example). If the cash purchase price for a piece of property is $1 million and the property produces a cash flow of $100,000 per year, the $1 million investment produces a 10 percent return. However, if the purchaser is paying the $1 million purchase price in equal installments over five years, even though the purchaser is required to pay interest to the seller, the return on investment to the purchaser in the earlier years is not significantly lower than if the purchaser paid all cash and did not incur the interest expense of the purchase money mortgage.

One thing the example indicates is why the seller would refuse to defer all or a significant portion of the debt service payments due on the purchase money mortgage. If the purchaser was able to accrue all the payments to the end of the fifth year, the purchaser would have received $500,000 in cash flow from the property for a $200,000 initial investment, while the seller would lose a similar amount of cash flow with no certainty that the balance of the payments would ever be made. Conversely, without a purchase money mortgage or the deferred payment of the purchase price, the seller would have received $1 million and the purchaser would have received the same $100,000 cash flow annually (10 percent return on investment).

In a transaction involving a purchase money mortgage, the purchaser is usually required to make a substantial, nonrefundable payment

EXAMPLE

The flexibility of purchase money financing is demonstrated in the following chart.

Year	Aggregate cash invested by purchaser	Aggregate cash flow to purchaser (rent)	Aggregate interest paid to seller	Annual return on investment to purchaser
1	$ 200,000	$100,000	$ 0	50%
2	400,000	200,000	80,000	21%
3	600,000	300,000	144,000	13.3%
4	800,000	400,000	192,000	10%
5	1,000,000	500,000	224,000	8.2%
6	1,000,000	600,000	244,000	8%

toward the purchase price (at least 25 percent) on acquiring the property, in order to:

- Provide the purchaser with equity in the property
- Reduce the likelihood that the purchaser would default because it has made a cash investment in the property
- Compensate the seller for its closing expenses, taxes and lost cash flow from the property
- Reduce the seller's financial exposure in the event of a subsequent default by the purchaser.

In the event of a default by the purchaser in making the deferred payments, the seller, to protect its interest in the property and to regain title, will be obligated to foreclose the mortgage or exercise its power of sale.

There is a particular risk to the seller in a purchase money mortgage that is frequently overlooked in the euphoria of selling the property. If the purchaser stops making the payments on the purchase money mortgage and continues to collect the rent or other income from the property while the seller is required to endure a lengthy foreclosure, the purchaser might be able to obtain several years of additional cash flow without any additional expense (see Example). Consider this scenario utilizing the example describing the five-year $1 million purchase price. If it takes the seller two years (after learning of the purchaser's failure to make the payment due after the first year) to foreclose upon and reacquire the property, then the purchaser owned the property for three years, received $300,000 in cash flow, and made the original $200,000 payment. To make matters worse, the purchaser may also defer paying real estate taxes and maintaining the property to increase its profit while it aggressively defends the foreclosure. This is the primary reason why the seller should receive an assignment of rents, income, and profits at the closing and make certain that it has the right to appoint a receiver as soon as the purchaser defaults. ·

A further risk to the seller is that its interest in the property could become subject to liens for unpaid real estate taxes or mechanics' liens, which could be superior to the purchase money mortgage, and thereby be payable prior to the purchase money mortgage from the proceeds of a foreclosure sale, or the seller could be required to pay them on reacquiring the property. To some extent, the seller could be protected against these risks by having the purchaser escrow taxes with the seller in advance of the payment date. However, this might place the purchaser at risk if the seller fails to pay the taxes.

Furthermore, the existence of a purchase money mortgage can benefit the purchaser and adversely affect the seller by providing the purchaser with a fund against which it can offset any damages it believes (and can prove) were caused by a misrepresentation by the seller in the agreement of sale or in the seller's failure to comply with its closing or postclosing obligations. Even if the purchaser is unable to prove that the seller misrepresented the property or did not perform its obligations, the threat of being able to do so could enable the purchaser to force the seller to agree to renegotiate the purchase price. To the seller, this postclosing negotiation reduces its profit, but avoids the expense and delay of a foreclosure or other lawsuit. Primarily, however, purchasers prefer purchase money mortgages because they enable the purchaser to acquire the property with a relatively small amount of cash, allowing the purchaser to conserve its capital to be available to directly benefit the property.

However, a purchase money mortgage and even a default by the purchaser may be beneficial to the seller. A default by the purchaser enables the seller to reacquire the property, which could provide the seller with a windfall. In such an event, the seller would again own the property and could retain any portion of the downpayment or the purchase money payments that it has already received.

Nevertheless, reacquiring the property would force the seller to have to deal with the same problems with which the purchaser was forced to deal. The seller would have to deal with the financing that the purchaser obtained subsequent to the sale. Unfortunately, the property may have less value at the time of the default than when it was originally sold because the real estate market has changed, or the property is in the middle of being developed or redeveloped, or a change has occurred in the demographics of the area in which the property is located or in the local competition. Moreover, the seller could be placed at a disadvantage if the operation of the property involves a certain expertise that the seller does not possess or requires a professional staff or an experienced purchaser. Under these circumstances, the seller might seriously consider assisting the purchaser with its problems by restructuring the purchase money indebtedness rather than reacquiring the property.

Although one would think that the seller should not have a problem deciding whether to reacquire the property, because it once owned the property, this is not necessarily the case. First, the seller's reason for selling the property may still exist. Second, the seller may have conveyed vacant land or a single-tenant retail store and could be getting back a partially completed or fully completed unleased large-scale commercial development or, worse yet, a property undergoing development. The expertise or financing involved in one enterprise is not necessarily the same

EXAMPLE

Based on the previous example, if the purchaser defaults after the
third year, the seller has received $600,000 in principal and $144,000
in interest and could then resell the property for its current market
value, which could be equal to or exceed the original $1 million
purchase price, thereby increasing the seller's profit on owning
the property.

as that involved in another. Furthermore, a project undergoing development may require large infusions of capital to complete or demolish it.

Negotiations over the business terms of a purchase money mortgage
(i.e., the interest rate, loan maturity, and payment and prepayment provisions) are usually less heated than negotiations over other provisions of
the original agreement of sale. The business terms are based upon the
relative negotiating strengths of the parties at the time the contract is
executed, but are usually within certain standard parameters. Moreover,
in many states, purchase money mortgages are exempt from the usury
laws, which allows the seller even more flexibility in structuring the
deal. However, interest rates are not usually excessive in purchase
money financing, because that might reduce the price of the property, as
well as the purchaser's ability to make the payments. The purchaser
usually negotiates to have the right to prepay the loan at anytime without penalty. Usually, purchase money mortgages require annual payments of principal and interest over periods of three to five years after
the sale. Occasionally, purchase money mortgages are standing loans
(i.e., interest only) with annual payments and a balloon payment on
maturity, or some or all of the interest will accrue and the principal and
interest will be due on maturity. However, the larger the payment due on
maturity, the greater the seller's risk that the purchaser will default.

One critical issue in a purchase money mortgage is whether the seller
will be obligated to subordinate its purchase money mortgage to development financing that the purchaser obtains from an institutional lender.
Subordination means that the purchase money mortgage would be made
inferior to subsequent financing regardless of the order in which the
mortgages are executed or recorded. Subordination is an important issue
for a purchaser who is acquiring unimproved property, because it determines whether the purchaser would be able to finance the construction of
the improvements without prepaying the purchase money mortgage or
would be required to first satisfy the purchase money mortgage. The need

for subordination of the purchase money mortgage is due to the fact that the developmental lender will usually insist on lien priority and, in fact, may be required to have a first lien on the property in order to satisfy the state banking or insurance requirements. Notwithstanding the risk involved to the seller, if the seller wants to obtain the highest sales price for the property, the seller may be forced to agree to subordinate its mortgage to construction financing. The sale may depend on the purchaser's ability to obtain the appropriate financing terms. Naturally, the seller benefits from subordination because the subsequent development will increase the value of the property and, therefore, the security for the purchase money mortgage.

However, subordination does require the seller to become reinvolved with the property in the event of a default by the purchaser in paying the superior indebtedness. If the purchaser defaults on paying the purchase money mortgage, then the seller should become immediately concerned with whether there is also a default on the superior financing. The purchaser's default in paying the debt service on, or performing the terms of, the superior financing would place the seller's purchase money mortgage and its interest in the property at risk of loss. Additionally, the seller has to consider whether taking control of the property and attempting to complete the development or otherwise resolve its problems would be acceptable to the construction or permanent lender or could make the seller personally liable for repaying the loan.

A purchase money mortgage also enables the seller to reduce its tax liability on the sale by enabling the seller to treat the sale as an installment sale and thereby allow the purchaser to spread the gain on the sale over the term of the purchase money mortgage. The availability of purchase money financing also enhances the seller's ability to sell the property at a higher price, thereby maximizing the seller's return.

If the purchaser is defaulting under either the purchase money mortgage or the superior financing, the seller can do a number of things to assist the purchaser other than forgiving the purchase money indebtedness or paying the superior indebtedness, which are two unacceptable alternatives for the seller. The seller could agree to a reduction in the debt service on the purchase money mortgage or a deferral or moratorium in making debt service payments or a reduction in making interest payments, or could agree to a modification of some of the limiting provisions in the purchase money mortgage or restrictions contained in the original deed for the property. If the seller sold the property with a deed containing a restriction that the property be used only for residential purposes and there is a residential glut on the market, the cost of resolving the problem may be for the seller to agree to permit commercial use of the property.

Even if the purchase money mortgage permits superior financing, then to protect the seller, the purchase money mortgage should contain specific limitations on the terms of the senior financing. The purchase money mortgage should also provide the seller with the right to review and approve the use of the funds, as well as the terms of the superior financing, providing that the seller does not unreasonably withhold or delay giving consent to the superior financing. The purchase money mortgage should specify the amount and purpose of any permitted construction or development financing, to prevent the seller from being required to subordinate its purchase money mortgage to a debt that bears no relationship to the value of the proposed improvements. For this reason, the seller would refuse to execute the subordination agreement until the construction loan commitment is obtained. The purchase money mortgage should provide the specific conditions under which the seller would execute the subordination agreement, to avoid potential problems created by the seller's refusing to execute the subordination agreement. The seller would also want to be certain that any funds in excess of those required for the development of the property would be used to prepay the purchase money mortgage. Conversely, the purchaser would want the terms of the subordination provisions to be self-executing so that the seller would not be involved in the process of the purchaser's closing the senior financing.

CONSTRUCTION AND DEVELOPMENT FINANCING

Construction and development financing is among the riskiest forms of lending. Thus, lenders are very cautious, and the borrower's actions are usually carefully scrutinized. During the period that the mortgage securing the construction and development financing is on the property, problems can arise for the owner, especially due to the possibility that (1) the construction costs could become excessive, (2) the permanent loan commitment could be terminated for reasons over which the construction lender has little or no control, and (3) the economic basis for the development could change radically, which could prejudice the ultimate use, sale, or other disposition of the property. The construction lender will be vigilant throughout the construction process to protect its interest in the property. The lender needs to be constantly reassured that the project is proceeding according to the plans and specifications and that the owner is maintaining the construction schedule, to avoid anything happening that could jeopardize the permanent financing or the ultimate disposition of the property.

One of the construction lender's biggest concerns is that the construction loan advances will be used according to the conditions specified by the lender. The lender wants to be certain that the property will not be encumbered by liens and that no problems (e.g., nonpayment or other default by the developer) will interfere with the contractors performing under their contracts. For that reason, prior to and throughout the construction, the construction lender will monitor all phases of the project.

Although land development financing and construction financing frequently are mentioned together, the kinds of financing represented by each term and the activities involved in each process are markedly different. Land development involves preparing unimproved land for construction and includes the following activities:

- Rating the land
- Planning the construction
- Obtaining the zoning approvals
- Installing utilities
- Grading and landscaping the land
- Installing streets, sewer and water lines, electric and other utility lines
- Installing drainage and retention basins and other similar physical improvements to the land.

Land development prepares the land for the subsequent construction of the improvements. Development financing is usually available on a short-term basis (less than two years) at an interest rate that is several percentage points above the prime lending rate and is usually provided by commercial lenders. The preconditions for a development loan differ from project to project and are based upon the following factors:

- The differing needs of each property
- The location of the property
- The amount of funds required
- The extent of the development work required for the particular location
- The anticipated use of the developed property
- The expertise and background of the developer.

Development lending requires the lender to supervise the development and be prepared to step into a project and immediately replace the developer if necessary. Although lenders are usually uncomfortable replacing the developer, by being prepared to take such an action, the lender is effectively reducing the developer's ability to hold the project hostage to its demands that the lender change the terms of the loan. Otherwise, the developer could use its importance to the project and the fact that the lender will almost certainly lose money if the developer does not obtain what it wants to maintain control. The developer could be seeking more control over the development, as well as the right to make changes that the lender believes are unwarranted, such as increased financing or better payment terms.

The issue of control frequently plays a role in negotiations between the lender and the developer due to the limitations that the lender will have structured into the loan documents. To protect its security in the property and to insure that the buildings are properly constructed, the development lender will have reviewed and approved the owner's development plans, and will retain the right to approve all changes to the plans, as well as the professionals and contractors the owner retains for the development. The land development agreement will also provide the lender with the right to approve all contracts entered into by the developer. Moreover, the loan documents will include an assignment to the lender of all agreements entered into with the contractors or professionals. In this way, the lender will be in position to take over the development in the event of a default by the borrower. The lender will also receive an acknowledgment by the contractors and professionals that, in the event of a default by the borrower, the lender would have the right to utilize the professionals' work products, plans, specifications, and drawings as long as the professionals are paid. The professionals and contractors will also agree to abide by the terms of their agreements, notwithstanding the fact that the lender was not a party to them. This prevents the professionals and contractors from attempting to negotiate their agreements after the default.

If the owner has financial difficulties during the development stage, because construction has not commenced and the development plans have not been finalized, the lender has the ability to step in and change the direction of the project. In this way, the development lender has more alternatives than the construction lender, who is usually required to finance the completion of the project in an attempt to protect its original investment. Because the development lender's role is so limited, such a lender is usually very experienced in the early identification and elimination of potential problems in a project. Moreover, prior to the development lender's attempting to solve a problem at the property by advancing additional funds, the lender would consider whether, because the owner is having significant problems or serious financial difficulties in the development stage of the project, it is reasonable to assume that construction should commence without a reevaluation of the likelihood of the project's success. The lender would also want to determine whether there is adequate financing and whether a permanent lender will be available to replace the construction lender upon the project's completion.

There is little doubt that construction financing poses the greatest degree of risk for the lender, because the property is generating no revenue while it is undergoing construction and, once the demolition and construction commences, there is little certainty that it will be properly completed and will have a use or a tenant. Moreover, once construction is under way, the lender has few alternatives but to finish the construction, if the lender has any hope whatsoever of having its loan repaid. In this regard, construction is like diving: The diver can change his or her mind until leaving the board; thereafter, there is no turning back.

Construction financing is the lending of funds for the actual construction of the project and includes the cost of the material, labor, overhead, and related costs. The risks to the lender (and the developer) include:

- Inclement weather
- Labor problems
- Poor planning
- Poor marketability of the project
- Changing neighborhoods surrounding the project site
- Adverse conditions in the national and local economy
- Unanticipated competition
- Changing consumer demands.

The reason that construction lending contains such a high degree of difficulty and risk is that the security for the loan is a building that is gradually being constructed as the loan is funded. Even if 90 percent of the building is completed, the lender will have, as its security, an asset that produces no revenue. For the construction lender to reduce its exposure in the event of a loan default, the lender will attempt to make certain that the loan proceeds are being used according to the construction loan agreement; the construction is proceeding according to the construction schedule; and the owner is complying with the conditions contained within the permanent loan commitment. There is little doubt that, at all times, the construction lender's paramount concern is that the permanent loan is in place and that the borrower does not default or violate any of its requirements. Primarily because the construction lender is a short-term lender who is looking to have its position purchased by the permanent lender within a relatively short term, the developer's strict compliance with the conditions of the permanent loan commitment are of paramount importance to the construction lender.

A construction loan is usually a high interest rate loan, which bears interest at several points above the prime lending rate or other standard rate and fluctuates with changes in the prime or other lending rate charged by large money center banks during the period that the loan is outstanding. The fluctuating interest rates tied to the prime or other lending rate are a major cause for default by construction loan borrowers during periods of highly turbulent interest rates. The other major reason for construction loan defaults is the funding of the construction loan by construction lenders prior to the borrower's obtaining permanent loan commitments, which leads to the borrower's default when permanent financing is unavailable and construction interest increases substantially. For example, if the prime lending rate increases by five points (500 basis points) during construction (from 7 to 12 percent), then the interest cost of a $10 million construction loan will increase by $500,000 per year. This increase will also create other dislocations in the economy, thereby reducing the likelihood that the completed building can be quickly or profitably leased or sold.

Furthermore, the fluctuations in interest rates on construction loans not only create problems in determining the amount of financing the property can carry, but also can create a usury problem if the interest rates increase substantially. This exposes the lender to the risk that the loan could be invalidated because the interest rate exceeds the maximum permitted rate. Accordingly, construction loans usually become unavailable as interest rates rise. The lender's concern is the risk of violating the usury laws and the belief that few projects can successfully carry extremely high interest rates.

Construction lenders also have to deal with construction delays and the possibility of significantly higher construction costs, either of which can cause the construction loan to exceed the amount of the permanent loan. Nevertheless, the problem that causes the most concern to the lender is the risk that excessive delay in completing construction could put the permanent loan commitment at risk, due to the fact that most permanent loan commitments have specific termination dates. Certainly, the termination date can be extended by the permanent lender, but only at the permanent lender's sole discretion. The construction lender must also be concerned with the marketing problems caused by the developer's inability to sell or lease the finished product and the possibility that the permanent loan might be conditioned upon the sale of a certain number of units or the lease of a certain portion of the finished product prior to the funding. The developer's profit will also be a concern to the construction lender, because once the project's costs exceed the developer's likely return, the developer's interest in the project will certainly wain, thereby increasing the risk of default for the lender.

The construction loan commitment will condition the lender's agreement to lend the funds providing the following stipulations are satisfied:

- The construction proceeds in accordance with the plans and specifications and in compliance with local zoning and building code requirements
- The borrower obtains a permanent mortgage commitment
- The borrower maintains adequate insurance
- The portion of the loan that the lender will withhold until final completion is always adequate to complete the construction
- The parties agree on the progress payments the lender is prepared to make during the loan funding
- The lender has the right to make payments either to the borrower or to the general contractor
- The interest is to be computed in an acceptable manner
- The collateral for the loan is adequate and secure
- Any guarantees the lender requires are received
- The condition of title is met before the lender makes each payment
- The borrower supplies the required opinion letters
- The borrower pays all the lender's fees and expenses involved in the loan.

The construction loan commitment defines the relationship between the borrower and the construction lender. The conditions contained in the commitment are then incorporated into the construction loan agreement, the construction loan note, and the construction loan mortgage. The construction loan agreement provides the framework for the construction loan, describes the relationship between the borrower and the lender, includes references to all the supporting documents, specifies the loan terms, establishes the funding procedures, and provides for the affirmative and negative covenants by the borrower. The construction loan agreement also permits the lender to have a certain degree of involvement in, and control over, the construction process and specifies the events that must occur and the conditions that are to be satisfied before the construction lender is required to advance any funds or continue making advances.

The basic provisions of the construction loan agreement include:

- An obligation by the borrower to complete the project within a specific period of time
- An agreement that the construction will be accomplished in a workmanlike manner
- A prohibition of the borrower's altering the plans and specifications for the development without receiving the lender's prior consent
- A requirement that the general contractor and the major subcontractors be bonded to assure their performance
- The obligation of the borrower to obtain lien waivers from all contractors and subcontractors covering the payment of all previously supplied labor and materials, to preclude the suppliers from placing a lien on the property that could have priority over the construction lender
- A requirement that proof be given that the improvements are being constructed within the borders of the property
- A certification from a title insurance company that there are no encroachments over the property line or easement lines that could adversely affect the buildings being constructed.

The construction loan agreement will also precondition any obligation by the lender to make loan advances under the construction loan agreement, unless the lender receives:

- Executed copies of the construction note, construction mortgage, guaranty (if any), assignment of leases and rents (if any), and permanent loan commitment
- The required insurance policies
- A fully paid title insurance policy containing coverage against mechanics' liens, without a survey exception; an undertaking by the insurer to provide the notice of title continuation; a pending disbursement clause; and affirmative insurance against any violation of any usury law
- The payment of the construction lender's legal and architectural fees
- Financial statements from the borrower, its principals, and the project

- Satisfaction by the lender's architect that the plans have been approved by all government authorities and the improvements are or will be in compliance with all zoning ordinances and regulations; that the general contractor is acceptable to the lender; and that all necessary roads and utilities have been planned for or have been installed
- Receipt and approval by the lender's architect of the plans and all change orders, as well as copies of the ordinances, maps, surveys, general contracts, permits, and licenses
- Satisfaction by the lender's counsel with all government authorizations, permits, and approvals
- A current survey indicating the location and perimeter of the buildings, all easements and rights of way, all existing building lines, the location and names of all streets abutting the premises, the existence and size of all encroachments, the acreage and square footage of all improvements, and the existence of contiguity, if the property contains several parcels
- A satisfactory opinion of counsel.

Each time there is an additional advance of construction funds, the borrower would be required to satisfy the lender that all the conditions for the initial advance have been satisfied and that the earlier documents, representations, and warranties continue to apply. The lender would also have to receive substantiation for the requisition of funds being made by the borrower, and the construction that is being funded must have been completed in satisfactory form. During the entire period that the construction loan is outstanding, the construction lender will insist on receiving copies of all agreements and documents being delivered to the developer from the contractors and major subcontractors. Thus, the lender can satisfy itself that the loan advances are being used properly and that the contractors and subcontractors are being paid. This reduces the risk that the contractors or subcontractors will have a claim against the developer or the project, or that the cost of construction will exceed the balance of the construction loan due to the improper use of the loan advances. To be certain that all the work required by the construction loan commitment has been accomplished in a good and workmanlike manner, the construction lender will also require that the borrower deliver a ratification from each of the professionals prior to any advances of construction loan proceeds.

The events of default under the construction loan agreement include:

- The borrower's failure to pay any amount required to be paid or advanced under the construction loan note or mortgage or the permanent loan commitment
- The borrower's failure to perform its obligations under the construction loan note, the mortgage, or the permanent loan commitment
- The construction not being carried out expeditiously or being discontinued
- The borrower's failing to disclose to the lender's architect the names of all contractors the borrower intends to utilize or has utilized on the project
- The lender's believing that the borrower will be unable to complete the buildings and improvements by the specified completion date (which is a date prior to the termination of the permanent loan commitment)
- Any lien being filed against the property and remaining unbonded or unsatisfied for 10 days
- The permanent loan commitment being canceled or amended without the construction lender's prior approval
- Any material adverse change in the condition of the borrower or the property.

An additional consideration is the courses of action available to the construction lender if the permanent lender fails to fund the permanent mortgage or the permanent loan commitment has terminated. Under such circumstances, the construction lender may attempt to obtain and sell, or force the owner to sell, the property to another developer prior to the lender's investing additional funds in the project. Alternatively, if the permanent lender is prepared to proceed with its loan once the conditions of the permanent loan commitment are satisfied, the construction lender can increase the amount of its loan to provide the funds for the developer to complete the project. However, even if the construction lender is going to advance an amount in excess of the amount being funded by the permanent lender, then it either has to arrange for the permanent lender to agree to increase the amount of its loan, or the construction lender will have to retain a second mortgage on the property behind the permanent lender.

The construction mortgage is similar to the permanent mortgage in many respects, except that the construction mortgage must also provide for partial release of the land, an opportunity to cure defaults, and future advances. Release provisions are particularly important in a construction mortgage due to the possibility that the borrower will develop the property into a subdivision or sell portions of the property. If the borrower anticipates subdividing the property and selling individual parcels, it is imperative that the borrower be able to have portions of the property released from the lien of the mortgage. If this is not possible, the borrower will be required to either sell all the parcels in order to close on the sale of any parcel or to refinance the entire mortgage when the borrower is ready to close on the sale of one or more parcels. These steps are unnecessary if the construction mortgage contains a mechanism for the release of individual parcels.

Nevertheless, the lender will want to be protected from being forced to release the most saleable parcels and being left with a lien on unsalable or unusable land. If noncontiguous parcels are released, the lender could be left with an interest in a checkerboard of parcels without access to the main roads or other amenities. Therefore, to protect itself, the lender will insist that no parcel can be released until a minimum number of continuous parcels are being released at the same time, which provide the unreleased portion of the mortgaged property with access to the public roadways, and that the release price for each parcel is at least 120 percent of the portion of the mortgage allocated to the parcel being released. In this way, the lender will have received the return of all its money when less then all the parcels have been sold, and need not be concerned with the borrower's inability to sell the least desirable parcels.

Lenders frequently attempt to reduce the risk incurred in a construction loan by syndicating the loan among a number of other lenders. The original construction lender acts as the lead lender and administers the loan on behalf of the group of lenders that acquire an interest in the loan. Thereafter, the lenders enter into a participation agreement, which establishes their interest in the loan, and requires each lender to provide a proportionate share of each advance and the expenses of administering the loan. The agreement would also provide the manner in which payments from the borrower are to be distributed and the manner in which decisions relating to the loans are to be made. In the event of a default by the borrower, the lead lender is required by the participation agreement to take all steps on behalf of the loan holders to protect their interests in the security for the loan and to either work out the default or foreclose the loan as expeditiously as possible.

The construction lender is interested primarily in receiving interest on its loan and being certain that it will be taken out of the loan by the permanent lender upon completion of the construction. The permanent loan is also important to the developer because the permanent loan will usually provide the borrower with a lower and fixed rate of interest and will enable the construction lender to obtain the profit portion of the financing. Occasionally, the construction lender will also be the permanent lender and will merely transfer the loan on its books, change the financial terms, and then become the permanent lender. However, more frequently, the construction lender will actually sell the loan to the permanent lender. Initially, the permanent lender will take part of the construction loan based upon its loan commitment, and the balance of the loan will be acquired by a bridge lender until the permanent lender or another lender is prepared to acquire the remainder of the construction loan.

To achieve these purposes, the borrower, construction lender, and permanent lender enter into a buy–sell agreement, which specifies the preconditions for the permanent lender's funding of the loan. The buy–sell agreement provides each of the parties with the knowledge that the other party is prepared to fulfill its function in the relationship. The buy–sell agreement provides the construction lender with confirmation that it will be taken out of the construction loan by the permanent lender and contains the permanent lender's conditions for taking out the construction lender. The borrower obtains comfort from the fact that both lenders are committed to the transaction and have privity with each other, which provides protection for the borrower if either lender defaults. The buy–sell agreement provides assurance to both the construction lender and the borrower that the permanent lender is obligated to proceed, and provides the permanent lender with the certainty that it will acquire the loan on the terms that have been negotiated. This also precludes the borrower from shopping around for a better permanent loan commitment once it has obtained the commitment from this permanent lender. Most importantly, the buy–sell agreement provides the construction lender with confirmation that the permanent lender is ready, willing, and able to fund the permanent loan. The agreement also contains the permanent lender's approval of the construction loan documents, as well as the plans and specifications for the project, the title insurance, the zoning, and all other relevant agreements prior to the construction loan funding.

An advantage of the buy–sell agreement is that it provides the procedures and time limits for funding the permanent loan and the closing between the lenders, the funds that will be utilized, and the notices that each of the parties will receive at various times. It also specifies that the permanent lender is not obligated to purchase the loan from the construction lender unless the conditions contained in the permanent loan commitment have been satisfied. Such conditions usually require funding of the loan prior to the expiration of the commitment, and preclude the construction lender from modifying the construction loan documents, releasing any security, accepting any prepayment of the loan, or selling the loan to any other lender without the permanent lender's consent.

PERMANENT FINANCING

Permanent financing is one of the most important attributes of real estate ownership. It provides the owner with the stability of a relatively long-term loan, usually with a fixed interest rate, which provides the owner with the comfort of knowing that, as long as it maintains the property's success, the owner will not have to seek alternative financing. For the lender, the permanent mortgage provides a relatively safe, fixed return on the lender's capital. The only complaint lenders have is that when interest rates decrease, the borrowers prepay the older, higher fixed-rate loans, which they never do as rates increase.

The ability of real estate owners to leverage their investments through long-term secured borrowing is what makes real estate an attractive investment. Leveraging is the ability of a real estate owner to purchase property valued at many times the purchaser's cash investment by using borrowed funds. The income to the purchaser or owner and the tax deductions accruing from the ownership of the property are frequently worth many times in excess of the cash purchase price. The difference between the fair market value of the property and the amount of mortgages on the property is the owner's equity in the property. Therefore, the owner's equity increases as the value of the property increases or the principal indebtedness of the mortgages decreases. Moreover, because the owner can usually borrow against his or her equity in the property, as long as the owner has equity in the property and a lender can be found, an additional mortgage can be placed against the property or an existing mortgage can be increased or refinanced to provide the owner with access to that equity.

The owner's access to his or her equity through mortgage financing without being required to sell the property, provides the owner with cash or credit with which to solve a property's problems or to renovate the property or acquire additional properties. However, at those times, when the value of the property decreases or the owner is unable to pay the debt service on the loan, thereby causing the accrued interest to be added to the principal indebtedness, which has the effect of escalating the owner's financial problems. Nevertheless, as long as the owner has equity in the property, he or she can obtain additional mortgage financing. The reason for this availability is the security that lenders feel by having a lien on real estate. The lender's security rises because it knows that if the borrower defaults on its obligations to the lender, the lender has the ability to obtain and sell the mortgaged property and use the proceeds to satisfy the indebtedness, the accrued interest, and the lender's expenses. Moreover, the borrower's other creditors could not attack the lender's right to the property, because the lender is a secured creditor.

A permanent mortgage loan usually requires the borrower to make regular monthly or quarterly installment payments of principal and interest during the loan term, with the loan either being fully satisfied on maturity (a self-liquidating loan) or requiring a large final payment on maturity (a balloon payment). However, the exact payment provisions of a particular loan will depend on the current market for loans and the borrower's negotiating strength. Borrowers frequently prefer loans that self-liquidate, which has the effect of increasing the borrower's equity in the property as the mortgage balance is reduced, whereas lenders prefer standing loans in which the borrower pays interest every month and still owes the entire indebtedness on maturity.

The following chart demonstrates the different amounts paid under self-liquidating and interest-only loans for the same $1 million loan with a 9 percent interest rate over a 30-year term:

	Self-liquidating loan	Interest-only loan
Monthly payment	$8,046.23	$7,500.00
Term in months	360	360
Total monthly payments	$2,896,641.42	$2,700,000.00
Final payment	-0-	1,000,000.00
Total debt service	$2,896,641.42	$3,700,000.00
Difference	$803,358.58	

Accordingly, by paying an additional $546.23 each month for 30 years ($196,642.80 in the aggregate), the borrower saves $803,358.58. The reason for the disparity in payments over 30 years has to do with the effect of the decreasing amount of interest on the constant monthly debt service payment. As the interest portion decreases, ever so slightly at first, the principal portion of the debt service increases—slowly for the first two-thirds of the loan, and then suddenly and dramatically faster. Moreover, when the loan matures and the balloon has to be paid, the borrower has an obligation to satisfy the indebtedness regardless of whether it has the money or is required to obtain the proceeds elsewhere. If the borrower is required to refinance the mortgage (i.e., obtain a replacement mortgage), the borrower will have to use all or a significant portion of the proceeds of the refinancing to make the balloon payment on the original mortgage and will then have a new continuing obligation to the new mortgage holder. It would therefore seem very apparent that it is in the owner's best interest to obtain a self-liquidating mortgage, or at least one with a small balloon on maturity.

Basically, a mortgage loan can utilize five different kinds of payment schedules, including:

1. Self-liquidating loans
2. Loans with balloon payments
3. Standing loans (in which only interest, not principal, is repaid during the term)
4. Accruing interest loans (in which all or part of the interest is not paid during the loan term and is then added to the principal balance of the loan, which can result in having a loan payable on maturity that is in excess of the original amount borrowed)
5. Reverse payment loans (in which each debt service payment is used to pay the principal rather than the interest, which has the effect of enabling the borrower to repay large amounts of principal in the early years, which decrease over time as the interest portion of the debt service payment increases; however, this loan type reduces the amount of available interest deduction for taxes in the early years).

The lender's decision as to whether it would prefer a standing loan, a balloon payment loan, or a fully amortizing loan, will depend upon the borrower's financial strength and the economic environment at the time the loan is made. Standing loans provide the lender with the biggest return, but entail the most risk of default because the principal balance is never reduced. Alternatively, a fully amortizing loan provides the lender with the smallest return, but involves less risk because the loan is automatically repaid over a period of time. This means that each month the borrower's equity in the property increases and the difference between the property value and the outstanding loan balance increases. The balloon payment loan, which provides for some amortization, is a compromise between a standing loan and a fully amortizing loan. It is usually utilized because the lender requires a shorter loan term to have the opportunity to adjust the interest rate on the loan to changing market conditions. The standing loan and balloon payment loan also provide the borrower with more cash flow from the property than the self-liquidating loan, because the cash flow would not be payable if it was used to pay principal amortization.

Nevertheless, the fact that a loan requires a balloon payment on maturity or a maturity date shorter than the end of the amortization schedule, does not mean that the loan will have to be repaid at that time. The shorter term provides the lender with the ability to renegotiate the interest rate at the point in time that the loan is repayable and enables the interest rate to adjust to market conditions at that point in time by the lender's either increasing the interest rate or refusing to refinance the property if the value has decreased. The interest rate on the loan and the form it will take will depend upon market conditions at the time the loan is paid. If the loan is funded when credit is tight, the interest rate will be high and the loan term may be for only a few years but with a lengthy amortization schedule. This means that the loan will mature relatively quickly, but the amortization portion of the monthly payments assumes that the loan will not mature for a longer period of time. Conversely, if the loan is funded when mortgage money is available, the interest rates will be low and borrowers will be able to obtain longer, self-liquidating terms. In periods of fluctuating interest rates, lenders will insist upon adjustable interest rates as a precondition for making loans, to protect themselves from losing money because the lender will be required to pay more to obtain funds from savers and the government than it is receiving on an earlier loan. The interest rates on variable interest rate or adjustable interest rate loans adjust automatically after specified periods of time (i.e., 1 to 5 years) in an attempt to reflect fluctuations in the prime rate, the bond rate, or another market index.

Debt service payments are the periodic payments that must be made in payment of a loan. There are four variables in calculating debt service: the amount borrowed, the interest rate, whether the loan will be amortized during its term, and the term of the loan. Each of the four variables can have a significant effect on the amount of the debt service payment. The higher the interest rate or the shorter the loan term or the faster the loan will amortize, the higher the constant payment will be. If $1 million is borrowed for different terms and interest rates, the monthly debt service payment for a self-liquidating loan (rounded to the nearest dollar) fluctuates as follows:

Interest	Term (Years)				
Rate	10	15	20	25	30
9%	$12,667	$10,143	$8,997	$8,392	$8,046
10%	$13,215	$10,746	$9,650	$9,087	$8,776
11%	$13,775	$11,366	$10,322	$9,801	$9,523
12%	$14,347	$12,002	$11,011	$10,532	$10,286

Moreover, the longer the loan term and the lower the monthly payments, the higher the aggregate debt service payment that will be made by the borrower over the life of the loan. If the $1 million is borrowed at 9 percent, the amount that has to be repaid increases from $1,520,160 if the loan has a 10-year amortization schedule ($12,667 per month for 120 months) to $2,896,560 if the loan is repaid on a 30-year amortization schedule ($8,046 per month for 360 months), whereas the payments on the $1 million loan at 12 percent increase from $1,721,640 if repaid in 10 years ($14,347 per month for 120 months) to $3,702,960 if payment is made over 30 years ($10,286 per month for 360 months). Accordingly, the lender can fluctuate the loan terms to provide the borrower with the monthly payment it desires while receiving more than the lender had originally planned to receive.

Alternatively, a number of variable interest rates can be utilized in a permanent mortgage that provide the lender with even more flexibility. The available variable rate loans include:

- *Adjustable mortgage loans* —The interest rate is based upon a particular index and fluctuates periodically as the index changes. To reflect the fluctuating interest, the loan term, debt service, and/or principal balance will change during the loan term.

- *Callable loans* —To protect its interest rate, the lender can call the loan periodically after an initial period, enabling the lender to reexamine the rates if a long-term rate no longer reflects the market.

- *Deferred interest mortgage* —To accelerate the payment of the debt, the principal is paid first and the interest rate accrues without interest and is paid after the principal.

- *Graduated payment mortgage* —To assist new entries into the borrowing market, the loan rate is kept low for one or more years and then increases in steps to a market rate of interest.

- *Shared appreciation mortgages* —The lender obtains a participation of the profit on the sale of the property to compensate it for lending the money at a below-market interest rate.

- *Variable payment mortgage* —This is a standing mortgage loan in which the interest rate fluctuates with the loan market.

- *Variable rate mortgage* —The interest rate fluctuates with the market interest rate, and the debt service payment fluctuates to maintain the same amortization schedule with the new interest rate.

The lender can also increase the return on its loan by sharing in the profitability of property secured by a mortgage through an equity participation. Properly negotiated, an equity participation provides a benefit to both borrower and lender, because the borrower obtains financing in a tight credit market and retains the full tax benefits of the property's ownership, control of the property, and a lower debt service payment, while the lender shares in the property's appreciation and success without losing its lien against the property. The equity participation can take a number of forms, including:

- A percentage of gross income over a certain threshold
- A percentage of net income
- A percentage of net income over a certain threshold
- A percentage of net operating income
- A share of the profit of the sale of the property or the refinancing of the mortgage.

The document describing the equity kicker should clearly define the basis for the lender's interest in the property, especially the meaning of the words *income* and *profit.* The borrower should also examine the effect of the equity kicker in the event the property is sold or the mortgage refinanced.

A precondition for the borrower's agreeing to a loan with an equity participation for the lender must be the borrower's certainty that it is unable to obtain the financing from another source without providing the equity participation for the lender. The borrower should also consider whether it would be more advantageous to pay a higher current interest rate to avoid the equity participation. To make this analysis, the borrower must consider the real cost of the equity participation, which must entail an analysis of the borrower's anticipation as to the rate by which the property will appreciate during the life of the loan and whether the cost of the equity participation when added to the actual interest that will be paid to the lender makes economic sense in relation to the benefit to the borrower from the funds that are going to be received by the borrower from the lender. The parties also have to consider the interest rate that will be included in the loan, together with the lender's participation in the property. The borrower must also consider what, if any, participation the lender will want to have in such critical decisions as to when to sell, lease, or refinance the property. The other issue with which the borrower must deal is whether the lender's equity participation will continue after the loan is satisfied or whether the borrower will have the right to buy out the participation for a fixed or otherwise determinable amount of money.

There are also complications for the lender in accepting an equity participation in lieu of a higher interest rate. The lender should consider whether it wants to participate in the ownership of the property due to the possible conflicts of interest that it will face in the event of a default by the borrower. The lender must also consider the likelihood that the property will appreciate sufficiently to make it worth its while to give up the certainty of a higher interest rate and a fixed term. The lender must also be certain that the equity participation can never cause it to be considered the borrower's partner or joint venturer rather than a creditor of the owner. This dilemma can become particularly troublesome if the property or the owner becomes insolvent or has to otherwise utilize the bankruptcy laws, and the other creditors of the property or the owner challenge the lender's status as a secured creditor.

Alternatively, the parties may want to consider convertible mortgages, which are loans that provide for a fixed interest rate for a number of years and then, at the option of the lender, can be converted into an equity participation in the real estate secured by the mortgage. The property owner obtains its money at a lower interest rate during the loan term, and the owner does not have a taxable event occur until the loan is converted to an equity position. The owner also receives the cash flow from the property during the initial years of the loan and all the tax benefits and is not required to make amortization payments. Another format for a convertible mortgage not only gives the lender the right to convert the mortgage to an equity position, but, in the interim, provides the lender with cash flow from the property through contingent interest, which could be based upon the success of the property.

JUNIOR MORTGAGES

A junior mortgage is any mortgage on the property other than the first mortgage. The first mortgage on the property is almost always held by an institutional lender (i.e., a bank or an insurance company) and usually secures an indebtedness equal to 50 to 80 percent of the property's fair market value. A junior mortgage can be a second mortgage, third mortgage, or any other inferior lien, that has as its primary consideration a concern that the property owner does not default on a superior indebtedness. Junior mortgages can be held by institutional lenders, but they usually charge a higher interest rate. For that reason, junior mortgages are held by specialized lenders, who are better equipped to gauge the risk involved in making the loan.

Junior mortgages are not usually considered permanent loans because they secure relatively short-term loans that provide the property owner with access to a portion of its equity in the property. Junior mortgages avoid the necessity of requiring the owner to refinance the existing indebtedness on the property or to sell the property to obtain capital for improvements to the property or for the owner's other purposes. A junior mortgage permits an owner, who has a need for additional funds and has equity in the property in excess of the existing indebtedness, to obtain additional funds from another lender, by providing the lender with a subordinate lien on the property.

Because the holder of a junior mortgage is accepting a greater risk than the holder of the first mortgage on the property, the lender would charge a higher interest rate, as well as points (i.e., fees) for making the loan. The increased risk is caused by the fact that a default and foreclosure of the more senior mortgage would eliminate the junior mortgage as a lien on the property unless the holder of the subordinate mortgage was prepared to cure the default or acquire the superior mortgage prior to, or purchase the property at, the foreclosure sale. How much higher the interest rate on a junior mortgage could be, would depend on what degree of risk is involved in the junior mortgage, how junior it would be, and what percentage of the equity is secured by the more superior mortgage. Nevertheless, it would not be unusual for a first mortgage to have an interest rate one to two points above the prime lending rate, while a second mortgage on the same property might bear interest at six to eight points above the prime lending rate. It is also not unusual for a second mortgage to contain a minimum interest rate to protect the lender in case the prime lending rate reduced substantially.

Borrowers frequently borrow against their property through junior mortgages, even if they are required to pay the higher interest rate, rather then refinancing the entire existing indebtedness. The reasons borrowers defer seeking a newer, larger first mortgage to include the amount they wish to borrow that is being secured by the junior mortgage include the following:

- The existing financing on the property may have more favorable terms (i.e., longer term or lower interest rates) than can be obtained on refinancing.

- The first mortgage precludes prepayment.
- The property may be unable to satisfy a new senior lender's debt-to-equity requirements for the entire indebtedness.
- A high prepayment premium is required on the existing indebtedness.
- The borrower desires to obtain tax-free funds quickly, because secondary lenders are frequently able to close loans faster than institutional lenders.
- Credit is not available from the institutional lenders due to government monetary policy or regulations.

Additionally, due to the increased risk, lenders are usually less flexible on the loan provisions contained in the junior mortgages. The lender will be reluctant to take any additional risk, even though each junior mortgage will be superior to any future amounts that the borrower may borrow from the present holder of an underlying indebtedness or any other lender, unless the preexisting indebtedness also secures future advances.

To protect itself, the junior mortgage lender frequently requires that the senior lenders provide it with notice of any default by the borrower in the senior indebtedness and allow the subordinate lender the opportunity to cure the default. A default by the borrower in paying the senior indebtedness or performing an obligation under the superior mortgage would be considered a default in, and cause acceleration of, the junior indebtedness. Moreover, the holder of the junior indebtedness will want to have the right to act with regard to insurance proceeds and condemnation awards, subject to the rights of the holder of the senior indebtedness.

WRAPAROUND MORTGAGES

A wraparound mortgage is a junior mortgage that includes in its principal balance the indebtedness secured by one or more mortgages that were liens on the property prior to the wraparound mortgage's encumbering the property. In a wraparound mortgage, the obligation to pay debt service on the mortgages that are senior to the wraparound mortgage become the obligation of the holder of the wraparound mortgage, and the principal balance of the wraparound mortgage includes the outstanding balance of the underlying mortgage plus the wraparound mortgage holder's equity in the wraparound mortgage. The holder's equity in the wraparound mortgage is the difference between the balance of the wraparound mortgage and the aggregate existing indebtedness secured by the underlying mortgages.

A property could become subject to a wraparound mortgage rather than a more traditional institutional mortgage in a number of ways. The property may already be subject to an institutional mortgage, and the owner is obtaining funds from a second mortgage lender; however, the second lender would rather reduce its risk by controlling the situation through a wraparound mortgage. Alternatively, a permanent lender may lend a sum in excess of the existing financing to the owner of the property, not prepay the existing indebtedness, and request the borrower to execute a wraparound mortgage rather than a first mortgage for the aggregate amount of loans on the property. In either event, the lender would have an obligation for satisfying the senior mortgages (see Example below).

The junior lender is willing to take a wraparound mortgage due to the increased financial benefit to the lender and the security this format provides to the holder of the wraparound mortgage. The wraparound mortgage provides the holder with control over whether there is going to be a default in the underlying mortgage and, if the owner is going to default, the holder of the wraparound mortgage can advance the sums itself to make those payments and avoid a default. Additionally, if the interest rate on the wraparound mortgage is in excess of the interest rate on the underlying mortgage or the term of the wraparound mortgage is longer than the term of the underlying mortgage, the holder of the wraparound mortgage will receive an effective interest rate far in excess of the interest rate described in the wraparound mortgage (see Example on page 140).

EXAMPLE

If the property owner wants to borrow $1 million more than the existing $2 million mortgage on the property, the lender has three options: (1) to loan $3 million and the borrower uses $2 million to satisfy the existing first mortgage; (2) to lend $1 million for a second mortgage; and (3) to lend $1 million, assume the obligation for the existing first mortgage, and obtain a wraparound mortgage which will secure an indebtedness of $3 million even though only $1 million is loaned. Thereafter, the property owner will make debt service payments to the holder of the wraparound mortgage on the $3 million indebtedness, and the holder of the wraparound mortgage will be obligated to make the debt service payments on the underlying mortgage.

EXAMPLE

If a property is encumbered by a $2 million first mortgage that bears interest at 9 percent per annum and the owner wants to borrow an additional $1 million at a time when the interest rate for such a loan is 10.5 percent, then the borrower understands that he or she will have to refinance the existing first mortgage and his or her monthly interest expense will increase from $15,000 (9 percent interest on $2 million) to $26,250 (10.5 percent interest on $3 million). If the new lender lends the owner the $1 million and leaves the existing $2 million indebtedness on the property, which it will service through its wraparound mortgage, the wrap holder will receive $26,250 per month and pay $15,000 to the existing lenders, thereby increasing its return on the $1 million it lent to $11,250 per month ($135,000 per annum). This is a 13.5 percent return on the $1 million it lent, rather than the 10.5 percent that is the going rate, and there is no increased cost or risk to the borrower.

The holder of the wraparound mortgage will have the right to refuse to make the payments on the underlying indebtedness unless the property owner has paid the debt service on the wraparound mortgage. To protect the borrower, the loan documents will frequently allow the property owner to make the payment on the underlying mortgage directly to the lender, if the wrap holder fails to do so by the payment date. Under such a circumstance, the property owner would be allowed to terminate the wraparound mortgage for the wrap holder's failure to pay the underlying mortgage. In considering a wraparound mortgage, the parties must carefully analyze not only the amortization schedule of the wraparound mortgage, but also the amortization schedule of the mortgages which it wraps around. This will enable the property owner to determine the actual long-term benefit to the lender.

The wraparound mortgage can also be a big disadvantage to the property owner, if the terms of the wraparound mortgage and the underlying mortgage or mortgages are poorly synchronized. For example, if the underlying mortgage is self-liquidating and the wraparound mortgage is a standing mortgage, then as the property owner makes its debt services payments, the wrap holder's equity in the wraparound mortgage is increasing as the balance of the underlying mortgage is decreasing and the balance of the wraparound mortgage stays the same. The property owner would then be obligated to repay the entire original principal balance on maturity, which the wrap holder would retain, because the underlying mortgage had already been fully amortized. It appears that the best position in wraparound mortgage financing is the wrap holder.

Because the wrap indebtedness includes the underlying indebtedness in its principal balance, the mortgage frequently provides that any reduction in the underlying indebtedness that reduces the obligation of the holder of the wraparound mortgage (i.e., insurance proceeds or condemnation awards that are used to reduce the mortgage balance) should also reduce the balance of the wraparound mortgage. Furthermore, prepayments of the wraparound mortgage in excess of the lender's equity in the wraparound mortgage should also be applied to reduce the principal balance of the underlying mortgage. Another issue that frequently arises in a wraparound mortgage is the lender's right to refinance the underlying indebtedness. To protect the borrower in the event of a default by the lender, the lender should not be permitted to finance more than an amount that can be self-liquidated during the term and with the debt service payments on the wraparound mortgage. The reason for this is that the property owner will be obligated to pay the underlying mortgage if there is a default by the holder of the wraparound mortgage, and the holder of the wraparound mortgage should not be obligated to pay more indebtedness than it would have had to pay under the wraparound mortgage.

Additionally, the parties should consider the issue of consent. The fact that the borrower obtains the consent of the holder of the wraparound mortgage to take a particular action relating to the property does not mean that the holder of the underlying mortgages will agree. Accordingly, their consent to the action would still be required.

7

Preventing a Mortgage Default

Recognizing that a property is having problems is the first step toward solving those problems. An owner who refuses to admit that his or her property is having problems and requires assistance to solve those problems is the most likely candidate to need to acquire a detailed understanding of the contents of Chapters 9 ("Defending against Foreclosure") and 10 ("Benefiting from Bankruptcy"). The sooner an owner realizes that the property has developed or is developing problems, the more likely it is that those problems can be dealt with in a satisfactory manner and the investment protected.

It is important to note that a problem can have many components and that a problem to one owner may not be considered a problem to another owner. For one thing, problems with properties include not only the potential loss of a property through foreclosure because it is not generating sufficient income to pay the operating expenses and the debt service on the mortgage, but also something as relatively inconsequential as a property that is not generating as much cash flow as it could produce if it were being properly operated.

Basically, there are three components to cash flow: *gross income*, which is the revenue that the property produces from its tenants; *net operating income*, which is the gross income less the property's operating expenses; and *cash flow*, which is the net operating income less the debt services paid by the owner on the mortgages encumbering the property. A property can be a financial disaster if either the gross income is too low or the operating expenses or the debt services are too high. Therefore, to improve the profitability of a property, the owner has to do one or more of the following:

- Increase the gross income
- Decrease the operating expenses
- Decrease the debt services
- Maintain an equilibrium among gross income, operating expenses, and debt services.

It may seem simplistic to say that these four elements are necessary to improve a property's profitability, but it never hurts to define one's goals. Too often an owner loses sight of his or her purpose in developing a grandiose scheme for the improvement of a property. For example, would it make sense to increase a property's operating expenses by $200,000 to generate an additional $150,000 in income? Probably not. The answer is *probably* not because there are always exceptions. For instance, the tenants of some properties have triple net leases and reimburse the landlord for their share of any increase in operating expenses, in which case the landlord can retain the increase in operating income, and the increased gross income will yield an increase in the property's cash flow. In most circumstances, however, increasing operating expenses to such an extent is inefficient.

It is therefore imperative for the property owner to keep his or her eye on the bottom line and make certain that the proposed changes for a property will result in an increase in the property's cash flow. Unfortunately, real estate investors too often hear of buildings being expanded or constructed on speculation, and a user, purchaser, or tenant ends up taking the property off the owner's hands and "rewarding" the investor for his or her foresight with a huge profit. However, the big successes are usually the ones that are publicized, not the colossal failures. It is a rare real estate investor who would pay a publicist to advise the public that the investor lost a large sum of money on a mistake. The great opportunities go to the investors who appear to be infallible, not the ones who are perceived to be patsies.

Moreover, it is not sufficient for an investment to simply survive if the property has the potential to be significantly more successful than it is and the owner is not taking the necessary steps to achieve that success. These steps include the same things that are required to make the property operate profitably in the first place—increased income, reduced operating expenses, and debt service. Accomplishing these changes may require a simple alteration or may involve highly complex and expensive modifications to the financial or operating structure of the property.

This chapter explores methods of increasing a property's gross income by changing the use or tenants of the property, by decreasing the debt service on the mortgages encumbering the property through refinancing, and by reducing the property's operating expenses. None of these steps should be taken without a careful consideration of the risks entailed and an understanding of all the things that could go wrong. No change should be undertaken without having contingency plans for dealing with the adverse consequences of the change.

ALTERING A PROPERTY

When the local real estate market is glutted with empty buildings or the cash generated by a particular use is not sufficient to maintain the property and pay the debt service and operating expenses, the owner may determine that it will take too much time for the real estate market to strengthen sufficiently to cure the property's problems. In those instances, the owner should consider changing the use of, or market for, the property as a means for increasing the likelihood of its success. Because changing a property could involve changing occupants or the size or configuration of the building, the issues are what it costs for the transfiguration and whether a different market for the property exists. The redevelopment of a property only takes time and capital to achieve. The result could be as simple as a change of tenant, or as complex as changing a shopping center into an office park, or an office building into a mixed-use apartment building with several floors of shopping, or a department store into a school, warehouse, factory, or even office space (see Example). The success of the new use would depend upon whether the selected use is already glutted in other parts of the locale.

The simplest change is to retain the property's original use, but change the marketing to attract a different tenant or economic group. Apartment buildings could be made more marketable by adding amenities or by combining smaller apartments to form fewer, more valuable larger apartments. The addition of medical offices or boutiques on the first floor of the building could also improve the property's marketability, and the rent generated by the commercial and professional use may be more than for the residential use. Another approach is to divide apartments into smaller, less expensive units, if there is a greater need for small apartments. Nevertheless, neither the owner nor the lender should consider making a change in the property's use without first

EXAMPLE

Smith determines that he is unable to attract any tenants to his strip shopping center because of the competition in the area, and the tenants he can attract are willing to pay only $5 per square foot. Smith may be able to spend $100,000 changing the fronts of the stores and lease the space as an office park or as offices for doctors, dentists, and related professionals at $15 per square foot. Alternatively, if Smith loses his anchor tenants, he can divide the space and create a mini-mall.

obtaining a current demographic study of the area to determine whether there is a market for the renovated facility. The parties should also obtain detailed cost estimates for reconfiguring the space. Furthermore, the owner and lender must also consider the time it will take to obtain the required municipal approvals and to reconstruct the space, as well as the possibility that during that time either the market for the current use will change or the market for the alternative use will become glutted. Under such circumstances, it would be better for the owner and lender to not change the property's use but to maintain it and wait for a change in the market.

Another change the lender and the owner might consider is a change in the form of ownership of the property. This can be accomplished by converting the building, regardless of its use, into a cooperative or a condominium and selling the stores, offices, or apartments rather than leasing the units or selling the entire project to a single purchaser. In such a conversion, the sum of the parts (i.e., the sale of individual units) is frequently worth significantly more than the current value of the whole property.

For the conversion to be successful, there would have to be an incentive for the tenant or purchaser to acquire the space. Fortunately, the economic benefit of purchasing rather than leasing space can be phenomenal, if the monthly payments toward debt service on the acquisition loan and the owner's share of common expenses are not significantly greater than the rent the purchaser would have paid. This benefit increases substantially when one considers that the purchaser would be building equity in the property instead of simply paying rent. Furthermore, the purchaser would share directly in the ultimate success of the property, be able to obtain refinancing proceeds, and participate in decisions regarding the operation and maintenance of the property.

Moreover, the ability of owners to obtain financing in the future will be adversely affected by the current problems in the real estate market and the lending industry. There is little doubt that, with all of the problems that the savings and loan associations, banks, and insurance companies are presently having with real estate loans, common ownership may very well provide a significant portion of future financing or property development and ownership.

Finally, the owner might consider the most frequently utilized method of increasing a property's popularity: leaving the property in its current condition, but providing incentives for purchasers or tenants to buy or lease. The incentives that an owner could provide to purchasers or tenants might include:

- Rent abatements
- Construction of additional amenities
- Reimbursement for tenant improvements
- Payments to a new tenant for breaking a preexisting lease
- Providing a new tenant with some form of equity to provide it with the opportunity to share in the ultimate success of the property
- Providing the tenant with a share of the proceeds that are ultimately received on the sale of the property.

Lowering the rent and increasing the incentives or amenities to attract tenants or purchasers may seem to be a simple solution (see Example). However, sometimes an owner becomes so bogged down in dealing with the problems of the property that he or she becomes unable

EXAMPLE

Jones, the owner of a garden apartment complex, is losing tenants to a new complex several blocks away, which is charging his former tenants a higher rent than Jones charged. Jones can increase the attractiveness of his property by installing a swimming pool ($15,000), turning storage space in the basement or elsewhere into a fully equipped health club ($15,000), installing new appliances in each apartment ($2,000 each), and improving the landscaping and exterior appearance of the property ($20,000), for which he should be able to charge a competitive rent with the newer facility. This make-over will cost under $200,000, but if Jones can increase his rent roll by $40,000 per year and retain his tenants, it is well worth the expense.

to make objective business decisions regarding the property, including being able to think of fairly simple solutions. Under those circumstances, the solutions might become more obvious to in a third party, who is asked to assess the situation.

The economics involved in changing a tenant depend entirely on the cost of replacing the existing tenant. If the tenant has defaulted or violated the terms of its lease, then the cost may involve only the legal fees incurred in obtaining a judgment against, and evicting, the tenant. If the tenant's lease is about to expire, the cost of replacing the tenant is only the cost of identifying a new tenant and paying for whatever work letter is required to interest the tenant in the space. However, if neither of these scenarios is available to the owner, then the cost of replacing the tenant might include a payment to the tenant to terminate the lease. Whether it will be worth it to the landlord will depend on the quality of the replacement tenant and the increase in potential rent (see Example).

Under certain circumstances, the quality of the tenant could make it worthwhile to replace the tenant with one paying the same or a lower rent. This would occur if the new tenant is likely to draw an improved clientele to the property, and thereby increase the rent that the other tenants are paying. This is the reason why the anchor tenant in a shopping center always pays significantly less rent than the local or regional merchants that lease the satellite stores. However, deciding whether to replace a tenant at the same or lower rent cannot be done in the abstract; it can be accomplished only in the context of a larger plan.

Obtaining an improved tenant can be accomplished in a number of ways. The best way is for the increased rental income to be earned by the property owner rather than the former tenant. A tenant with a lengthy lease or the right to renew the lease for several additional terms and the right to sublease the leasehold or assign the lease, for example, can generate the profit on the lease by conveying its leasehold interest in the property to the new tenant. Although the landlord continues to receive the original rent, the old tenant makes a profit on the sublease or assignment.

EXAMPLE

> Ross owns a shopping center in which a shoe store is paying rent of $2 per square foot with five years remaining on its lease. Ross is approached by a liquor store owner who would pay $10 per square foot for the store. It would pay Ross to buy out the remainder of the shoe store lease for a payment equal to the discounted current value of half the additional rent Ross will receive from the liquor store owner.

If the lease was a below-market lease, this possibility is an unfortunate turn of events for the landlord. However, if the landlord realizes that the rent is a below-market rent and the tenant does not actually need or utilize the space to its full capacity, there is no reason why the landlord cannot approach the tenant about a payment to terminate the lease. Thereafter (or, more likely, while that negotiation is proceeding), the landlord would approach the potential tenant about leasing the property. The tenant may realize what the landlord is doing and attempt to sublease the property or assign the lease, but even in a lease that permits the tenant to sublease or assign the lease, there are limitations on what a tenant can do without the landlord's consent. For example, a subtenant or assignee interested in taking over the space must obtain the landlord's consent to make any alterations in the space. Under these circumstances, however, the landlord is not likely to give consent.

Another question the landlord needs to consider is how much to pay the tenant to terminate the lease. The simple answer is, as little as possible! However, the actual solution depends on the increased rent the landlord is going to receive from the new tenant. The amount paid to the old tenant should be less than the present value of the increased rent the new tenant will pay over the remaining term and renewal periods of the old tenant's lease, and should be discounted based upon the present cost of borrowed funds. A sum paid to the tenant that is larger than the present value of the additional rent means that the new tenant will obtain the benefit of the new lease without any risk that the payments will not be made.

The mathematics become significantly more complicated if the landlord does not have a replacement tenant waiting to take over the space, but is speculating that a tenant will be identified when the space is available. The other complication occurs if the new tenant is an inducement to getting other tenants to lease space at higher rents. In that circumstance, the landlord must include in the calculation a factor for the value of the increased rent from the other space being leased. However, the former tenant should not receive full credit in the calculation for the increased rent the landlord will receive.

It is possible that the new tenant will want the space so badly that the new tenant will reimburse the landlord for the cost of removing the original tenant. In that case, the landlord needs to find out how much the new tenant is willing to pay to obtain the space. But even then, a problem exists. In all likelihood, the new tenant's cost of obtaining the space will reduce the amount of rent the new tenant is willing to pay the landlord for the space. Therefore, the landlord is reimbursing the new tenant for the cost of removing the old tenant, but it is payable in monthly installments over the term of the lease by limitations on the rent the new tenant is willing to pay.

Unfortunately, in the current real estate market, a landlord is less likely to be faced with a replacement tenant interested in paying a higher rent, than with an existing tenant approaching the landlord and demanding the right to pay a lower rent. This problem could arise either when the lease is due to expire or if the tenant has no other assets but is a wholly owned subsidiary of a larger, more affluent corporation. In this event, the landlord has three alternative courses of action. The landlord can attempt to negotiate with the tenant to pay a reduced rent and be grateful that at least the cash flow from that tenant will continue. Alternatively, the landlord can point out to the tenant that the tenant can leave, but will have to pay the costs of moving and preparing the new space, as well as making up for the time lost in planning and executing a move to another location with its attendant loss of productivity and the new space may not be as adequate as the old space. Finally, the landlord can refuse to renegotiate the rent and, instead, look for a new tenant and at the same time examine the tenant's corporate structure to find a way to have the parent corporation made responsible for the subsidiary's unpaid rent. The last alternative, however, works only if the tenant is breaking the lease, not if the lease is terminated on its own terms. Under those circumstances, the landlord's safest course of action is to agree to the lower rent, but either for a reduced term or with increases built into the lease or tied to the Consumer Price Index. (See Example).

EXAMPLE

Peter owns an office building that has 10,000 square feet leased for seven more years at $35 per square foot to Jones Leasing Corp., a wholly owned, but nominally funded subsidiary of Jones Industries, Inc. Jones advises Peters that because it can rent comparable space at $20 per square foot, it intends to abandon the space unless Peters lowers the rent to $25 per square foot for the balance of the lease term. Since a judgment for the rent against Jones Leasing Corp. will be worthless and Peters can rent the space for only $20 per square foot (assuming that information is true), it makes sense for Peters to agree to the reduction.

REFINANCING THE MORTGAGE

The property owner can accomplish several goals by refinancing the mortgage, each of which can have significant long-term benefits for the owner. If interest rates are lower when the loan is refinanced or a substantial portion of the original mortgage has been amortized, refinancing the mortgage will result in a reduction in the debt service payable by the owner, which increases the property's cash flow. Alternatively, if the property needs improvements or refurbishing or the landlord needs money to pay a departing tenant and obtain a better tenant, refinancing can produce those funds. (See Example below.)

The savings are just as effective if the mortgage has been heavily amortized and the interest rate is higher (see Example on page 151).

In any event, in the short run, refinancing the mortgage can certainly reduce the debt service and increase the cash flow. The issues are whether the owner wants to pay the price and whether the additional financing is available.

Permanent mortgage financing is available from many sources, many of which depend upon the availability of money throughout the economy.

EXAMPLE

If a property is encumbered by a $5 million mortgage that bears interest at 12 percent per annum and is self-liquidating over 15 years, the annual debt service payment of $720,100 can be reduced and the cash flow increased in the following ways:

- If interest rates are reduced to 9 percent, the debt service payment would be reduced to $608,559.
- If the term was extended by 10 years, the debt service payment would be reduced to $631,934.
- If the loan was interest only, rather than self-liquidating, the debt service payment would be reduced to $600,000, but the full $5 million would be due on maturity.
- If the interest rate was reduced to 9 percent and the term extended by 10 years, the debt service payment would be reduced to $503,517.

Therefore, the debt service payment can be reduced and the cash flow can be increased by up to $120,000 per year through refinancing.

EXAMPLE

An original mortgage of $5 million bearing interest at 9 percent has been reduced to $2 million. The $608,559 annual debt service payment can be reduced to $218,088 per year if the property is refinanced for another 25 years at 10 percent per annum. Therefore, there is a savings of $390,470 per year merely by extending the term of the loan, even if the interest rate is higher. However, over the term of the refinanced loan, a significantly greater amount of interest will be paid.

The availability of funds for mortgages depend, to a large extent, on the economy in general, and on whether the Federal Reserve Board decides to make credit available. Traditionally, the largest sources of funds have been commercial banks, insurance companies, savings banks, pension funds, mortgage companies, Real Estate Investment Trusts, and savings and loan associations; however, this is rapidly changing due to the financial difficulties the lenders are having and the changing regulations issued by the regulators. Nevertheless, the availability of permanent financing usually depends upon investment decisions by the lenders, and is usually based upon current interest rates, the relative risk to the lender from a particular kind of real estate loan, and the demand for credit from different segments of the economy. Moreover, each lender participates in the mortgage market based upon its own internal lending criteria and the amount of money the lender has to lend for real estate. The lenders' concerns range from the rate of return they need to achieve a required loan-to-value ratio to their interpretation as to how different segments of the economy are likely to perform over the short and long term in different geographic centers. They also want a diversified loan portfolio.

Furthermore, the funds that the lenders have available for permanent loans and the loans' terms depend upon (1) what the lenders are required to do to attract funds from their depositors or policy holders, (2) what is happening in the economy, and (3) whether the federal reserve is making money available. They also depend on whether the lenders are comfortable in tying up their capital for extended periods of time. Lending institutions frequently prefer short-term corporate borrowing rather than long-term real estate loans because the short-term loans are more sensitive to fluctuations in the interest rate market. They also provide the lender with the ability to constantly reevaluate its loan portfolio. Nevertheless, lenders still lend against real estate because secured real estate loans provide greater security than unsecured business loans and the relatively fixed rates on real estate loans provide the lenders with protection when the interest rate market declines. Lenders also prefer business loans because, unlike corporate borrowers, real estate borrowers do not usually maintain significant bank balances. Real estate borrowers usually utilize all the money they borrow for new deals immediately upon receipt of the loan proceeds. Moreover, due to the soft real estate market, real estate loans recently have become a more complicated decision than short-term business loans in terms of credit risk.

When the government reduces the availability of funds, the lending institutions reduce their real estate loans to be able to continue providing liquidity to their corporate borrowers. When funds are not readily available, interest rates rise and the banks require larger downpayments and shorter mortgages and terms; points from the borrowers; and, occasionally, an equity interest on the sale or refinancing of the property. Alternatively, when money becomes available, mortgages are available at lower interest rates and with smaller downpayments and longer terms.

The federal government has established the secondary mortgage market to maintain the availability of funds for the purchase of housing. This market includes the Federal National Mortgage Association ("Fannie Mae"), the Federal Home Loan Mortgage Corporation ("Freddie Mac"), and the Government National Mortgage Association ("Ginnie Mae"):

- Fannie Mae, a private corporation, is regulated by the Department of Housing and Urban Development. It borrows money by issuing debentures, notes, and bonds, and then purchases mortgages from lending institutions, thereby providing liquidity to the institutions that loaned the money in the first place.
- Freddie Mac purchases mortgages from the banks and resells mortgages and issues debt instruments.
- Ginnie Mae uses money from the United States Treasury to purchase and resell mortgages at a discount to Fannie Mae and also has a program in which mortgage bankers put mortgages together in packages and issues debentures against the package which are guaranteed by Ginnie Mae.

The secondary mortgage market also includes the sale of pass-through mortgage securities, which are insured by private mortgage insurers, and the sale by savings and loan associations of bonds collateralized by their mortgage portfolios.

Permanent mortgage financing is also available from life insurance companies due to the relative security of the loans and the lender's need to receive long-term income from the premiums to pay the insurance proceeds when required. One reason that life insurance companies are so active in real estate loans is that, unlike a bank or other lending institution, a life insurance company is unable by law to become involved in many aspects of commercial banking and general unsecured lending. Pension funds also have a need to make long-term investments to be certain that funds will be available to fund retirement benefits.

Permanent real estate loans are also available from mortgage banks. Mortgage banks have their own sources of capital that are used to originate real estate loans, which they then sell to institutional lenders. Frequently, a mortgage bank will seem more interested in making loans than other institutional lenders because mortgages are the mortgage bank's only business. Moreover, after the loan is made, the mortgage bank is able to dispose of the mortgage, receive back an amount in excess of the amount advanced, and make a profit on the servicing of the loan. Mortgage banks are more active lenders due to their familiarity with real estate and the different loan criteria. For these reasons, they are more willing than other lenders to make a loan and take the risk of either finding an interested lender or holding the loan until market conditions improve. Private investors, real estate investment trusts, and credit unions are also frequently interested in making permanent mortgage loans because it is a secure long-term investment providing a minimum of risk and a strong likelihood of receiving the principal and interest payments.

Mortgage brokers and mortgage bankers play an important role in obtaining financing for real estate, even where the subject property is in default. A mortgage banker seeks listings from particular property owners to obtain mortgage funds. The mortgage banker will review the property and the proposed transaction and advise the owner of the property as to the kind of financing it can obtain, the interest rate, amortization period, prepayment provisions, points, and other terms. The owner then enters into an agreement with the mortgage banker and pays it a fee to obtain the requisite financing. Mortgage bankers are usually correspondents (i.e., have relationships) with several institutional lenders. As a correspondent, the mortgage banker plays an important role in identifying good investments for the lenders and assisting the lenders by servicing the loans that the mortgage bankers have placed for the lender. The mortgage banker prepares a detailed loan package, which it sends to the lenders it feels would be most likely to lend against the subject property. This determination is based upon the criteria established by the lender. The mortgage banker's submission to the lender includes an application, an economic analysis of the project, an appraisal of the property, a review of the security for the loan, and biographical information on the borrower. The mortgage banker also provides the lender with follow-up information relating to the proposed loan and the collateral.

A mortgage broker also seeks financing for an owner, but it does not act as a correspondent for any lenders and does not have permanent relationships with particular lenders. Mortgage brokers offer the loan to many diverse lenders throughout the country to find the best deal for the borrower. Although the mortgage banker is usually able to quickly arrange the financing, owners sometimes prefer dealing with a mortgage broker because the broker is seeking the lowest rates from a broader market, whereas the mortgage banker may be more interested in protecting its relationships with the lenders for whom it is acting as a correspondent. Generally, however, the mortgage banker can obtain excellent rates from the lenders with whom it regularly does business, because the lenders feel more secure placing a loan with one of its correspondents.

Seeking permanent financing begins with the borrower's preparation of a written mortgage application. The application provides the lender with information upon which to make a preliminary credit analysis. The borrower uses the lender's application form, which is considered an offer by the borrower to the lender to borrow the funds, and is not binding on the lender until executed by the lender and accepted by the borrower. The loan application requires a great deal of information about both the borrower and the property, including:

- The identity of the borrower, its principals, and their business background and real estate experience
- Financial statements, credit history, and tax returns for the borrower and its principals
- A detailed description of the property
- Copies of any leases or lease commitments that have already been executed
- A survey of the property
- A title report for the property
- An environmental inspection report for the property
- Photographs of the existing site
- Renderings of the completed improvements
- The amount and terms of the requested loan
- A current appraisal of the property by an independent appraiser
- Information relating to the zoning and taxes for the property.

Each lender usually has its own criteria as to whether to make a mortgage loan, which it applies according to the lender's own procedures and standards. The lender begins by making a general determination that:

- The borrower is someone with whom the lender wishes to do business
- The property is located in an area that appears to be growing
- The improvements are adequate and are or will be properly constructed
- The tenants or proposed tenants are sufficiently creditworthy
- The location of the property is appropriate for the anticipated use
- There is a demand for space and a low enough vacancy rate in the area for similar space.

As part of its review, the lender will determine the total property value for its purposes and the maximum amount it will be prepared to lend with the property being used as security. The property value can be determined in a number of ways, including comparing the property to a similar property that recently sold, determining the cost of replacing the improvements on the property, and capitalizing the current and anticipated income from the property. The capitalization method is accomplished by calculating the net operating income produced by the property (i.e., the gross income less operating expenses) and capitalizing the net operating income based upon prevailing market rates for a return on an investment in real estate. Value is calculated by dividing the capitalization rate into the property's net income. Therefore, if the current capitalization rate is 11 percent and the net income from the property is $400,000 a year, then the property value would be $3,636,363 ($400,000 divided by 11 percent). The higher the net operating income produced by the property or the lower the capitalization rate, the higher the value of the property and the amount that can be borrowed by a mortgage. Accordingly, when interest rates rise, the capitalization rate would also rise because an investor in real estate would be able to earn a higher return on a bank deposit if the interest rate is higher then the capitalization rate. Interest rates and capitalization rates also fall together.

After the lenders determine the value of the property, they apply their own loan-to-value ratios to the value to determine the amount they are willing to lend against that value. Lending institutions are subject to self-imposed lending limitations, as well as those limitations that are imposed by the federal and state banking authorities. These ratios were once up to 90 percent, but now are frequently no more than 75 percent of a property's value. The lenders frequently increase their required loan-to-value ratio if other criteria are met, including:

- The relationship between the loan amount and the gross rentable area
- The amount of the loan as a multiple of gross income
- The amount of the loan as a multiple of net income
- The dollar value of rentals from credit tenants compared with the actual operating costs and debt service of the property
- The relationship of cash flow to debt service
- The relationship of debt service and operating expenses to gross income.

If the loan-to-value ratio is satisfactory and the other loan criteria are satisfied, the lender would issue a loan commitment at such time as the permanent lender has determined that (1) it will have the funds available to make the loan, (2) the property provides adequate security for the loan, (3) the borrower's credit is satisfactory, and (4) the borrower will be able to repay the loan and interest in a timely fashion. The written loan commitment assures the borrower that if the conditions of the loan commitment are met and the lender obtains a valid security interest in the property, the loan will be funded. The loan commitment usually contains the loan terms (the loan amount, the property to be mortgaged, the interest rate, the maturity date, the monthly payments, and the expiration date of the commitment), as well as the lender's closing requirements. A condition of the loan commitment is that the borrower will pay a commitment fee to the lender when the commitment is issued. The amount of the commitment fee depends on the size of the loan and the nature of the interest rates. A fixed interest rate usually requires the payment of a higher commitment fee than an adjustable rate to compensate the lender for the risk its taking in the event of a fluctuation in the market prior to the loan funding.

The permanent lender usually attempts to keep the term of the commitment as short as possible to avoid being committed to lend funds at a certain interest rate if, due to fluctuations in the loan market, the rate becomes unattractive prior to the funding. The lender then would be unable to obtain the required funds or would be forced to sell the loan in the secondary market at a significant discount. If the lender is acquiring the construction loan, the construction lender will want a permanent loan commitment to remain in effect for as long a term as possible to provide the borrower with sufficient time to complete the project. The borrower should also be concerned with the financial conditions relating to the funding of the loan. If the loan is conditioned upon the borrower's entering into a certain number of leases or a certain number of tenants occupying their space before the loan will be funded, there is a risk to the borrower that, in the event the market becomes soft, the lender will not fund the loan.

The loan commitment contains all the important provisions of the loan and describes the documentation that the borrower needs for the closing. It includes the following provisions:

- The borrower's name, address, and business affiliations
- Whether the borrower is a partnership or a corporation, the state in which it is incorporated or filed, and whether it is qualified to do business in the state where the property is located
- Whether the lender is making the loan based upon any security in addition to the property, including a guaranty by the principals of the borrower or the corporate parent of the borrower
- Whether the loan is conditioned upon the execution of certain specific leases or of a construction loan commitment, and the required terms of such leases or construction provisions
- The payment provisions of the proposed loan, including the loan amount, loan term, interest rate, payment provisions, and prepayment limitations
- The name of the lender's counsel and the fact that the borrower has to pay the lender's counsel's fees
- The default provisions that will be included within the loan documents
- The requirement that the borrower accept the commitment by a certain date and close the loan by a certain date or the commitment expires
- A brief description of the property to be mortgaged and the fact that the loan is conditioned upon the lender's receiving a first lien on the land and buildings and improvements, without any liens or security interests affecting the lender's position
- The fact that the borrower will obtain title insurance on behalf of the lender at the borrower's cost and that the title will be good

and marketable and the mortgage will be a valid first lien on the property

- The obligation that the borrower provide an "as built" survey to the lender, demonstrating that the property abuts a public street or has access to a public street and indicating the location of all buildings, improvements, easements, and other limitations

- The obligation of the borrower to supply certificates of occupancy or the local equivalent permitting the property to be used in the manner in which the borrower intends to use it

- Proof that the property is in compliance with all federal, state, and local environmental requirements and that there are no toxic or hazardous substances on the property or in the buildings

- Evidence that the property has received the proper local zoning approval or that a subdivision map has been filed or that local approval is not necessary

- Copies of all executed lease, as well as an assignment of the leases to the lender

- Satisfactory evidence that the borrower has authority to enter into the loan and execute the loan documents

- Conditions relating to the borrower's financial condition

- The fact that all real estate taxes must be paid at the closing, and the fact that tax escrows must be established to pay future taxes

- Satisfactory proof that the property is covered by required insurance, which usually includes fire with extended and additional coverage, sprinkler, boiler, rent or business interruption, public liability, plate glass, flood, and any other relevant insurance to the business, including workman's compensation

- The fact that the loan will not close if any part of the property is subject to a condemnation proceeding

- The lender's right to declare the loan in default if the borrower attempts to sell the property or to place any additional liens on the property

- The borrower's confirmation that the lender has the right to cancel the commitment if any of the provisions of the commitment or the application turn out to be incorrect, or if there is a material adverse change in the borrower's or tenant's financial condition, or if that property is damaged in any way, or if any litigation exist that could have an adverse financial position on the borrower

- A provision that the loan commitment cannot be assigned without the lender's consent
- The borrower's counsel supplying an opinion to the lender.

REDUCING OPERATING EXPENSES

Reducing a property's operating expenses presents the owner with a dilemma. Although the owner can always reduce the operating expenses, the issue is at what point the reduced operating expenses and curtailed services to the tenants adversely affect the income being generated from the property. Earlier in this chapter, it was indicated that the bottom line must not be forgotten and that the important number is the cash flow being paid to the owner. Therefore, the important criterion is not how low operating expenses can be reduced, but what minimum expenses are necessary to support the property's current income level. The owner must also consider whether the reduced operating expenses will inhibit the increase in gross income in a larger amount than the amount saved by reducing the expenses.

The cautious owner can do many things to reduce operating expenses; however, some require an expenditure before the owner can achieve the benefit of the reduced expense, and others do not actually reduce expenses, but keep them from increasing. One such expense saver is preventive maintenance. It is quite possible that, by having an engineer periodically inspect the property and expending sums to maintain the various components of the property prior to their breaking or leaking or otherwise failing to perform their function, the owner can save the significantly higher costs of replacing the item altogether. This holds true whether the item to be replaced or repaired is the roof; the exterior walls; the plumbing; the heating, electrical, or air conditioning systems; or any other aspect of the building.

Another way to save money by spending money is to determine that replacing a component with something more energy efficient will save the ever-increasing cost of energy in the future. This could entail changing the heating system to one that is more energy efficient, even if it is only newer. This could also involve automating portions of the property to reduce the cost and inefficiency of manual labor.

The owner can also reduce the property's operating expenses by assuming the role of managing agent or leasing agent. That role assumption can work very well, providing the owner is capable of handling those tasks, and the tasks are not taking him or her away from a task that is more important or profitable.

Furthermore, operating expenses can be reduced by retaining professional consultants to examine the operation of the property and make recommendations as to more cost-efficient ways of operating the property. Every property is different, so each proposal will be different. However, there are probably changes that can and should be made to every property to reduce the short- and long-term costs to the owner, and therefore increase profitability and reduce the likelihood that the owner will require financial assistance.

8

Restructuring the Debt

The cornerstone of real estate ownership is the owner's ability to borrow against his or her equity in a property at the time the property is acquired and throughout the ownership cycle. Financing is part of the very essence of the acquisition, development, improvement, and disposition of real estate. Financing can be one of the fundamental causes for many owners' problems with their real estate investments, as well as part of the cure for many of the problems that affect real estate. Even if an owner's problems were not caused by excessive financing, because debt service is usually one of the property's largest expenses, a temporary or permanent restructuring of the property's indebtedness is an expeditious method for increasing the owner's cash flow and assisting him or her in surviving the downturn.

Restructuring the debt that encumbers a property can facilitate the borrower's survival in a difficult time. This restructuring involves an agreement by the lender to a temporary or permanent change in the loan terms to prevent the owner from being forced to sell the property at a distressed price, file for bankruptcy protection, or defend a mortgage foreclosure action. The idea behind a debt restructuring is that it is a joint attempt by the borrower and the lender to salvage a valuable property and avoid the delays, expense, and negative publicity generated by a foreclosure or a bankruptcy proceeding. The basis of a debt restructuring is an acknowledgment by the owner and the lender that their best interests are to attempt to avoid a real estate meltdown.

A debt restructuring assumes that it is in the best interests of both the owner and the lender to cooperate with each other, to find ways to compromise, and to make concessions. For a debt restructuring to be successful, both the owner and the lender must realize that they have to take reasonable steps to protect the value of the property, to maximize its ultimate worth and thereby protect the investment in the property of both the owner and the lender. There is no correct manner of restructuring a debt. A debt restructuring is the creation of the borrower and lender in response to problems arising with a particular property. It is the reaction of the borrower and lender to a sudden and dramatic reversal in the fortunes of a property. The similarity between all debt restructurings is that both the owner and the lender share an optimism that under the correct set of circumstances the property can become successful. Alternatively, the debt restructuring can be taken as a pessimistic acknowledgment by the parties that they have no other hope of protecting their investment in the property.

Even if this seems like the only solution to the property's problems, however, the parties should still be extremely cautious as they proceed. The lender will agree to cooperate in a debt restructuring only if the lender believes that the problem property has a chance for success, even if the chance is small. The lender will believe that if it attempts a debt restructuring of a property that is in such dire straits that success would be impossible, the lender would be wasting its time and may be further compromising the security for its loan. The result of attempting to restructure the debt of a property that has no chance to succeed, would only postpone the inevitable, make it more difficult for the property to be sold at a price that would provide the lender with a return of its loan, and could connect the owner with an unsuccessful property for a longer time than is necessary or desirable. Moreover, the more involved the lender becomes with a property that is going to fail, the more likely it is that the borrower or another creditor will attempt to use the lender's actions as the basis for claiming a lender liability defense to the lender's foreclosure or otherwise using it in an offensive manner in a lawsuit against the lender. The lender's risk of a lender liability defense or a claim of equitable subordination becomes even more problematic if the borrower follows its default with a filing under the Bankruptcy Code.

Nevertheless, regardless of what the lender does, there is little to stop the borrower from raising defenses to the lender's foreclosure action, which can probably prevent the loss of the property for at least a year, and does not preclude the borrower from then filing a bankruptcy petition prior to a judgment of foreclosure being rendered and thereby obtain additional time to reorganize the property. The borrower may even be able to use the bankruptcy to force the lender to agree to better terms on the loan which is referred to as a "cram down." However, foreclosure and bankruptcy are last resorts for the owner and the lender because they both carry a stigma for the owner and the property. Years after the problem is resolved, the property will be remembered for having had serious problems and not for its subsequent success. These delays become a real incentive for the lender to find an acceptable alternative and thereby resuscitate its loan.

Moreover, a debt restructuring is a far more preferable solution than foreclosure and bankruptcy, which would result in the loss of the property and the recapture of income tax losses by the owner's investors or partners. Regardless of the outcome, the result of foreclosure or bankruptcy will be an adverse impact on the owner's credit rating, could result in the loss of the owner's equity in the property, and would produce an antagonism to the lender as well as to the owner's investors. Accordingly, restructuring of the property's debt provides the owner with the best means of salvaging its investment in the property and its reputation with its investors, lenders, and other creditors.

Once the parties determine that restructuring the property's debt is an appropriate method of solving the property's problems, it becomes imperative for the parties to act as quickly as possible to identify and solve the problems before the situation deteriorates further. From the owner's perspective, restructuring the debt is the best solution to the property's problems, particularly in a depressed real estate market. If the debt restructuring is successful and the property subsequently prospers, the owner's credit history will not be adversely affected, the property will command higher rent, the owner may eventually be able to generate a significant return on its original investment when the property is ultimately disposed of in a stronger market, and the lender will again have a loan that is performing.

PRELIMINARY CONSIDERATIONS

For any negotiation between the property owner and the lender to be successful, the owner must put itself in the position of the lender and analyze the situation and consider solutions in the same manner as the lender. Therefore, the initial consideration for the owner and the lender, before attempting to restructure the debt on a particular property, is to make a precise determination of the direct and indirect as well as the primary and secondary causes of a property's problems. Only then will the parties be in a position to determine whether the restructuring can solve the problems and make the property self-sufficient and profitable. This preliminary analysis requires a complete review of the owner and the property to determine whether the problems were caused by the owner, the economy, the property, or a combination of factors. This analysis will entail the same due diligence as that made by a lender or purchaser prior to investing in, or lending against, the property. For the review to be meaningful, the lender must become fully familiar with the property and the owner and the advantages and disadvantages of rescuing the property. Accordingly, the lender's review will include an analysis of all aspects of the property, including leases, promissory notes and mortgages, agreements relating to the development, construction and operation of the property, and all title, survey, environmental, engineering, and demographic reports relating to the property that are in the possession of, or available to the owner and the lender. Moreover, if time is available, the lender will also consider obtaining a current property appraisal.

The probable result of this review is that the lender may realize things about the property that were obvious at the time the loan was originally made, but were considered immaterial or insignificant. The loan was made when the economy was strong and the parties were optimistic; the loan commitment was issued, and the loan closed as quickly as possible. However, for the review to be meaningful, the lender must acknowledge the problem, and identify the cause and its involvement in order to deal with the current situation. The result is that, notwithstanding the owner's potential default, the lender will have to decide the best manner of proceeding to protect its loan.

Lenders believe that this due diligence review is essential for determining whether to participate in a debt restructuring and for identifying the components of a solution. However, the resolution of the problem must entail more than the lender's postponing loan payments. The lender's judgment would subsequently be questioned if its response to the owner's default was to allow the borrower to continue making all the decisions relating to the property without any supervision. There is little doubt that, notwithstanding the default, the owner would continue to have the best understanding of the property and the cause of, and solution to, the property's problems. Nevertheless, the lender may believe that the owner's priorities are different from those of the lender, and the owner's concern is probably not the security for the loan. Unfortunately, the owner might continue to believe that the property is perfect and will still succeed, if given an opportunity, which usually translates into additional time and financing. Every owner also believes that his or her handling of the property is above reproach. Therefore, the lender must make a realistic assessment of the situation and decide whether the property can succeed under current circumstances, in its present condition and without a change in ownership. Alternatively, the lender can utilize the owner's weakened financial condition as the catalyst for making changes that it reasonably believes are necessary.

The lender's initial consideration is whether to foreclose its mortgage or to otherwise take control of the property and thereafter replace the owner. The lender should never make this decision without a detailed consideration of the advantages and disadvantages of such an action, especially whether such an action would place the lender at risk. Alternatively, the lender could provide the owner with incentives to execute and deliver a deed in lieu of foreclosure, which would provide the lender with absolute control over the property's future without the risk of litigation by the owner. Although few lenders would consider this to be a preferred alternative, if the lender has no confidence in the owner's ability to operate the property, the lender may have little choice other than to obtain control.

To a large degree, the success of the property after the debt restructuring will depend upon the owner's ability to resolve the property's problems with additional capital or additional time. Thus, it is important for the lender to feel satisfied that the owner has acted and will continue to act in a prudent and businesslike manner and in good faith. It is likely that, initially at least, the lender will view the owner with suspicion and assume that the owner is to blame for the property's problems. The basis for the lender's assumption will be that the problems were caused by the owner's faulty perception of the property or its use or the owner's inability to recognize a change in the market or bad timing or dishonesty. If the owner is to remain in control of the property and carry it to fruition, the first issue with which the owner must deal has to do with the owner's integrity, diligence, prudence, and good faith. If the lender continues to have no confidence in the owner, the lender's perception of a solution to the property's problems will be to find a new owner for the property and then restructure the debt or dispose of the property entirely. However, notwithstanding their initial discomfort with owners, most lenders would prefer to leave the original owner in control of the property in order to benefit from the owner's expertise and his or her business relationships. Nevertheless, if the lender believes that the owner has acted improperly or dishonestly, the owner will not be able to overcome the lender's perception. Accordingly, the owner's actions in response to the property's problems are of paramount importance in altering the lender's perception of the owner's competence and integrity.

The most important thing that the owner can do to impress the lender and increase the likelihood of a debt restructuring is to make certain that the lender learns of the property's problems from the owner shortly after the problems develop. The lender would prefer to be advised by the owner that the property is having problems as early in the process as possible. The lender would not want to learn of the problem from the absence of debt service payments for several months. This is not to say that the owner must contact the lender immediately after perceiving the potential problem, rather than wait to see if a problem really develops. The lender would understand a delay due to the owner's honest belief that the situation is temporary and would be quickly resolved. Nevertheless, as soon as the owner determines that the problem is more then a temporary shortage of cash, the lender or the loan correspondent should be advised of the situation. Unfortunately, delays frequently occur because the owner is embarrassed by the sudden appearance of a problem after having been optimistic about the particular project, and it takes a little time for the owner to acknowledge the problem. However, it is never too early or too late to advise the lender that the property is having a problem.

The lender's perception of the situation will also be affected by local and national economic conditions. In a recession, the lender will be less surprised to hear that the property is having financial problems and the owner requires assistance. Conversely, if the owner has the only failing property in an otherwise successful area, the lender would certainly reconsider the owner's ability to resolve the problem. Once the lender learns of the property's problem, the first thing the lender will do is attempt to determine the cause of the problem and whether it can be resolved by the lender in any of the traditional ways of handling defaults. Because the lender will want to be certain that the owner acted expeditiously and in good faith, the lender's investigation of the owner and the property will focus on obtaining answers to the questions posed in the following sections.

The Owner

- When did the owner first recognize that there was a problem and should the owner have learned of it earlier?
- Could the problem have been reduced or averted if the owner had been more diligent?
- Who actually discovered the problem?
- How did the lender learn of the problem?
- Has the owner satisfied its obligations under the loan documents?

- Did the owner advise the lender of all information it had at its disposal?
- Did the owner attempt to solve the problem before it advised the lender?
- Did the owner attempt to cover up the problem?
- Did the owner act in good faith?
- Is this an isolated problem, or are all the owner's properties having similar problems, or are many properties in the area having similar problems?
- What has the owner done to solve the problems?
- Did the owner's financial statements and projections accurately reflect the deteriorating situation at the property?
- Why did the owner's independent certified public accountant fail to identify the property's problems sooner?
- Have affiliates of the owner been retained to perform services and, if so, were the prices paid to the affiliates competitive?
- Has the owner previously defaulted on this or any other loan?
- What other creditors have claims against the owner or the property?
- Have the owner's investors and/or partners been advised of the problems?

The answers to these questions indicate the manner in which the owner acted when it learned of the problems. The lender is seeking to determine that the owner learned of the problem as early as possible, to satisfy itself that the owner remained fully informed regarding the property. The lender also wants to know that the owner advised it of the problems as soon as possible, although there is nothing wrong with the owner's believing that the problem was manageable and attempting to resolve it before advising the lender. Nevertheless, the manner in which the owner reacted to the problem will provide the lender with a great deal of information as to whether the owner should remain in possession of the property and be given the opportunity to resolve the problems. The lender also wants to know whether this property is an isolated situation or whether other properties in the vicinity are also having difficulties.

The lender also wants to know what involvement third parties had in the property's problems. If the owner failed to disclose information to the lender or the owner's accountants were unable to identify the problem or the owner is using income from this property to support another property or is paying inflated prices to affiliates who are providing services to the property, the lender would be less inclined to trust the owner. Moreover, the lender may be more interested in working with the owner in resolving the problems if the owner has other assets or partners who could provide additional capital to assist in the recovery. Finally, the lender would be concerned about the owner's integrity if it was misled or misdirected by the owner.

The Condition of the Property

- What is the physical condition of the property?
- Are the real estate taxes currently paid?
- Is the insurance currently paid? Is the coverage adequate? Is the lender named as an additional insured?
- Does the property require additional construction?
- Are there unleased portions of the property?
- Have the tenants complained about the operation or condition of the property?
- Are the tenants currently paying rent?
- What actions has the owner taken to fill vacancies?
- Is the owner involved in litigation with tenants, the local government, or third parties?
- How successful are the surrounding properties?
- Is the owner currently paying its bills for the property?
- Are there any liens against the property?
- Has the owner filed current income tax returns and paid taxes that are currently due?
- Are there subordinate mortgages on this property?
- Should the other lenders participate in any discussions? Would they be willing to advance additional funds?

Answers to this group of questions provide the lender with information regarding the property's physical condition, the satisfaction of the property's tenants, and whether the owner has complied with local laws and paid the property's real estate taxes and operating expenses. The answers to these questions provide the lender with an understanding of the actions that must be taken to protect the property, which should always be one of the lender's paramount concerns. If the property is fully leased and properly maintained, and the real estate taxes and insurance are paid, the lender's only concern is to deal with the financing and find ways to improve the property's cash so that the debt service will be paid.

The lender must deal with much greater problems if the property is not being properly maintained; if the tenants are terminating their leases, vacating the property, or withholding their rent; or if the real estate taxes or insurance are not being paid. Moreover, the lender may be required to advance additional cash into the property to protect the security for its loan. Being required to take such an action would be highly objectionable to the lender and would reflect negatively on the owner.

Lender's Internal Review

- What is the status of the tenant's security deposits?
- Have the owner's employees been paid? Have the property's withholding taxes been paid to the government?
- Has there been a recent environmental audit of the property?
- Does the lender have copies of the current leases and contracts that affect the property?
- If the property has been subdivided and parcels sold, how have the purchase prices been allocated? Where are the deposits for the parcels that are subject to contracts that have not closed?
- Is the property secure to avoid vandalism?
- If the property is a leasehold, what is the status of the ground lease? Has the ground rent been paid? How will the lender's actions affect the ground lease?
- What are the lender's rights and remedies under the loan documents?
- Is the owner's default technical or material?
- Is there any additional collateral for, or guaranties of, the loan secured by this property?
- What are the lender's rights under local law?
- Has the lender provided the owner with the notices required under the loan documents?
- Has the lender received a current title insurance report for the property?
- Has the lender received an assignment of the owner's interest in the leases and/or the contracts affecting the property?

Responding to this category of questions requires the lender to review its files to make certain that its documents are accurate and that it has received everything it will need to proceed with a debt restructuring or a foreclosure. The lender should review its files before commencing any proceeding or taking any action, and not after the owner and lender have become adversaries.

Each of these questions provides the lender with detailed information as to how the problems developed, how the owner reacted, whether the owner should remain in possession of the property, whether it is likely that the owner or anyone else can resolve the difficulties, and whether the lender or the property is at risk of loss. Naturally, this review would not be required if the lender had been carefully monitoring the property from the time the loan was funded; however, because it is not feasible for the lender to monitor loans that carefully, the lender must rely on the owner's business judgment and integrity in keeping the lender informed and making the appropriate decisions regarding the property. Nevertheless, lenders should never forget that even the most diligent and honest owners can be overwhelmed by events. If the lender overreacts by immediately replacing the owner or foreclosing the mortgage, the lender's actions could damage the property permanently.

For that reason, it is prudent for the lender to take its time in performing its assessment and making a decision as to whether to continue working with the owner. Fortunately, most lenders are inclined to leave the original owner in place and are opposed to taking over the property because they do not have the time or expertise to operate and manage the property. Their attitude is that, as long as the owner acted in a reasonable manner, it is likely that the owner can do a better job than the lender of resolving the problems and the lender will not force a disposition of the property.

CAN THE PROPERTY BE SAVED?

After the questions relevant to the particular situation have been answered, the lender utilizes the answers to derive a full understanding of the current status of the property, the people or entities with an interest in the property, and the alternative courses of action available to the lender. Finding a workable solution to the property's problems and determining whether a debt restructuring will help are complicated issues with no simple answers. The following sections describe important considerations.

The Nature Of the Default

The initial question is whether a default has actually occurred, or the owner is threatening to default, or the lender perceives a default as a possibility. The speed with which the lender reacts and the nature of its reaction will depend on the answer to these questions. If the owner has ceased paying the debt service, the lender would have to determine the amount that is owing to the lender and the other creditors having a lien on the property and decide whether anything would be gained by immediately commencing a foreclosure; or whether to charge the owner with the default rate of interest, penalties, and legal fees permitted under the loan documents; or whether to simply accrue the unpaid interest. It is not uncommon for lenders, in order to force an owner to recognize that it is having a serious problem and motivate it to work toward a resolution, to initially start accruing the late fees, default interest, and other expenses permitted in the loan documents. Nevertheless, the lender is aware of the fact that, as part of the ultimate resolution of the problem, the unpaid amounts may have to be waived or rolled into the outstanding principal balance of the indebtedness.

An important factor in the lender's decision as to how to proceed involves determining whether the defaulting property is the only one of the owner's properties having problems or whether it is in the vicinity of other properties having financial problems. The lender will want to understand the reasons for the default and whether it was directly or indirectly caused or worsened by anything the owner did or should not have done or whether the problem was the result of problems in the local, regional, or national economy. It would be best for the owner if the lender determines that the borrower was simply the victim of bad timing, rather than the developer of an ill-conceived, poorly constructed, or mismanaged project.

The lender will also analyze the manner in which the owner responded to the property's problems. The lender understands that how it responds could affect other properties that are owned by the owner or are under common control with the owner, some or many of which may be financed by the same lender. The lender will examine the other properties it has financed that are owned by the same or a related owner, as well as the other properties financed by the same lender that are located in the immediate vicinity of the property that is having difficulties. This additional review could alert the lender to other potential problems and thereby provide it with an opportunity to act in advance and resolve the problems before they get out of control. The lender will also discuss with its professionals its rights and remedies pursuant to the loan documents and local law.

Loan Documentation

The lender will do an audit of the loan documents to make certain that the loan closing was properly documented and all the documents are accurate, that the lender's lien was properly perfected and recorded, that the title insurance policy has been issued, and that any modifications to the loan documents have been properly executed and recorded. In the internal review, the lender will also verify who holds legal title to the property and make certain that the lender has copies of the certificates of occupancy, and other documents, licenses, and permits related to the use and operation of the property; plans and specifications and other construction documents; leases and assignments of leases; and assignments of other documents that would enable it to take control of the property if necessary. The lender will also examine its relationship with the borrower and owner to make certain that the lender cannot be accused of violating the borrower's or owner's rights or taking an inappropriate action. The lender will review the correspondence and records of conversations between the borrower, the owner, and the lender, as well as the actions the lender has taken, to identify any exposure the lender might have. If there is a risk that the lender has acted improperly, the lender will consider what actions it can take to reduce its liability. The lender should also obtain a current title insurance report to be certain that its lien continues to have the priority that it had at the time the loan was funded.

The lender should not attempt to proceed against the owner without recognizing that the owner will be aggressive in its defense to protect its interest in the property and will attempt to avoid losing the property until the real estate market can improve. Undoubtedly, the lender can probably overcome any impropriety that it can be accused of, by taking the correct precautionary steps prior to attempting to foreclose the loan. The lender may even consider that restructuring the debt may provide it with adequate protection from any accusation that it has acted improperly toward the owner or the property.

The Property's Physical Condition

Prior to seeking assistance from the lender, the owner should realize that the lender will seek a great deal of information regarding the property before it decides how to proceed. The lender will not consider whether to foreclose its mortgage or restructure the debt without carefully considering the property's physical condition. If the property is still under construction, determination must be made based on what is required to complete the construction, what it will cost, and whether it can be accomplished using the balance of the original construction loan. Under these circumstances, the construction lender will want to be certain that the permanent loan commitment has not been jeopardized and that the owner has not violated the terms of the permanent loan commitment.

The physical inspection of the property also entails determining that the already constructed portions of the property have been constructed in compliance with local building codes and the plans and specifications. The lender will have its architect or engineer review the condition of the buildings and improvements on the property to assure the lender that the developer has acted properly. The lender will also want to determine the status of the lease-up of the newly constructed space and whether the lease terms or conditions have been violated by the owner. The lender will attempt to resolve any problems with the tenants to reinstate the lease. The lender will also seek to determine that the property's insurance coverage is adequate and is being maintained by the owner with an acceptable carrier.

If the property was to be subdivided and sold, then the lender will also review the owner's sales efforts to determine whether the terms and conditions of the contracts comply with the release provisions in the mortgage and whether the owner has violated the conditions of the contract. The lender will also want to make certain that the prices for the portions of the property are not significantly below the property's fair market value. The lender's concern is that the owner has attempted to sell all or portions of the property to its friends for below-market prices. Additionally, the owner's financial problems might be causing it or forcing it to sell the parcels at discounted prices. For this reason, it might be advantageous for the lender to require the owner to stop making sales while the property's deficiencies are corrected so that the market value of the parcels can be increased when sales resume.

The fact that the property is not in the process of being constructed will not deter the lender from analyzing the property's physical condition to determine the amount of deferred maintenance, the necessity for capital improvements, and whether a renovation or improvement of the property would increase its income. If the lender determines that the property is so badly deteriorated that major capital improvements are required, a restructuring of the debt might not be feasible unless the owner had a source of available capital to correct the problems or the lender was prepared to increase its investment in the property.

Changing the Property's Use
The lender will also review the property's use and consider whether a change in the use is required to increase the property's value and income. A change in the market to which the property is being directed or the tenant mix could improve its short-term cash flow and its long-term viability.

Claims to which the Property Is Subject

The lender will take no action without determining the effect of a subsequent bankruptcy filing by the owner. Thus, the lender will seek to determine what its position would be if the owner filed a bankruptcy petition or if another creditor commenced an involuntary bankruptcy proceeding against the owner. This review would require that the lender determine whether there are any other secured creditors and, if so, whether they would be senior or junior to the lender and whether the lender's position could be affected by the filing. The lender would also want to determine the names and claims of the general unsecured creditors, the trade creditors, and anyone else having a claim that may have a priority on the property, such as mechanic's lienors, governmental agencies having unpaid taxes or assessments liened against the property, and the local utility companies. If the lender identifies any weakness in its position, it may decide to help the owner resolve the property's problems rather than to allow the property to deteriorate further, which could result in an unfavorable bankruptcy filing. Alternatively, the situation may be so hopeless that the lender decides to accelerate the foreclosure to obtain control over the situation as quickly as possible.

Parties with an Interest in the Property

Determining the parties with an interest in the property is one of the most important considerations for the lender in determining whether to proceed with a debt restructuring. The lender will also determine whether the borrower has partners or stockholders or other equity owners involved in the property who may be willing to provide additional capital to the project to help resolve the problems. It may be worth it to the borrower's partners to advance a small amount of additional capital to save the capital they have already invested in the property and avoid the far more serious tax consequences of a foreclosure or forced sale at a distressed price.

The lender will also want to identify the individuals with an involvement in the property other than the owner. These would include the owner's employees who manage or maintain the property, as well as the property's professionals, including the managing agent, sales agent, attorney, accountant, and engineer. The lender will also want to be certain that these individuals are experienced in a real estate transaction and a debt restructuring. Even if the owner's experience is limited, this may not be a handicap if the owner is surrounded with experienced advisers. There is little double that a lender would feel more comfortable working with an owner who has experience in real estate but has not experienced the necessity for a debt restructuring than with an owner who has frequently been forced to participate in debt restructuring. Nevertheless, the lender will be more concerned with the owner's general experience in real estate and business and reputation for integrity than with the owner's prior involvement with a debt restructuring.

If it is required to take any action with regard to the property, the lender would also want to contact those individuals who provide goods and services to the property and whose participation is required to support the property. Regardless of whether the lender intends on foreclosing its mortgage, accepting a deed in lieu of foreclosure, or attempting a debt restructuring, the lender would want to know the basis of the relationship between these third parties and the owner and whether it can count on, or should count on, the participation of the third parties in helping to facilitate the resolution.

The Owner's Performance of Agreements that Affect the Property

Unless the owner intends on replacing everyone involved with the property, the lender will require the assistance of third parties to successfully restructure the debt or operate the property properly. The lender will therefore want to be certain that any agreements that affect the property remain in full force and effect regardless of the owner's financial difficulties. This requires the lender to identify the important documents, which include the following:

- Ground lease
- Occupancy leases
- Master lease
- Management agreement
- Franchise agreement
- Construction contracts
- Loan commitment
- Agreement of sale.

The review of these agreements would include determining their current status and whether the other parties to the agreements would recognize the lender's ownership and continue to provide the goods and services that have been provided, if the lender was to take control of the property. The lender would also seek to determine whether similar services could be provided by other purveyors at a better price or on better terms.

The lender would pay particular attention to the documents that actually affect the real value of the property. In the event the land is leased, then the ground lease is critically important to the lender since, without it, the lender would have no security for its loan. Additionally, the occupancy leases would have to be examined because if they are at above-market rents, the lender would not want the borrower to take any action or fail to take any action that might jeopardize the leases. Moreover, even if a lease is at a below-market rent, if it is with an important tenant that draws other tenants, it would be an important asset of the property. Furthermore, if the property is being utilized as a hotel, motel, or restaurant as part of a national chain, the franchise or management agreements with the operating company become important property assets. If the property is undergoing construction, the most important sets of documents are the construction loan, the permanent loan commitment, and the construction contracts. If any of these agreements are in default due to the owner's actions, the lender will have serious problems in resurrecting the project and protecting its loan. At the very best, the other party to these important agreements should be notified and advised to contact the lender if anything happens or fails to happen that could cause a default under the agreement.

Additional Assets Available to the Lender

The lender's due diligence review also involves determining whether the owner has sufficient equity in the property to refinance the mortgage for a higher amount and thereby provide additional equity for the resolution of the property's problems. It involves making a determination as to whether the borrower has other assets that are presently unencumbered or additional collateral that might be available to provide the lender additional security for the risks it is taking in agreeing to restructure the debt. This analysis would include a review of the owner's partnership or shareholders agreement to determine whether the limited partners, other general partners, or shareholders are subject to an additional assessment or capital calls. This would provide the property with additional funds with which to cure the property's problems. This review would also entail examining the financial strength of the guarantors to determine if they have available capital to invest in the property in order to limit their guaranties, reduce their guaranties, or avoid the necessity of a call against their guaranties.

This search for additional sources of capital would include asking a contractor to provide the financing to complete the project or wait to be paid. This will enable the owner to provide the contractor with the work to complete the construction or renovation, and the contractor would share in the property's appreciation. The lender would feel more comfortable providing additional funds for the property knowing that those who would benefit from the ultimate success of the property would be absorbing part of the lender's risk in postponing the inevitable.

Controlling the Owner

The lender would also examine what actions it could take or controls it could put into place to protect its position and preserve the property. This might involve putting financial limitations on the owner as to payments it can make and bills it can pay without the lender's consent. This would include requiring the owner to make more frequent and detailed financial reports to the lender and placing controls on the way money is obtained and spent by the owner. The controls imposed on the owner could include changes in the owner's management structure to make certain that the key personnel have sufficient expertise in their areas to avoid a further deterioration of the situation. The lender would also want to be certain that the property's real estate taxes are paid prior to their becoming a lien, that the withholding taxes are paid on time to the government, that the insurance payments are current, and that the property is properly secured and maintained.

Nevertheless, the lender cannot lose sight of the fact that one problem for the lender in imposing controls over the owner and the owner's operation of the property is the risk of a lender liability claim against the lender. The owner or another creditor could subsequently raise the claim that the owner has become an instrument of the lender and that the lender should be liable to the other lenders for anything that happens to the property. Thus, the lender must be careful to suggest controls that merely improve the monitoring of the owner and the property and not to suggest controls that provide the lender or its designees with the ability to make decisions relating to the operation of the property.

The Cost of Restructuring the Debt

The lender should not restructure the debt without determining the lender's actual long-term cost of restructuring the debt. The cost of debt restructuring includes the following:

- The cost of completing the construction or renovation of the property
- The cost of resolving any regulatory problems
- The costs of the architects, engineers, accountants, attorneys, and other professionals

- The marketing costs
- The costs to the lender of not receiving current interest on the mortgage
- The costs of monitoring the property.

The lender may consider that the costs of resolving the property's problems will be so large that it makes more economical sense for the lender to foreclose upon its lien, take a loss on the sale of the property at the discounted value, and avoid any further losses. In such an event, the lender will consider the advantages and disadvantages of proceeding before committing itself to spend more money in an ill-conceived attempt to protect the investment it has made in the property. It is possible that, regardless of how much additional money the lender invests in the property or how much additional time it provides the owner to resolve the property's problems, the property will not be successful and the loan will not be paid. Under such circumstances, it would be less expensive and less time-consuming for the lender to take its loss at this point rather then to continue to advance additional funds.

Unfortunately, the situation may be even worse. The lender, in its investigation, may determine that the property has such severe problems that the lender's best action would be to abandon its security, sue the borrower on the promissory note, and not even attempt to resolve the property's problems. This could occur if the lender learned that the property contained serious environmental hazards, which would have to be removed. If the lender merely has a lien on the property and does not become involved in the actual management, control, or ownership of the property, the lender would avoid any risk that it would be liable for the cost of the cleanup. Conversely, foreclosing the mortgage and bidding its mortgage at the auction, and thereby acquiring the property, could cause the lender to be liable for the astronomical cost of the cleanup.

Lender Liability

The lender will carefully analyze the possibility that it could be subject to a liability claim based on a theory of lender liability. The lender would determine what actions it should take to minimize the risk that such a claim could be made, or that a defense could be raised by the owner against the lender. This analysis would involve an examination of the lender's relationship with the owner and borrower so that a determination could be made whether the lender has violated any laws regarding financial institutions or the owner has violated any securities, tax, or environmental laws that could be used against the lender. The lender would also need to confirm that its actions were taken in good faith and were prudent. The lender would want to avoid an accusation that it harassed the owner or a claim that the owner could be held to be an alter ego of the lender.

The lender will also determine as to whether its actions could be misinterpreted in a bankruptcy proceeding as an attempt to defraud or obtain a preference over the other creditors. The lender should also confirm that the borrower has paid all its payroll taxes and that there are no hazardous wastes on the property. If the lender can be accused of any wrongdoing, it will delay acting to foreclose the loan until it takes the necessary steps to cleanse the record and avoid the likelihood of such a claim's being successful.

Once the lender determines that the owner is having financial difficulties, the lender will assume, as it takes each step to assist the owner or to obtain the collateral, that the owner will ultimately file a petition under the Bankruptcy Code. Therefore, the lender will consider how its actions would look when subsequently examined. The lender will make certain that its files contain all necessary documentation and memoranda reflecting everything that transpired in the relationship, even if the memoranda are self serving. All conversations, telephone calls, and decisions will be followed up by, and confirmed with, correspondence to the other party. Anything the lender does or says will be examined in the worst possible light, which makes the lender all the more cautious in its dealings. The lender will retain all records that substantiate that its action was taken in good faith or had a legitimate business basis. The owner should therefore be just as cautious in its dealings with the lender to be certain that it can rebut the lender's recollections.

The result of the lender's examination of its position and that of the owner and the property, will be to decide whether to foreclose its mortgage (Chapter 9 describes defenses to the foreclosure) or to restructure the debt. The lender should complete its analysis as quickly and as early in the default scenario as possible, to provide the lender with sufficient time to complete the debt restructuring before the property has deteriorated to the point where it cannot be saved. If it is apparent from the lender's analysis that a debt restructuring is unlikely to be successful, the lender's speed in accelerating the loan and foreclosing on its mortgage, or accepting a deed in lieu of foreclosure, or going after the guarantor or the obligor on the note, will improve the likelihood that it can maximize what it will receive.

RESTRUCTURING THE DEBT

A debt restructuring has to be designed and tailored for the needs of a specific property. No two restructurings are identical because every loan is different, every property is different, and every property that is having a problem requires a different solution. Adjacent properties can require different solutions because they are constructed differently, have different uses, have different tenants, or attract a different kind of purchaser. Dozens of factors can come into play in determining whether a property will be a success or a failure. Therefore, each property requires a different format for the debt restructuring, although several might work successfully. The owner, lender, and other interested parties will determine which kind of debt restructuring would be most beneficial.

Whether restructuring has been successful will become apparent only over time, if the property can operate without further financial assistance. Ultimately, the property will be considered successful if the lender's loan is repaid, even if the loan is repaid because the lender was able to arrange for the property to be sold and the loan repaid from the sale proceeds. The property will also be considered successful if the lender restructured the debt service and, thereafter, the borrower was able to keep the loan current. Certainly, the lender would prefer to have the loan repaid as quickly as possible to minimize its exposure to risk and to minimize the interest it will be deferring. However, most properties having financial problems are not saleable except at a huge discount, which would probably result in a price that would be insufficient to repay the loan. It must be assumed that a property that needs to have its debt restructured has potential value that requires the right financing to enable the property to ultimately be sold or released.

The alternatives available to the owner and the lender are quite extensive and include the following actions, which are not necessarily mutually exclusive and are certainly not the only available remedies:

Alternative No. 1. Lender takes no action.

Description	The lender leaves the owner in control of the property, allowing the owner to continue making all operating decisions.
Advantage	This alternative causes the least disturbance to the property and has the least immediate negative effect on the owner. It indicates that the lender either has supreme

confidence in the owner's ability to resolve the problems or has absolutely no hope that the property can be salvaged and does not want to be blamed when the situation deteriorates.

Disadvantage   This alternative leaves the solution of the property's problem to the owner's ability and the lender's patience. This cavalier attitude may be difficult for the lender to explain later if the property fails and the lender has not taken any action to protect the security for the loan. If the lender indicates no interest in assisting the owner, it might indicate to the tenants and the other creditors that there is no likelihood that the property can succeed, and thereby exacerbate its decline.

Alternative No. 2. Lender convinces owner to sell the property.

Description   The lender believes so strongly that the property cannot succeed while it is owned by, and is under the control of, the owner, that the lender convinces the owner to sell the property as quickly as possible. The sales price might be sufficient to repay the loan and, if not, the new owner might have sufficient capital or ideas to improve the situation.

Advantage   If a price can be obtained that is at least close to the unpaid balance of the indebtedness, it provides the lender with a fast and relatively risk-free resolution of the problems. Not owning a property that is foreclosed protects the owner's reputation and credit history.

Disadvantage   This alternative could leave the lender open to a subsequent claim that the owner was the subject of duress or harassment by the lender to force the owner to sell the property. This alternative also increases the likelihood of the owner's filing a bankruptcy petition prior to the sale, in order to protect the asset. Moreover, if the price received is less than the principal and accrued interest, the lender must recognize its loss at the time of the sale, while the owner is forced to recognize the negative tax consequences of the sale and may still be sued by the lender for the difference between the sales price and the indebtedness.

Alternative No. 3. Lender extends the loan term to reduce the amount of debt service paid toward amortization.

Description	The lender agrees to modify the loan terms by extending the maturity date, which reduces the amortization of the debt service and provides the owner with more time to satisfy the loan.
Example:	If a $10 million loan bears interest at 10 percent per annum and is amortized over 15 years, the debt service would be paid at the rate of $1,289,526 per year. If the same loan was repaid over 25 years with the same interest rate, the debt service would be reduced to $1,090,440 per year. However, although the borrower saves $199,086 during each of the first 15 years (totaling $2,986,290), over the term of the loan, the savings would be more than offset by the owner's being required to pay the $1,090,440 annual debt service for an additional 10 years (totaling $10,904,400), which results in an increased cost to the borrower and an increased return to the lender of $7,918,110 over 25 years.
Advantage	This alternative results in the lender's receiving the return of its entire loan and more interest than it would ordinarily have received due to the longer payout period, while reducing but lengthening the payment provisions for the owner. It also provides the owner with a 15 percent reduction in the debt service during the earlier years, when it most needs the assistance.
Disadvantage	The lender must retain its involvement with the property for an extended period of time and, if the debt restructuring is not successful, the lender will have to make future concessions. In exchange for lower debt service initially, the owner will be forced to pay significantly more interest over the term of the loan.

Alternative No. 4. Lender eliminates the amortization.

Description	The lender agrees to convert a self-liquidating loan into an interest-only loan with a balloon payment.
Example:	The owner would save $144,763 per year in debt service payments if a $5 million loan, bearing interest at 10 per-

cent for 15 years was converted from a self-liquidating loan to an interest-only loan. However, the owner still has to pay the $5 million principal balance on the maturity of the loan.

Advantage   The owner's monthly payments are reduced by 22 percent at a time when it needs the cash flow to operate the property. The lender still receives its interest currently and receives more interest because the principal balance is not reduced during the term of the loan.

Disadvantage   The owner is required to pay $5 million on the maturity of the loan, rather than an additional $12,666 per month for 15 years ($2,171,446). The change therefore costs the owner an additional $2,828,554 because monthly payments were reduced from $53,730 to $41,666.

Alternative No. 5. Lender reduces the interest rate.

Description   The lender agrees to reduce the interest rate in an attempt to reduce the owner's payments and thereby enable the owner to maintain a current payment schedule.

Example: Reducing the interest rate from 14 percent per annum on a $10 million loan to 9 percent per annum would save the owner $500,000 per year in interest.

Advantage   If the new interest rate is not below the current market for interest rates, the lender will not be significantly adversely affected, whereas the owner will receive immeasurable assistance by being able to pay a lower amount of debt service without being tied to a subsequent increase. The lower interest rate would still provide the lender with a reasonable return for its loan. Moreover, the lower interest in the earlier years can be offset by the lender's receiving a higher interest rate in the later years or even a percentage of the cash flow after the property becomes successful.

Disadvantage   The lender would lose a portion of its profit on the loan and may be required to pay a higher interest rate on the money it borrowed to make the loan. The lender would also be subsidizing the owner after the property becomes successful and would be hurt further if interest rates increase and the rate is tied to a low-interest loan. However, the lender could be protected by shortening the maturity date of the mortgage, thereby requiring the owner to refinance earlier.

Alternative No. 6. Lender provides moratorium on payments.

Description   The lender would provide the owner with a moratorium during which loan payments accrue but need not be made until after the property's performance improves.

Example: If the lender permits one year's debt service payments on a $10 million loan that bears interest at 11 percent per annum and self-liquidates over 30 years to be deferred and then repaid over the next five years, the owner would save $1,142,788 during the first year, but the owner's debt service would increase by $228,557 per annum during the next five years if the deferred does not bear interest. If the deferred amount bears interest at 10 percent, the owner's debt service would increase by $291,370 per annum during the next five years. If the deferred payments did not bear interest, the owner would obtain the benefit of the accrual without an increased cost. If the owner has to pay interest at the rate of 10 percent on the deferred amount, the aggregate increased cost to the borrower would be $314,067, payable over the five years.

Advantage   This alternative provides the owner with an opportunity to resolve its problems with the property without a long-term adverse effect on the lender's return or subsequent increases to the owner's debt service.

Disadvantage   The lender does not receive any payments during the moratorium (although the lender did not receive payments prior to the moratorium either), and the owner would be required to make significantly higher payments after the moratorium to compensate the lender for its loss during the interim.

Alternative No. 7. Lender capitalizes the accrued interest.

Description   The lender agrees to defer the payment of the debt service that was not paid and add it to the principal balance to be repaid on maturity of the loan.

Example: If the owner fails to make $1 million in debt service pay-
                ments, which is then included in the outstanding princi-
                pal balance of a loan bearing interest at 9 percent per
                annum and due in 25 years, the increased cost to the
                owner (and the increased return to the lender) would be
                $100,703 per annum, or $2,517,589 over 25 years.

Advantage   This alternative eliminates the need for the owner to
                find a source to repay the debt service that it has not
                paid during the default and provides the lender with a
                method to recover said sums.

Disadvantage   This alternative increases the owner's monthly debt
                service payments during the remaining term of the
                mortgage, and thereby increases the possibility of a fu-
                ture default.

*Alternative No. 8. Lender restructures the debt service so that it is not in
excess of the net operating income.*

Description   The lender agrees to reduce the components of the debt
                service (interest rate, amortization period, term of loan)
                so that they adjust monthly to maintain the aggregate
                payment at a level lower than the income produced by
                the property.

Example: In this alternative, if the net rental income from the
                property is $350,000 per annum and the real estate
                taxes, utilities, repairs, and other operating expenses
                equal $200,000 per annum, the debt service would be
                $150,000. If the income increased or the operating ex-
                penses decreased, the debt service would be increased.
                Similarly, if the income decreased or the operating ex-
                penses increased, the debt service would decrease.

Advantage   This is the easiest alternative for the owner to handle be-
                cause the debt service will never exceed what the prop-
                erty can produce. It is then impossible for the owner to go
                again into default. If the property becomes successful,
                this alternative would produce a phenomenal return for
                the lender since it would receive the bulk of the profit.

Disadvantage   This is one of the least desirable methods for the lender
                to utilize, because it provides no motivation for the

owner to improve the performance of the property, increase income, reduce expenses, or make the operation of the property more efficient. It also eliminates the lender's ability to terminate the mortgage in the future. It also causes the loan to have nominal value because the interest rate will bear no similarity to the market rate of interest. If this formulation is used, the lender would probably not agree to its use other than for a relatively brief period of time, while the owner acts to make the property more successful.

Alternative No. 9. Lender reduces the principal amount of the indebtedness.

Description   By reducing the outstanding principal balance of the loan, the lender can adjust the amount the owner has to pay in debt service payments during the term of the loan and on maturity.

Example: If the lender agrees to reduce the indebtedness by $250,000 on a self-liquidating loan, it would reduce the debt service on a 15-year loan bearing interest at 12 percent per annum by $36,005 per annum or $540,075 over the term of the loan.

Advantage   This method provides the owner with a lower monthly payment and a smaller amount that has to be repaid on maturity, thereby making it easier for the owner to sell the property without financing or to refinance the lender out of the loan.

Disadvantage   The lender is waiving any right to repayment to a portion of its loan, even if the property increases substantially in value. What the lender is doing in this alternative is providing the owner with equity in the property. It would be significantly less expensive for the lender to waive the payment of debt service on the $250,000 for several years, than to permanently reduce the indebtedness. A reduction in the principal indebtedness may be necessary, however, to facilitate the sale of the property and the immediate repayment of the balance of the loan by the purchaser. This decision should not be made until a purchaser is identified and the lender can review the facts and circumstances of a particular transaction.

Alternative No. 10. Lender advances additional funds to the owner.

Description	The lender lends additional money to the owner because the lender determines that if the property is improved, its prospects for increased tenants or higher rent might also increase, which makes the property and the loan more valuable.
Example:	The lender increases the indebtedness by the amounts reasonably required by the owner, and thereby increases the monthly debt service payment to the lender.
Advantage	If the property needs capital improvements or other important bills (i.e., utilities, taxes, repairs, insurance) must be paid, this action will provide the owner with the money with which to make the payments.
Disadvantage	The lender would be concerned as to whether it is throwing good money after bad and subjecting itself to criticism if the property fails regardless of the additional loan funding. If the interest rate is high, the increased principal balance might be difficult for the owner to pay currently, thereby reducing the likelihood that the property will survive.

Alternative No. 11. Lender obtains additional collateral.

Description	The lender obtains additional collateral for the loan, and either increases the amount of the loan or restructures the debt service payments.
Example:	The lender could use the owner's equity in other property to collateralize the lender's advance to the owner of funds necessary to pay debt service or other operating expenses.
Advantage	This is probably one of the lender's favorite ways of dealing with the problem because it facilitates the resolution of the problem, while providing the lender with additional security.
Disadvantage	The lender must be concerned about the value of the additional collateral, and the owner must be concerned about tying up additional collateral, which it might need to liquidate to make payments.

Alternative No. 12. Lender obtain guaranties.

Description	The lender insists on and receives a guaranty of the entire loan or only the additional funding, as the basis for advancing additional proceeds.
Advantage	The lender is able to assist the owner in resolving its problems without incurring any extraordinary risks and, in fact, might be reducing its risk.
Disadvantage	The owner might have a difficult time finding someone with the wherewithal to guaranty any part of the loan who is prepared to accept the risk without a substantial payment by the owner.

Alternative No. 13. Lender establishes controls.

Description	The lender requires that operating or financial controls be placed on the property and the owner, which may include requiring the owner to hire different professionals, advisers, or contractors.
Advantage	The lender is provided assurance that the money it is advancing or the actions it is taking will be in the best interests of the property and will not be wasted. The lender then receives first-hand information as to what is really happening at the property.
Disadvantage	The controls could hamper the owner's ability to function by replacing people with whom the owner may have a long-standing relationship with inexperienced people. If the lender has too much involvement in the day-to-day operations, it could expose the lender to liability for actions taken by the owner.

Whether one or more of these alternatives could be used successfully for a particular property would depend upon a number of factors, including (1) the likely result from changing the structure of the existing loan or advancing additional funds, (2) the lender's ability to restructure the loan, and (3) the possibility that the owner will be successful in resolving the property's problem if the lender agrees to make the proposed changes. The purpose of each alternative is based upon the concept that, because the debt service is the largest component in the property's operating expenses, reducing or temporarily eliminating the debt service would provide the owner with the time and financial ability to cure its other problems. The lender would undoubtedly want to negotiate a method to be repaid the lost or deferred interest from future profits if the property is ultimately found to be successful.

Restructuring the debt service is usually the basis for a solution to a property's problems, because it provides the owner with an opportunity to examine the operation of the property, rather then merely seek money to continue to make debt service payments or attempt to avoid the lender altogether. The restructuring offers a moratorium on the original payments, giving the owner time to analyze the property's other problems and thereby increasing the likelihood that the owner will be successful in its attempt to resolve the operating problems.

The restructuring does not preclude the lender from requiring the owner to sell the property. A precondition to the lender's agreeing to the restructuring may be an agreement by the owner to immediately place the property on the market for sale at a reasonable price after the loan is restructured. The lender would have the loan repaid shortly, or the lender's refinancing of the property would result in the property's being purchased by a financially stronger owner. The lender would find the repayment of the loan in the near future an appetizing prospect. This would lead the lender to be more amenable to restructuring the debt service payments to enable the owner to focus on leasing or selling the property.

Because projects under construction are usually prime targets for financial problems, they are of particular concern to lenders. The usual turn of events is that midway through the construction, the owner runs out of money and is unable to finish the development. The construction lender's immediate concern is that the permanent lender will not acquire the property and the tenants will terminate their leases because the construction will not be completed on time. To preclude this from happening, the construction lender might increase the amount of its construction loan. This would provide the owner with sufficient funds to complete the construction, and thereby enable the construction loan to be repaid by the permanent lender. This will be a preferred alternative for the construction lender. Even if the permanent lender is committed to taking only part of the construction loan, the construction lender will be left with only a small second mortgage on a property after the bulk of its loan has been repaid by the permanent lender. Otherwise, the construction lender will be left with a partially completed, untenanted property in which the permanent lender refuses to close the permanent mortgage due to the incomplete status of the property and the absence of operating tenants.

Alternatively, the owner could provide the lender with a deed in lieu of foreclosure as an additional incentive to the restructuring. The deed in lieu of foreclosure would be delivered at the time of the restructuring to be automatically recorded if the property does not achieve certain levels of performance by a specific date. This deed would save the lender a great deal of time and aggravation if the debt restructuring or other solutions are not successful. Nevertheless, nothing could prevent the owner from subsequently taking the position that the lender still has to foreclose, stating that the deed in lieu of foreclosure was invalid or that it was really a mortgage. Moreover, if the borrower sees that it has no alternative, nothing can prevent the borrower from seeking an injunction or filing a bankruptcy petition proceeding to prevent the deed from being recorded. The fact that the borrower has stated in the debt restructuring agreements that it would not file a bankruptcy petition is irrelevant because such a provision would be unenforceable and would not prevent the borrower from filing a petition. Alternatively, the lender could exercise a certain degree of control over the owner if it agreed to waive any guaranties of the loan and to not enforce a deficiency judgment, as long as the owner does not renege on its delivery of the deed.

One common solution to the property's problems might include a combination of these alternatives. The owner might be given preferential loan terms or additional financing to be able to complete or improve the property and thereby facilitate a sale. Alternatively, the lender may condition additional financing on the owner's providing additional collateral or a mortgage on other property or an additional guaranty. This method provides the lender with the comfort of knowing that the owner is committed to resolving the problems and is willing to increase its exposure and risk. Many lenders do not consider the guaranty as an important document because they assume that the owner is broke or has legally shifted its assets prior to, or simultaneously with, the default.

Nevertheless, the additional collateral or guaranties will provide the lender with a certain degree of additional protection. Likewise, the new guarantor may agree to guaranty only the amount of the additional financing rather than the entire indebtedness, or the lender might be persuaded to release the mortgage on the additional property at such time as a certain portion of the original indebtedness is repaid. However, the additional guarantor is provided with motivation for assisting the owner by the fact that its liability will be limited in the event the debt restructuring is not successful. Moreover, this limitation on claims against a subsequent guaranty should not be a serious problem for the lender, because the lender will be placed in no worse position.

The numerous structuring alternatives for the lender and the owner depend on many factors, including the relationship of the parties and the confidence that the lender has in the property and the owner. The lender's confidence in the likely success of the property will be directly related to the past and present dealings between the owner and the lender and the lender's projections of the project's likelihood of success. If the lender loses confidence in the owner's ability to resolve the problems, the lender may negotiate to have the owner sell the project to someone whom the lender believes is more likely to succeed. In exchange for the sale, the lender will provide the owner with a release from liability on the guaranty or other consideration. The lender will identify an acceptable purchaser to whom the lender may offer financing as an incentive for agreeing to resuscitate the property. The lender's thought in such a case is that it would be worth releasing a probably insolvent owner from liability if it avoids the time and delays of a foreclosure or a lawsuit over the relationships and the property. The owner may also find conveying the property to a purchaser selected by the lender an acceptable alternative. The owner loses the property, but the owner protects its reputation and credit rating and also avoids the time and expense necessary to resolve the matter through litigation.

Just because the lender finds a purchaser for the property, however, does not mean that the lender will not be required to restructure the loan. Part of the arrangement to obtain the right purchaser is an agreement by the lender to provide restructuring and additional financing to assist the new owner in salvaging the property. However, the lender might find this to be an attractive alternative to relying on an owner who has already proven that it cannot operate the property successfully.

Alternatively, the lender might agree to take no action for a certain amount of time. If the owner is then unable to resolve the property's problems on its own, the owner would convey the property to the lender, an affiliate of the lender, or a third party produced by the lender. Accordingly, the owner is provided with an opportunity to correct the problems and, if unsuccessful, it would convey the property to someone else, who would attempt to resolve the problems. The lender would certainly be amenable to providing the owner with a moratorium on payments or modifications to the loan during this period. Moreover, this additional time would also reduce the likelihood that the owner could successfully raise a lender liability defense in a subsequent litigation between the owner and the lender. However, to protect itself from a change of mind, the lender would probably insist that the owner execute a deed and other conveyance documents to be held in escrow pending the owner's success or failure in resolving the problems.

The key to any successful debt restructuring is time. Debt restructuring provides the owner with the time to resolve its problems with the property. It also provides the property with time to find the market and time in which the local and national economy can improve. It also provides time for inflation to increase the value of the property. Hopefully, the rent that is accruing from the property would also increase to a level at which the property can be self-sufficient. Restructuring the debt also provides time for the glut of office space, retail space, industrial space, or residential space that is adversely affecting the property to be absorbed, thereby creating a demand for the troubled property.

9

Defending against Foreclosure

The time may come when, notwithstanding the owner's best attempts to keep the mortgage on the property in good standing, the owner defaults and the lender decides to take an aggressive position to gain title to the property as quickly as possible. In such an instance, the lender would accelerate the indebtedness and commence an action to foreclose the mortgage, or exercise the power of sale contained in the deed of trust, or take the equivalent action under local law. Unfortunately, national and local economic conditions in general and the real estate recession and banking crisis in particular, have turned borrowers and lenders into adversaries in ever-increasing numbers. Foreclosures are now commonplace, whereas, until recently, they were the exception.

Because many lenders now believe that the first response to a problem is to commence a foreclosure, rather than to negotiate a workout, borrowers must now consider their defensive positions in mortgage foreclosure actions in order to delay and possibly defeat the lender's attempt to terminate the owner's interest in the property. The mortgagor must consider an aggressive response to have an opportunity to retain the mortgaged property until the real estate market improves, or the property can be put to a better use, or the owner can identify a tenant who is willing to rent the space for a higher rent, or a purchaser can be found. Other reasons for the owner to attempt to delay the foreclosure is to protect the owner's creditworthiness, to avoid personal liability, and to delay the recapture of previously taken tax deductions.

If a foreclosure is commenced, the borrower basically has three options: to do nothing and allow the property to be lost; to file a Chapter 11 reorganization proceeding to obtain time to try to resolve the difficulties; or to act aggressively to defend against the foreclosure (and, if unsuccessful, file for Chapter 11 protection). This chapter describes several methods the borrower can consider in defending against a foreclosure. However, notwithstanding an aggressive defense, the borrower should not lose sight of his or her goal in raising defenses, which is to obtain time for the situation to improve and not simply to defeat the foreclosure. Although some of these approaches may ultimately be successful in terminating the foreclosure or even (more remotely) in eliminating the mortgage as a lien on the property, in most instances, the borrower's defensive posture is intended only to delay the foreclosure. Nevertheless, this delay might enable the owner to find a way to resolve the property's problems or provide time for the real estate recession to end. Also, during this time, the lender may decide that it is easier to negotiate a restructuring of the indebtedness or agree to take a deed in lieu of foreclosure on favorable terms for the borrower than to attempt to proceed with the foreclosure. After all, the lender is, first and foremost, a businessman.

One of the critical things for the owner and the lender to remember is the effect of the owner's equity of redemption on the lender's actions. The equity of redemption is a concept of English common law that has been adhered to for over 800 years. The equity of redemption permits the property owner to reclaim the property, notwithstanding the default, upon the repayment of the debt to the lender. The owner has this right regardless of the size of the default or the length of time the mortgage has been in default or the foreclosure has been pending. Therefore, until the completion of the foreclosure and the sale of the property, the owner can save the property if it can pay the indebtedness to the lender. Therefore, the longer the owner can delay the foreclosure, the more time the owner has to satisfy the indebtedness and retain the property. Accordingly, time is on the owner's side. The only disadvantage to the owner from the delay is that interest continues to accrue; however, that can also be part of the final negotiation.

LENDER'S REASON TO FORECLOSE

Initially, the owner should consider the lender's reason for proceeding to commence a foreclosure action. It is possible that the lender does not actually want to obtain possession of the property, but rather to force the owner to pay attention to a problem at the property or to have a receiver appointed to prevent the owner from using the rents and profits generated by the property for purposes other than preserving the property. If nothing else, the acceleration of the indebtedness secured by the mortgage and the commencement of the mortgage foreclosure action are very effective methods for the lender to take control of the situation. However, the situation is even more complex than that.

Currently, each state has its own foreclosure law, based on one of three theories: the common law or title theory, the intermediate theory, or the lien theory. Title theory states that the lender is given the right to have possession of the property when the loan is made. Intermediate theory states that the lender is precluded from obtaining possession of the property until the owner has defaulted. Lien theory states that the lender is unable to obtain possession of the property due to a default by the owner, and the owner retains legal title to the property until the mortgage is actually foreclosed.

None of the states' current mortgage foreclosure laws allow the lender to have control over the mortgaged property or to obtain the income from that property until, at the very earliest, the foreclosure action has commenced. At that time, the lender can move to have a receiver appointed. The court-appointed receiver provides the lender with a certain indirect degree of control over the property. Until the receiver is appointed, the owner can collect rent from the tenants leasing portions of the mortgaged property and, instead of using the rent to pay the debt service on the mortgage, the real estate taxes, the insurance premiums, and the costs of repairing and maintaining the property, the mortgagor can keep the money or spend it on anything that it wants even if it is unrelated to the property. Accordingly, the lender's biggest fear is not that the property is currently having a problem or that the owner has failed to make the debt service payments, but rather that the owner's action or inaction will cause the value of the security to deteriorate. The deterioration can be the result of the lender's being required to pay the taxes from its own funds, thereby increasing the amount of its lien on the property; or having to deal with an uninsured casualty loss or liability claim; or being required to make major repairs to the property. Therefore, at the very least, the commencement of the foreclosure allows the receiver to be appointed and, in theory, serves to preserve the lender's security. In the same regard, if the lender can be assured that the value of the security will not deteriorate and that the rents and other income will be spent on the property, even if the debt service is not being paid, the lender will be more inclined to allow the owner to remain in control of the property during the pendency of the foreclosure.

The commencement of the foreclosure also permits the lender to reexamine the economics for the loan and determine whether it will permit the owner to merely cure the default or require the owner to repay the entire indebtedness. The equity of redemption allows the owner to retain title to the property if it repays the entire indebtedness; there is no theory in the law, other than the owner's persuasion, that requires the lender to reinstate the indebtedness. The persuasion can occur when either the owner threatens to create a protracted dispute with the lender if the loan is not reinstated or a judge in the foreclosure action indicates that the foreclosure may be placed at the beginning or the end of his calendar, if either party fails to act in a reasonable manner. In fact, the possibility of a fast or slow foreclosure is a very effective method of providing the owner and the lender with a rationale for resolving the matter expeditiously, assuming that the owner has the ability to cure the default.

Additionally, the commencement of the foreclosure forces the owner to pay attention to a problem because it changes the passive lender into an active participant in the future of the property and the owner's continued interest in the property. Before the indebtedness is accelerated and the foreclosure commenced, the owner can either deal with a problem or ignore it; afterward, the owner must consider and consult with the lender to be able to retain the property and be able to deal with the problem in its own way. These events force many owners who believe that the problem either is insignificant or will take care of itself to immediately focus on eliminating the problem as quickly as possible.

FORECLOSURE DEFENSES

Basically, a foreclosure is an equitable action in which the property owner loses legal title to the property. Because foreclosure is an equitable action, all defenses available to a party in any other equitable action are available to the owner in a foreclosure. Although the mortgagor cannot utilize defenses that are inapplicable to the facts of the particular case, the owner can utilize any other facts that relate to the mortgage, including issues involving the execution of the mortgage documents and the granting of the original loan. The only preclusion from raising a particular defense would occur if the owner had previously waived a matter relating to the mortgage, which precludes the matter from being raised again at this time.

The foreclosure of a mortgage and the exercise of a power of sale contained in a deed of trust are extremely technical actions and require that the lender comply with every provision of the applicable law of the state in which the property is located. The slightest variance from complete compliance with the least significant provision of state law could require that the foreclosure action be recommenced, even if the discrepancy is identified after the property has been sold. Thus, the owner's first action in response to the commencement of the foreclosure should be a detailed examination of the terms of the promissory note, mortgage, and other loan documents, as well as the mortgage and foreclosure laws of the jurisdiction in which the property is located. This review should include a detailed examination of the execution of the loan documents, the events leading up to their execution and the default, and the continuing relationship between the owner and the lender prior to, and subsequent to, the default. Such an investigation may uncover actions that the lender failed to take or, if taken, may not have accomplished in the proper manner or the proper order, which will provide the owner with the basis for a legitimate defense.

The first requirement for a mortgage to be foreclosed is that the mortgage was executed by the current owner of the property; that it was properly acknowledged by a notary public or other local officer of the court; that the applicable mortgage tax was paid, if any; and that the mortgage was properly recorded as a lien against the legal title to the property. A mortgage that was not properly executed or recorded cannot be foreclosed, regardless of the lender's reason for attempting to foreclose the mortgage. Additionally, because a mortgage is only a security interest in property that secures a promissory note, the promissory note must contain all the salient business terms of the mortgage and make specific reference to the actions or inactions by the owner that would be considered a default, which could give rise to a foreclosure.

Next, the owner should determine that the action that the lender claims the owner took or failed to take as the basis for the foreclosure, is in fact an event of default under the mortgage. Although the owner's actions could be terribly detrimental to the property or the lender's interest in the property, if the mortgage and the promissory note do not delineate them as events of default, the lender will have a very difficult time attempting to use them as the basis for a mortgage foreclosure action. Traditionally, events of default include:

- Failure to make timely payments of the interest and principal on the promissory note
- Failure to pay the real estate taxes and assessments when they become due
- Failure to maintain adequate casualty, liability, and required insurance on the improvements
- Permitting the property to be encumbered by any other liens

- Violating any local, state, or federal laws, rules, or regulations
- Failure to pay utility charges
- A casualty or condemnation of the property regardless of the owner's fault
- The owner's sale of its interest in the property
- The owner's failure to comply with any of the leases on the property
- The lender's determination that it believes it is "insecure," which could mean anything if the lender's insecurity is an event of default under the mortgage.

The lender's ability to proceed with the foreclosure could also be hampered by ambiguities in the promissory note, mortgage, or other loan documents. The mortgage must specifically provide that a certain activity or failure of the owner violates the terms of the mortgage, or the lender cannot use the owner's action or failure to act as the basis for foreclosing the mortgage. For instance, the lender cannot accelerate the indebtedness and foreclose the mortgage due to the owner's failure to pay real estate taxes or maintain insurance unless the mortgage specifically states that such actions are an event of default. Regardless of how absurd the owner's actions might be, unless they are specifically precluded by the terms of the mortgage, they cannot be the basis for a foreclosure.

In most jurisdictions, for the foreclosure sale to be binding on all parties having an interest in the property, every entity with an interest in the property must be named as a defendant in the foreclosure action, even if their interest in the property is inferior to the mortgage. Accordingly, if the lender fails to include an interested party as a defendant in the foreclosure, the lender may have to recommence its foreclosure action, or the title the purchaser receives at the foreclosure sale will be subject to claims by parties who were not named in the original action to foreclose the mortgage. Therefore, if the owner realizes that a necessary party was not named in the foreclosure, the owner could notify that party or the court of the omission, after the foreclosure is well under way. This would necessitate a delay while the lender amends its complaint to include the necessary party and must then serve that party and give it time to answer. In some jurisdictions, it can take over six months for the court to rule on the lender's motion to amend the complaint and add a party.

Another method for the owner to frustrate the lender's ability to foreclose the mortgage is to claim that the lender has waived the default or has implicitly or explicitly agreed to not foreclose the mortgage. This is a cunning defense, because it is based on the lender's actions, which usually include providing the owner with an opportunity to resolve the property's problems before proceeding to foreclose the mortgage. However, the owner will argue that this delay was an implicit agreement by the lender to refrain from proceeding with the foreclosure. Although the owner and the lender may have entered into a supplemental agreement in which the lender agrees to forebear foreclosing the mortgage while the owner diligently attempts to resolve the property's problems, that agreement will almost definitely provide the lender with the right to proceed to foreclose the mortgage if the owner fails to act diligently or if the supplemental agreement is violated by the owner. If the owner has not defaulted in satisfying the terms of the supplemental agreement, than the lender could be stopped from proceeding with the foreclosure. The disagreement will revolve around the subjective issue of whether the owner has defaulted in fulfilling its obligations under the agreement and the mortgage.

If there is no agreement between the parties and the lender has simply delayed commencing the foreclosure, it is more difficult for the owner to rely on the lender's delay. Nevertheless, the waiver claim, unless founded on a specific document, provides the owner with something of almost infinite value in a foreclosure—a delaying tactic. If the owner can make a reasonable argument to prevent the lender from quickly obtaining a judgment of foreclosure, which entails raising issues of fact that require a trial, the owner may be able to obtain sufficient time to resolve the property's problems.

As a defense to the foreclosure, the owner can utilize the fact that it has made the required payment or performed the required act that the lender is using as the basis for foreclosing the mortgage. However, the parties can have a difference of opinion as to whether the owner's performance was total or partial and satisfied the requirements of the mortgage. The owner can argue that the lender had agreed not to proceed to foreclose the mortgage as long as the owner took the limited action that it took. Nevertheless, the owner would still have to prove that it was required to take only a limited action. The lender would not be able to foreclose the mortgage if the owner made the entire payment or performed the entire action that was required. The issue is whether the owner's less-than-complete performance is sufficient. Alternatively, if the required action is subject to a subjective determination, the issue is whether the owner's performance was satisfactory. The issue that will entail a great degree of delay is determining whether the lender's request for the owner's performance of a specific action is reasonable in light of the terms of the mortgage and can be interpreted as required by the mortgage. If the lender fails to meet these requirements, then the owner's action or failure to act cannot be utilized as the basis for a foreclosure.

Moreover, the court could inquire into whether the owner could reasonably have believed that the lender would have accepted a partial performance in lieu of a complete performance and not foreclose its mortgage. Was there some indication, regardless of how slight by the lender, that it would accept the owner's partial performance? If so, the lender might be precluded from proceeding with its foreclosure. The owner's ability to raise these issues would delay the lender from being able to proceed with the foreclosure.

Another defense, although very difficult to utilize, is that the statute of limitations has expired. Two statutes of limitation are involved in a mortgage foreclosure, one for the promissory note and another for the mortgage. A separate statute would begin to accrue at the time the owner defaults in fulfilling the terms of each document. Utilizing the statute of limitations defense is very difficult because the lender would have to defer bringing the foreclosure of the mortgage or an action to collect the indebtedness for several years after the default in order for the owner to successfully argue that the statute of limitations has expired. Although many lenders delay in commencing the action, it is highly unlikely that a lender would wait several years to proceed to enforce its rights.

A similar defense would be based on the concept of laches. Laches is a theory in which a party is required to proceed to enforce a legal right within a reasonable period of time, or it is precluded from enforcing the right. Unfortunately, a mortgage foreclosure is an equitable right, and laches is not usually available in equitable actions. Moreover, as long as the foreclosure is commenced within the applicable statute of limitations period, laches could not be raised as a defense. However, laches could be raised by the purchaser at a foreclosure sale against the holder of an inferior mortgage where the parties believed that the prior mortgage had been extinguished, but it had not. If the original lender failed to raise the prior mortgage as an objection for an extended period of time after the sale, it would lose its right to proceed against the property.

The lender's attempt to charge excessive or usurious interest could also be the basis for precluding the lender from foreclosing the mortgage. However, the use of this defense would be subject to the vagaries of the law of the state in which the property is located, as well as federal preemption of interest rates in certain circumstances. Usury, the charging of excessive interest, must usually be raised as a defense by the original obligor on the promissory note and not by an assignee or subsequent owner of the property. Each state has its own law as to the effect of charging usurious interest, which could result in either the reduction of the interest or the loss of the interest or principal on the loan. Additionally, based on local law, the fees charged by the lender may also be considered additional interest on the loan, which increases the risk of a usury defense against the lender. However, every state also has exclusions from its usury laws, which allows excessive interest to be charged for business loans, loans for sums above a certain amount, loans secured by real estate, purchase money financing, or loans to entities other than individuals.

Fraud or misrepresentation by the lender in the owner's granting of the original mortgage is another defense that could be raised in the foreclosure. The elements of fraud include the fact that someone other than the property owner executed the mortgage and the owner did not authorize the granting of the mortgage. The defenses of fraud or misrepresentation could not be raised by a subsequent owner of the property if the fraud or the misrepresentation related to the owner's original acquisition of the property or the original execution of the loan documents, rather than to a subsequent event. The defenses of fraud or misrepresentation could be raised in the foreclosure of a purchase money mortgage if the original purchase involved a fraudulent act even though the mortgage was not fraudulent. The defense of fraud could also be raised by a junior lienor in an attempt to protect its position by eliminating the more senior mortgage.

The purchaser of a property, on discovering the fraud or misrepresentation by the seller, would probably be required to elect whether to deliver the property back to the seller (the lender) and demand recision of the transaction or to retain the property and sue the seller for fraud. It would seem unlikely that the courts would allow the purchaser to retain the property and to be repaid all its money. Nevertheless, the purchaser's retaining the property should not deprive it from being able to recover part of its payments due to the fraud. This would include cancellation of all or part of the mortgaged indebtedness. The damages for fraud or a material misrepresentation could be the actual expenses the fraud caused the purchaser or the reduced value of the property due to the fraud. If the owner was aware of the fraud or misrepresentation at the time the property was acquired, the fraud or misrepresentation could not be raised in an attempt to defeat a mortgage foreclosure action. To successfully defend the foreclosure based upon a claim of fraud, the owner would have to demonstrate that a material fact was misrepresented to it prior to its purchase and that the purchaser relied on such facts and was justified in relying on such facts under the circumstances. Moreover, the seller or lender would not have had to actually be aware of the true facts if the seller or lender either knew the facts to be untrue or made a reckless statement with or without having the intent to deceive the purchaser, the result of which was harmful to the purchaser. However, it is unlikely that vague statements by the seller as to the potential appreciation in the property's value could be the basis for a claim of fraud. The exception to this would be proof by the purchaser that the seller's or lender's assurances went beyond general statements and were very specific.

Another defense would be based on the Uniform Fraudulent Conveyances Act, which provides that a conveyance of property that results in someone's being rendered insolvent, is fraudulent if the conveyance is made without fair consideration. The actual intent of the parties is irrelevant. Additionally, if a conveyance is made by a party with the actual intent to hinder, delay, or defraud creditors, it would be considered fraudulent. Moreover, a conveyance made without fair consideration when the person making it intends to incur debts beyond its ability to pay would also be considered fraudulent. Accordingly, a creditor that is adversely affected by a fraudulent conveyance would have the right to raise it as a defense in the foreclosure action. A mortgage placed on a property by someone related to the owner in an attempt to defeat the rights of other lenders would also be considered a fraudulent conveyance and be subject to attack as such. The basis for a claim against a fraudulent conveyance is an absence of fair consideration for the indebtedness.

Another defense that could be used to delay the foreclosure of a mortgage, would be a default based upon the breach of a duty by the lender. This defense could be raised only if the lender actually owed a duty to the owner to perform in a certain manner and failed to perform the act. In such an event, the lender would not be able to utilize the effect of the lender's failure to perform as a basis for a foreclosure action against the mortgage. An example of the lender's failure to fulfill a duty would include (1) its failure to advance funds that it was obligated to advance or (2) to take certain actions that it failed to take or (3) not take certain actions, which it did in fact take and which harmed the owner.

The owner could also argue that the mortgage was originally executed under duress. The lender's threat to take certain actions against a third party unless the mortgage is executed would be a basis for a defense of duress. If the owner could support its claim of duress, the claim could be raised as a defense in the foreclosure action and, if successfully asserted, the mortgage would be void. However, a claim of duress would ordinarily be raised by the owner shortly after the execution of the mortgage. It is important to note that the lender's threat to exercise its right to foreclose the mortgage if the owner failed to perform its obligations under the mortgage, would not be considered duress.

The owner could also raise a defense to the foreclosure action by claiming that the transaction was illegal. To effectively pursue such a defense, the illegality would have to be based upon a critical provision in the agreements or the basic relationship between the parties. It would not be sufficient for the claim to be based upon a particular irrelevant provision that was contained in the note or mortgage, which may be illegal due to a technicality. Likewise, the lender's unconscionable conduct with the intent to cause a mortgage default by the owner would be a legitimate defense in the foreclosure action. A determination that the lender's actions were unconscionable or taken in bad faith would also be the basis for a defense in the foreclosure. Such a defense could include the lender's unreasonable interference with the owner's tenants or blocking the owner from leasing portions of the property.

Payment is the most effective defense that an owner can raise and should extinguish the lender's right to foreclose the mortgage. The payment need not be made by the owner or made directly to the lender; if it was made to the lender's agent or pursuant to previously received instructions from the lender, the action would be sufficient. Payment is a complete defense against a foreclosure. The fact that the lender refused to accept the payment of the indebtedness should preclude the lender from being able to proceed with its foreclosure of the mortgage. Additionally, the owner's payment of the amount due at the time the foreclosure is commenced would also terminate the foreclosure and allow the owner to retain ownership of the property. Whether payment has been made could also become an issue if the owner has a number of obligations to the lender and the lender insists that payments be applied to the various obligations in a certain order, whereas the owner claims to have made the payments toward different obligations. Usually, the owner can indicate to the lender the manner in which the payments are to be applied. If the lender fails to adhere to such directions, the owner would be able to raise a defense of payment. Payment could also be raised as a defense based upon the lender's application of insurance proceeds or condemnation awards.

Failure of consideration could be raised by the owner as a defense in the lender's attempt to foreclose on a purchase money mortgage if the property that the lender sold to the owner and upon which the lender holds a mortgage is worth significantly less than what the owner paid for it, and the difference is due to a material misrepresentation made by the lender to the owner. However, except under unusual circumstances, a lender does not guarantee the value of a property. Nevertheless, in a situation where the owner executed the note and mortgage based upon certain promises made by the lender, upon which the lender reneged, there would be an absence of consideration, and the mortgage could be voidable.

Another defense to a foreclosure action could be based on estoppel, the act or statement of one party on which the other party relies. The defense of estoppel is intended to provide fairness between the parties. The theory of an estoppel defense is that the lender should not be able to foreclose a mortgage if the owner's default was caused by the owner's reliance upon the words or actions of the lender, which were misleading. An estoppel defense is made based on a false representation or a concealment of material facts by the lender and an intention or expectation by the lender that the owner would rely on such facts to its detriment. Accordingly, the lender may be estopped from foreclosing the mortgage, if it precluded the owner from resolving the problem by indicating that it would not proceed to declare a default or foreclose the mortgage. The basis of estoppel can also be caused by the false execution of an estoppel certificate or by the acts or omissions of the lender, which mislead the borrower or purchaser. For example, if the owner made tax and insurance payments to the lender and the lender failed to properly dispense the payments, the lender could not subsequently use the failure to make such payments as the basis for declaring the loan in default or commencing a foreclosure.

The owner could also interpose as a defense that the relationship between the owner and lender was that of partners or joint venturers, and not merely creditor and debtor. If the owner can demonstrate from the loan documents that the relationship between the parties was other than merely borrower and lender, the owner may be able to impede the expeditious foreclosure of the mortgage. Under such circumstances, the mortgage could not be foreclosed without discovery and a trial regarding the true relationship between the parties. However, to maintain this defense, the owner must have some shred of proof to support this claim.

A junior lienor could also raise a defense in a foreclosure action commenced by the senior lienor that the action is intended to improperly eliminate the junior lienors' liens on the property. Such a defense could be based on a claim that the senior lienor is taking actions that are unfair to the junior lienors and that such actions are being taken without their knowledge or consent. Defenses that could be raised by the junior lienor would include committing waste on the property or allowing the owner to commit waste, which would reduce the value of the property and make it less likely that the junior lienor will be able to receive a payment from the proceeds of the foreclosure sale. Notwithstanding the foregoing, the junior lienor would be unable to object to the senior lienor's actions, which are commensurate with its rights as the senior lender. The fact that the junior lienor does not approve of the senior lienor's actions or would be adversely affected by them, does not mean that they are improper or the basis for a defense against the foreclosure.

A junior lienor could also raise a defense to the foreclosure that the junior lienor's interest in the property is actually senior to the mortgage being foreclosed. This claim could be raised by an owner of the property, whose position is superior to the mortgagor. It could also be raised by another lender that believes that its mortgage is senior to the mortgage being foreclosed but that the complaint in the foreclosure action does not describe the relevant priorities correctly.

CLAIMS AGAINST THE LENDER

A recently developed approach to dealing with lenders that are attempting to foreclose a mortgage is to seek damages against the lender based upon the evolving concept of lender liability. The owner's best defense is a good offense. Moreover, the borrower or the owner of the property would be able to use the lender liability defense even if the lender is not attempting to foreclose the mortgage or is not even a secured creditor and has no mortgage to foreclose.

Although the lender liability defense is frequently raised, it is not usually successful. Nevertheless, the consequences to the lender of losing a lender liability claim can be so harsh that borrowers will increasingly consider making the claim in an attempt either to preclude the lender from proceeding with the foreclosure of the mortgage or to uncover sufficient evidence of wrongdoing by the lender to actually cancel the indebtedness or obtain damages. Generally, lender liability is based on the theory that if the lender's actions were taken in bad faith, the borrower or the borrower's creditors should be able to assert a claim for damages against the lender, or the lender should be precluded from benefiting from its actions by not being able to obtain a judgment against the borrower.

The problem for a lender is not merely avoiding situations in which it can be accused of some act of wrongdoing, but finding ways to make credit decisions and protect existing loans in this environment. Notwithstanding the lender's good intentions, the more the lender does to protect the loan or assist the borrower in surviving an economic downturn, the more likely it is that the borrower, one of the borrower's creditors, or even the Internal Revenue Service could attempt to utilize the assistance as the basis for a lawsuit based upon the concept of lender liability. The lender's lender liability exposure is directly related to the amount of influence or control the lender exercised over the borrower. The lender's influence could result in a claim that the lender should be responsible for the borrower's debts.

The risk of a lender liability claim places the lender in a quandary. At the time that the borrower is having financial difficulties, the lender considers acting to protect the loan, the collateral for the loan, and the lender's relationship with the borrower. Unfortunately, it is when the borrower is most in need of the lender's assistance that the lender must act most carefully in considering its alternatives. If it acts and the owner fails, the lender could be accused of lender liability for accelerating the failure. Conversely, if the lender fails to act, the likelihood that the debtor will fail increases dramatically. The lender's response could be based on whether it wants to protect itself from a potential claim of lender liability and increase the likelihood that the loan can be repaid. Although most lender liability cases are eventually dismissed, not all lenders are free of blame, and some lenders' actions have caused borrowers to collapse. Perhaps, one day, this theory will require the lender to act to assist a borrower in trouble.

Claims have been raised against lenders and other creditors in many instances, including:

- The lender's failure to issue a written loan commitment
- The lender's failure to comply with a loan commitment
- The lender's attempt to terminate a loan commitment
- The lender's control over the debtor, which results in the lender's being responsible for the debtor's debts
- The lender's being the borrower's partner
- The lender's failure to disburse a loan according to its commitment
- The lender's breach of a fiduciary duty to the borrower
- The lender's failure to act in good faith
- The lender's interference with the debtor's business
- The lender's controlling the debtor
- The lender's attempt to improve its position prior to a bankruptcy filing
- The lender's fraud, duress, or tortious interference
- The lender's misuse of the loan collateral
- Usury

- Environmental liability
- Securities law violations.

Notwithstanding the foregoing list, not every action by the lender can lead to a claim of lender liability. The possibility of success will depend on the particular case.

The issue of a lender's liability can be raised either offensively or defensively after the borrower has defaulted, because such a claim can be used to slow or defeat a lender's attempt to accelerate a loan or realize upon the collateral for the loan. A defaulting borrower, believing that the best defense is a good offense, could begin to negotiate a debt restructuring with the lender by implying or stating that, unless the lender agrees to a moratorium in the debt service or makes additional advances or restructures the debt, the borrower will either sue or defend the lender's foreclosure by claiming that the lender was the debtor's alter ego or was guilty of:

- Bad faith
- Fraud
- Interference with business relationships
- Breach of fiduciary duties
- Negligence
- Conflict of interest
- Duress
- Misrepresentation
- Agency.

However, the lender will probably be safe as long as the lender acted in good faith and was merely supervising the administration of the loan. Moreover, if the lender acts properly to protect the loan or the collateral for the loan or is foreclosing upon the collateral, the lender probably will not be found liable to the debtor or a third party for the lender's actions or inactions. Nevertheless, if the lender directly or indirectly assumes control over the borrower or its business, the lender risks increasing its chance of losing a claim of lender liability. The problem for the lender and the opportunity for the borrower are based on identifying the line between merely supervising a borrower and taking control of the borrower's business. The borrower can utilize a number of theories of lender liability and defensive actions in defending itself from accusations against the lender.

THEORIES OF LENDER LIABILITY

The recent development of the defensive and offensive use of the concept of lender liability arises from the longstanding use of similar doctrines in the general business environment. Although lenders have been relatively successful in responding to this new weapon by borrowers and their creditors, there have been losses, especially in the lower courts. To utilize these theories in defending against mortgage foreclosures or threatening the lenders if they fail to cooperate, the real estate owner must understand the basis of the concept of lender liability. Although these theories might not seem directly applicable in the abstract, they may be very useful in defenses against specific actions taken by a particular lender.

One of the oldest theories of lender liability is based on the instrumentality doctrine. This doctrine provides that if one corporate entity exercises control over another, the exercise of control should also impose liability on the controlling entity. The reason for this theory is that the corporate identities of the two corporations should be disregarded and one corporation held liable for the debts of another corporation, regardless of the absence of fraud, deceit, or misrepresentation. A corporation can become liable for the debts of another corporation in either of two ways. First, the dominant corporation can indicate either implicitly or expressly to the creditors of the subservient corporation that the former will stand behind those debts as a guarantor. Alternatively, the dominant corporation may be held liable for the debts of the subservient corporation when it misuses that corporation by treating it as a conduit for the purposes of the first corporation. According to this theory, the subservient corporation's debts should then belong to the dominant corporation. In these instances, courts will look through the form of a transaction or the relationship between the parties to the realities of the relationship between the two entities.

The relationship between the dominant and the subservient corporations is frequently described using the *identity theory*, in which the separate corporate identities are ignored and the two corporations are treated as a single entity, or the *instrumentality theory*, in which the subservient corporation is described as being the instrument, agent, adjunct, branch, or dummy of the dominant corporation. For there to be liability under the instrumentality theory, the dominant corporation must have had control over the subservient corporation, and the dominant corporation must have caused the harm through misuse of this control. An important part of the test to determine if lender liability exists is to demonstrate the connection between the dominant corporation's activities and the harm to the subservient corporation.

The basis for liability under the instrumentality theory is the extent of control that must exist. The ownership of the subservient corporation's stock by the dominant corporation is insufficient to establish liability. Liability depends upon the degree of control that one entity exercises over another entity, regardless of whether the control is based upon one party's owning the other party's stock or one party's being a creditor that made large advances to the debtor. The absence of stock ownership also is not determinative. Even if one party does not own stock in the other party, liability could exist if the two entities had common stockholders and directors or if one party managed, operated, or otherwise controled the other party.

Under the instrumentality theory, a creditor–debtor relationship between the parties by itself will not be considered control by one entity over another entity. One entity's loan of money to another entity would not make the lender liable for the borrower's acts. The most important factor between the parties is the control of one entity over another. If a lender becomes so involved with the debtor's activities that it is actively managing the debtor's affairs, then the degree of control necessary to support a claim of liability under the instrumentality theory may be achieved. An examination of the instrumentality theory involving debtor–creditor relationships demonstrates that what is usually required for liability to exist is a strong showing that the creditor assumed actual, participatory, and total control of the debtor. The concept of control is also open to interpretation. The lender's participation in the management of the debtor is not automatically considered control. For there to be instrumentality liability for the creditor, the subservient corporation must be used to further the purposes of the dominant corporation. For liability to exist, the subservient corporation in reality must have had no separate, independent existence of its own.

For the instrumentality theory to prevail, the dominant corporation must exercise such control over the subservient corporation that it totally dominates the subservient corporation. To some degree, the subservient corporation would be found to have had no separate corporate identity. For liability to occur, there must also be present a misuse of the control by the dominant corporation for its own purposes, even if it does not intend to defraud the creditors of the subservient corporation. The instrumentality theory is based on the concept that the party responsible for the loss should be liable for the loss. For a lender to be found liable pursuant to the instrumentality theory of lender liability, the lender must have actually exercised control over the debtor, and the loss must be based upon the misuse of the control by the creditor over the debtor. One must also assume that the control must be over a relevant and significant portion of the debtor's business.

The *agency theory* of lender liability is based upon the concept that, when one corporation completely controls the activities of the other, the subservient entity is actually the agent of the dominant corporation. Like the instrumentality theory, success in utilizing the agency theory requires that the other creditors demonstrate that the dominant corporation abused its fiduciary duty and acted in bad faith and that the dominant corporation's intention was to further its own purposes, rather than to act in the best interests of the subservient corporation.

Nevertheless, under both the instrumentality theory and the agency theory of corporate liability, a lender is not precluded from exercising some degree of control over the debtor's finances in order to protect its loan. However, the lender cannot attempt to exercise total dominion and control over the debtor's entire business, effectively making it a subsidiary operation of the lender.

The lender's bad faith is a particularly fertile area of claims over lender liability. The lender can be held responsible for a creditor's debts if the lender has acted in bad faith, and the result is a deterioration of the debtor's financial condition or a financial loss to the debtor. Bad faith includes fraud, deceit, self-dealing, misrepresentations, or interference with the debtor's contractual relations. A lender is not required to violate a written affirmation that it will act in good faith. Every agreement contains an implied covenant of good faith and fair dealing between the parties.

A lender's threat to terminate a loan commitment if its conditions are not met, would not be considered an act taken in bad faith. However, bad faith would exist if the lender refused to perform the loan commitment unless entirely new or different conditions were met. Bad faith requires that one party to an agreement, either willfully or by mistake, demand of the other party a performance to which it has no right under the agreement. Bad faith requires that the lender demand that, unless its altered demands are met, it will not render its promised performance.

For an anticipatory breach to be considered an action taken in bad faith, the lender must make a clear and unequivocal declaration that the agreed-upon performance would not be forthcoming. However, to be successful, the nonrepudiating party must have the ability to perform all its obligations under the agreement. If the party could not or would not have performed, that party cannot recover damages for the other party's nonperformance or repudiation. The dispositive issue is not only the lender's refusal to perform, which could have been motivated by bad faith, but also the borrower's inability to perform at the time the borrower demanded that the lender perform.

Bad faith can also be demonstrated by a lender's inducement of, and knowing participation in, a breach of fiduciary duty. The elements for inducing or participating in a breach of fiduciary duty are that the claimant must prove that (1) there was a breach by a fiduciary of an obligation to the claimant, (2) the fiduciary knowingly induced or participated in the breach, and (3) the claimant suffered damages as a result of the breach. Generally, if one party knowingly participates with a fiduciary in a breach of trust, that party will be liable to the beneficiary for any damages caused by the breach. Moreover, once a party is put on notice of the existence of the fiduciary duty, it must investigate and determine whether the parties were authorized to act.

A fully secured lender also has a requirement of good faith to provide notice to a borrower prior to refusing to advance funds under a financing agreement. Unless it is presumed that a lender's actions are limited by an obligation to act in good faith, even if the loan agreement does not provide for good faith performance, the debtor's continued existence would be left entirely at the whim or mercy of the creditor. The concept of good faith or the absence of bad faith does not have to be stated in the loan documents for the lender to be obligated to exercise good faith in its dealings with its borrowers.

Even if the agreement between the borrower and the lender allows the lender the right to payment on demand, the lender must act with a certain degree of reasonableness and fairness. Although it is not necessary that a lender be correct in its understanding of the facts and circumstances pertinent to its decision not to advance funds, there must be at least some objective basis upon which a reasonable loan officer in the exercise of his or her discretion would have made a valid business judgment to call the loan. The lender must act in a reasonable manner in accelerating the loan, especially if it was fully secured and would not have been hurt by the debtor's potential financial problems. The alternative is that the debtor would be damaged by the lender's precipitous actions.

Although a promissory note may grant the bank the right to repayment on demand, that does not mean that the agreement could simply be terminated at the whim of the parties. The right of termination or acceleration is subject to the limitations contained in the other loan documents. The lender could be found to have not acted in good faith in abruptly terminating a line of credit, when the borrower was not in default, its overall financial position had not changed, and the lender had not previously complained about the conduct of its business. If the lender anticipates that it will terminate a line of credit, the lender should advise the borrower that it would not lend additional funds and that it expected repayment of the outstanding balance at the earliest possible date.

The lender may not be found to be bound by an officer's oral promise to make a long-term financing commitment, if the borrower had no reason to rely on a statement by an employee of the lender that the loan would be made, if it is obvious that the officer did not have the authority to make the decision. This is especially true if the lender gives the borrower sufficient-warning that the loan would not be made. The liability for bad faith denial of a contract occurs when the party not only breaches the contract, but also denies that the contract existed. It should also be noted that neither preliminary negotiations nor an agreement for future negotiations is the equivalent of an actual agreement to lend money. Moreover, reliance by a borrower is irrelevant without justification, and a borrower's misguided belief in relying on a statement on which no reasonable person would rely is not justifiable reliance.

A lender can be found liable for a borrower's problems if the debtor or its other creditors can prove that the lender gained from deceit, duress, or a material or fraudulent misrepresentation. This defense is similar to a lender's bad faith, although it implies that the lender took an affirmative action that placed the borrower in a significantly worse position than if the lender had not acted. This is not simply the improper accelerating of a loan or failure to make a loan without complying with the terms of its agreements, but rather a situation where the lender took steps that were actually improper. Bad faith is a question of judgment and requires a subjective determination, whereas deceit, duress, or material misrepresentation is obviously improper. A decision in favor of a borrower could be based on the conclusion that if the lender conveyed incorrect information to the borrower, the lender then had an obligation to correct the information given to the borrower. However, ordinarily, failure to disclose material facts known only to one party is not actionable fraud unless there is a fiduciary or confidential relationship imposing a duty to disclose.

A claim of fraud may not be based on a promise to perform an act in the future or on a representation as to future matters, because there is no right to rely on such statements. The prerequisite to reliance is a relation of trust and confidence that exists between the parties. Alternatively, fraud can exist if the speaker, at the time of making the representations, had the present undisclosed intention not to fulfill his or her promises. Not only must the party claiming fraud have relied on the allegedly false statement, but such reliance must have been reasonable and, more importantly, must have been detrimental to the debtor.

Misrepresentations and omissions are grounds for fraud only if they were material and designed to induce the other party into taking actions that the party would have refrained from taking if it had been aware of the actual facts. Moreover, the courts are usually disinclined to believe that a lender has breached a fiduciary relationship to a borrower unless (1) the relationship goes beyond each party's operating for its own best interests, (2) the borrower and the lender must have a common interest and rely on trust and confidence in each other, and (3) one party has the ability to control the other party. However, a fiduciary relationship could arise between a borrower and a lender under certain circumstances, such as when (1) the applicant has deposited escrow or other funds with the lender; (2) the borrower and lender have a special confidential relationship; (3) the lender fails to keep an express or implied promise; or, (4) the lender becomes the broker for or an agent of the borrower. Finally, for a claim of negligence to exist, the borrower must demonstrate that the lender owed it a duty of care that it breached, and that breach was the approximate cause of harm to the borrower.

10

Benefiting from Bankruptcy

Bankruptcy is the ultimate threat. It can be used by either the debtor or the creditor to accomplish the same goal—to resolve the property's problems—but with different results. The debtor (i.e., the property owner) will want to stop the creditor (i.e., the lender) from obtaining the property, whereas the creditor wants to protect the property and get it away from the debtor. At the least, bankruptcy is a way of dealing with a debtor's problems in an orderly fashion with the intention of protecting the creditors. However, not infrequently, the debtor is the one who receives the most protection, because, in many instances, the largest number of creditors will be protected if the debtor is given an opportunity to remain in business and resolve its problems as a going concern.

Bankruptcy is one of the most effective and flexible tools available to both the debtor and the creditor to force a reasonable resolution of problems with a property. However, as with any threat, the party must be prepared to follow through and, therefore, must understand the concept. To a large extent, bankruptcy is a very effective tool because it is a harsh solution to the property's problems and, most importantly, because the bankruptcy court has such great authority to alter and terminate agreements that most debtors and creditors would rather compromise than risk involvement with the bankruptcy court.

Bankruptcy is extremely complicated and provides the bankruptcy court, the trustee (if one is appointed), and the parties such latitude that, in many instances, the creditor can achieve a faster, less expensive, and more equitable solution to its relationship with the debtor by working with the debtor to avoid bankruptcy. The large corporate bankruptcies of the last few years have made bankruptcy an acceptable method of doing business. The days are gone when bankruptcy was considered a last resort and was postponed until the debtor had no alternative but to liquidate. Today, bankruptcy is one of the first solutions considered by business people to solve what seems to be an otherwise unsolvable problem. Bankruptcy has now become as popular in real estate as in any other business.

During previous recessions in which overbuilt and overleveraged real estate adversely affected the market, the debtor and its creditors knew that the debtor could always file a bankruptcy petition; however, neither side suggested bankruptcy. The word was never uttered in polite conversation. Today, not only is the word *bankruptcy* used, but debtors and creditors assume that the debtor will file a voluntary petition (or the creditor can file an involuntary petition), and both sides plan their strategy around the potential filing. This propensity of debtors to choose the bankruptcy alternative has caused creditors to become so concerned about the resulting delays, expense, and loss of control that secured lenders have paid debtors for providing a deed and a general release, so the creditor can take control of the property and avoid a further deterioration in the property's value. (See Example.)

EXAMPLE

Powers owns a shopping center encumbered by a $5 million first mortgage and a $1.5 million second mortgage. He is in arrears in paying both mortgages because the operating costs have accelerated dramatically during the past few years and several tenants have defaulted in making their rent payments. The lenders commence foreclosure actions. Powers defends, but the lenders move for summary judgment of foreclosure. Powers then files a petition to commence a Chapter 11 reorganization. At that moment, the lenders' foreclosure actions are stayed (i.e., suspended) while Powers attempts to reorganize the business and obtain new tenants. Because the lenders are stayed, they have two choices: to cooperate with Powers to restructure the loans and the operation of the property or to continue to make motions to lift the stay in order to foreclose their mortgage. If Powers can delay long enough, the lenders may eventually agree to cooperate in order to move the matter along.

In the current environment, the owner of real property must have a working understanding of the Bankruptcy Code to determine whether solutions to its problems are contained within the Code. At times, bankruptcy will be the perfect solution to an owner's problems; at other times, it should be avoided at all costs; and in most instances, the owner should be prepared to threaten to utilize its provisions, but should stay away from bankruptcy. This chapter contains an overview of the Bankruptcy Code and the aspects of it that affect or benefit real estate. However, this chapter does not contain any certain advice as to when and how to utilize the Bankruptcy Code and does not replace the need to obtain competent legal assistance.

Each owner must determine when and to what extent the Bankruptcy Code can be used advantageously in each situation. The real estate owner can undoubtedly benefit from a filing under the various chapters of the Bankruptcy Code. The benefits arise from the automatic stay that goes into effect on the filing of the petition, which precludes any creditor from proceeding against the estate's property while the proceeding is pending. Moreover, the delays and expense involved provide the creditors with reason for cooperating with the debtor in finding solutions to its problems. There are also benefits for the creditors, because the Code provides for an orderly solution to the owner's problems and protection for the assets of the estate.

OVERVIEW

The basis of the federal Bankruptcy Code is Article I, Section 8, Clause 4 of the United States Constitution, which mandated that Congress "establish uniform laws on the subject of bankruptcies throughout the United States." Congress enacted the first bankruptcy act in 1800, and has regularly revised the bankruptcy law to keep the law consistent with the changing nature of American society. As used in this chapter, *Bankruptcy Code* refers to the federal Bankruptcy Code, as amended. The Bankruptcy Code currently contains eight chapters which, for historical reasons, are not numbered sequentially.

Chapters 1, 3, and 5 apply to all cases filed in bankruptcy. Chapters 7, 9, 11, 12, and 13 contain provisions that apply only to the particular chapter and cannot be used for cases arising in another chapter. The following is a brief description of the chapters:

- *Chapter 1* contains the general provisions of the Bankruptcy Code.
- *Chapter 3* deals with the administration of the bankruptcy cases as they proceed, including the institution of the bankruptcy case and

the rights, obligations, duties, and compensation of the fiduciaries; retention and compensation of professionals; creditors meetings; debtor's examination; and issues relating to the conversion of a proceeding from one chapter of the Bankruptcy Code to another and the dismissal of a case.

- *Chapter 5* deals with creditors, the debtor, and the estate, and provides for the rights and obligations of the debtors and creditors, the filing of proofs of claim, establishing priorities, determining whether or not a creditor is secured, providing for the subordination of certain claims, delineating what property is included within the bankruptcy estate, and acting upon preferences, and fraudulent transfers.
- *Chapter 7* deals with the liquidation of a debtor's assets and liabilities and provides for the appointment of a trustee to liquidate the debtor's assets for distribution to its creditors and the discharge of all dischargeable debts.
- *Chapter 9* deals with the adjustment of debts by a municipality.
- *Chapter 11* provides for the reorganization and rehabilitation of a business and allows the debtor to remain in possession of its property while a plan is worked out, which is subject to approval of the court and the creditors.
- *Chapter 12* deals with the adjustment of debts of a family farmer with regular annual income.
- *Chapter 13* deals with the rehabilitation of an individual.

The Federal District Courts have exclusive jurisdiction of all cases filed under the Bankruptcy Code. They also have jurisdiction over all civil proceedings arising in or related to a bankruptcy, even if they relate to a matter usually arising in a state court. Accordingly, the bankruptcy court has the authority to hear all the following issues relating to a bankruptcy:

- Matters concerning the administration of the debtor
- Allowance or disallowance of claims against the debtor
- Claims by the debtor against creditors
- Orders for the debtor to obtain credit
- Orders to turn over property of the debtor
- Proceedings to determine, avoid, or recover preferences
- Motions to terminate, annul, or modify the automatic stay
- Proceedings to determine, avoid, or recover fraudulent conveyances

- Determinations as to the dischargeability of particular debts
- Objections to discharges
- Determinations of the validity, extent, or priority of liens
- Confirmation of plans
- Orders approving the use or lease of property
- Orders approving the sale of property
- Other proceedings affecting the liquidation of the assets of the estate or the adjustment of the debtor–creditor relationship.

The bankruptcy court thus has a great deal of latitude over which matters it wishes to hear and which it wishes to delegate to a state court for a hearing. Although the issue being heard by a bankruptcy court must be relevant to the federal issue or the viability of the creditor's claim, even within these limitations, the bankruptcy court has the ability to set its own agenda.

A bankruptcy proceeding can be commenced in one of two ways: through a voluntary proceeding, filed by the debtor, which is the most common, or through an involuntary proceeding, filed by creditors.

A principal reason for a debtor to commence a proceeding under the Bankruptcy Code is to obtain the benefit of the automatic stay. The automatic stay halts all proceedings against the debtor and provides the debtor with the time to organize its affairs and permit an orderly reorganization or liquidation. Until the stay is lifted, the automatic stay also accomplishes the following:

- Protects the debtor from any creditors' attempts to collect debts that arose prior to the commencement of the bankruptcy proceeding
- Prohibits the commencement or continuation of any litigation against the debtor
- Prohibits the seizure of any of the debtor's property
- Prevents any attempt to create, perfect, or enforce liens against the debtor's property.

SELECTING A CHAPTER

The debtor can choose among five different proceedings under which it can commence a bankruptcy proceeding, although not every proceeding is available to every debtor. The proceedings, described by their chapter number, are Chapters 7 (liquidation of the debtor), 9 (adjustment of a debtor's debts where the debtor is a local government entity), 11 (reorganization of a business), 12 (adjustment of a family farmer's debts), and 13 (rehabilitation of an individual). This section highlights the availability of each chapter, as well as its advantages and disadvantages.

Chapter 7 provides a relatively inexpensive method for a debtor to liquidate its assets under the supervision of a trustee. The Chapter 7 proceeding is what most people think of when they hear that a business has filed for bankruptcy protection, because a Chapter 7 proceeding results in the sale of the debtor's assets and the distribution of the proceeds to the creditors. It is utilized in business situations when there is no likelihood that the debtor's business can be reorganized and made able to survive and, for example, is most apparent by the advertising of liquidation sales under the supervision of the bankruptcy trustee.

The presence of the trustee in the Chapter 7 proceeding assures the creditors that none of the debtor's assets are being hidden or secretly disposed of through other means. The trustee also protects the debtor from attack by creditors and protects the debtor's property that is exempt from the liquidation unless some of the debtor's debts turn out not to be dischargeable. The concept of a discharge is one of the purposes of a bankruptcy filing, because it extinguishes the debtor's personal obligation to pay dischargeable debts that accrued prior to the filing of the bankruptcy petition and allows the debtor, if it is an individual, to start over again. However, certain debts may not be dischargeable, and the debtor will still have to pay these even after the completion of the Chapter 7 proceeding.

The disadvantage of a voluntary Chapter 7 proceeding is that, after the proceeding is commenced, the debtor may learn that not all of its debts are dischargeable and the debtor may not be able to retain property that it expected to be able to retain. Property that is not exempt will be sold by the Chapter 7 trustee and the sales proceeds distributed to the creditors. If the debtor is a business and commences a voluntary Chapter 7 proceeding, the business will be terminated and the trustee will liquidate the assets of the business. The trustee will also examine the books and records of the business, which may result in the trustee's commencing lawsuits against the officers, directors, shareholders, or partners of the debtor based upon any available cause of action under either state or federal law. Another disadvantage of a voluntary filing arises from the fact that bankruptcy is a public record, and the debtor must be prepared to be examined under oath and must be willing to make its finances public.

A voluntary Chapter 7 proceeding is commenced by the debtor's filing of a petition. Within 15 days thereafter, the debtor must file a schedule of its assets and liabilities, current income and expenditures, a statement of its financial affairs, and a statement of its currently unfulfilled obligations. A Chapter 7 proceeding can be filed by either a business enterprise or an individual. However, for an individual to file a voluntary proceeding, (1) the individual and his or her spouse must have noncontingent, liquidated, and unsecured debts of less than $100,000 and noncontingent, liquidated, and secured debts of less than $350,000; (2) the individual cannot be a stockbroker or commodity broker; and (3) the individual must have regular income that is sufficiently stable and regular.

Chapter 13 is a voluntary bankruptcy filing in which an individual with regular income can obtain time to adjust his or her debts. The advantage of Chapter 13 is that an individual is able to discharge all debts except alimony, support payments, and certain priority payments, which must be paid in full. A Chapter 13 filing does not prevent a debtor from being able to obtain a discharge in a bankruptcy case within six years after a prior discharge. The Chapter 13 allows a debtor to retain its assets and enables the debtor to stop a mortgage foreclosure action on its residence. The Chapter 13 filing also has the advantage of extending the automatic stay to anyone who has guaranteed a debtor's obligations.

Chapter 12 is another voluntary bankruptcy proceeding. Its applicability is limited to an individual and his or her spouse who are engaged in a farming operation (or a corporation or partnership in which one family owns more than 50 percent the equity and the family controls the farming operation) and (1) whose aggregate debts do not exceed $1.5 million; (2) at least 80 percent of whose debts, excluding the debt for such individual's principal residence, arise out of the farming operation; and (3) who receive more than 50 percent of their gross income from the farming operation. Under Chapter 12, the farmer files a plan of reorganization, which can include modifying the terms of a mortgage on a residence. Unfortunately, in Chapter 12, some debts are not dischargeable, and the debtor could be required to dedicate all disposable income for three to five years after filing the petition to payments to creditors. The court also has the authority to review whether the debtor is using all of its disposable income in good faith. Moreover, the debtor is required to obtain court approval for all business transactions, including leases and sales that are not in the ordinary course of business.

The most popular form of bankruptcy filing for business enterprises is the Chapter 11 proceeding, which allows the business to continue operating while the owner attempts to reorganize its debts. The Chapter 11 proceeding is what major industrial corporations have begun to use to limit the effect of negligence lawsuits, avoid the effect of unfavorable contracts, and enable the business to survive a temporary downturn in the economy.

A Chapter 11 proceeding can be commenced by any individual, partnership, or corporation, and there is no requirement that the debtor be insolvent or unable to pay debts as they mature. Pursuant to Chapter 11, the debtor remains in possession of its assets (and becomes a debtor-in-possession, or DIP) unless a trustee is appointed. Usually, however, a trustee will be appointed only if it is in the best interests of the creditors or if there is a realistic belief that the debtor has been involved in fraud or gross mismanagement. Accordingly, during the pendency of most Chapter 11 proceedings, the debtor remains in possession of its assets and operates its business as a DIP, while obtaining the benefit of the automatic stay. Chapter 11 provides the debtor with the time to rehabilitate or reorganize its business, and obtain confirmation of a plan of reorganization that provides for the creditors to be paid.

The purpose of Chapter 11 is the creation of a plan of reorganization, which, after confirmation by the court, is binding on all creditors, even those who voted against the plan or refrained from voting. Moreover, the confirmation of the reorganization plan discharges the debtor and the debtor's property from most debts that arose before confirmation of the plan. Nevertheless, the confirmation of a Chapter 11 plan does not discharge a debtor if:

- The plan provides for liquidation of the debtor's property and the debtor does not engage in business after the consummation of the plan
- The debtor has transferred, removed, destroyed, mutilated or concealed property within one year before or at any time after the date the petition is filed
- The debtor knowingly and fraudulently made a false oath or presented a false claim or withheld information
- The debtor failed to satisfactorily explain any loss of assets or deficiency of assets
- The debtor refuses to obey any court order on the grounds of privilege against self-incrimination after the debtor has been granted immunity.

The disadvantages of a voluntary Chapter 11 filing are the expense incurred by the debtor and the possibility that, if the creditors do not accept a plan of reorganization or the court does not approve the plan, the matter may be dismissed or converted to a Chapter 7 liquidation. A voluntary Chapter 11 proceeding is commenced by the debtor's filing a petition, together with a list of the names and addresses of each creditor or a schedule of liabilities and the names, addresses, and claims of the twenty largest unsecured creditors and, within 15 days after the filing of the petition, the debtor must file a schedule of assets and liabilities, a statement of financial affairs, and a statement of its executory contracts and unexpired leases.

In addition to voluntary proceedings, an involuntary proceeding can be commenced under either Chapter 7 (liquidation) or Chapter 11 against anyone except a farmer or a corporation that is not a moneyed, business, or commercial corporation. An involuntary proceeding can be commenced by three creditors executing the petition if there are twelve or more creditors, or one creditor if there are fewer than twelve creditors. However, the aggregate amount of the unsecured claims must exceed $5,000 after subtracting the value of any liens held by the creditor, and the petitioning creditors must hold claims that are not contingent or subject to dispute. An involuntary proceeding can continue only if the court determines that the debtor is not paying its debts as they become due or if a custodian has taken charge of the debtor's property and the debtor is insolvent.

Creditors should not commence an involuntary proceeding before determining whether the debtor is, in fact, insolvent and whether the proceeding should be in Chapter 7 or Chapter 11. Two concerns the creditors should have prior to filing the involuntary petition are that if the petition is subsequently dismissed, the creditors will have the expenses to pay, and if it is determined that they acted in bad faith, the debtor could obtain punitive damages. The creditors should also be concerned about:

- The expense of a Chapter 11 proceeding
- Whether commencing the involuntary proceeding will cause them to lose control of the situation or force the liquidation of the debtor's assets
- Whether filing a petition will create a hardship for the creditor, because the automatic stay immediately goes into effect, which precludes the creditor from being able to obtain and collect on a judgment during the bankruptcy proceeding.

If the creditor is secured, there is no reason to commence an involuntary proceeding. A secured creditor should proceed to foreclose its lien and obtain its collateral.

The discharge of debts contained in Chapters 7, 11, 12, and 13 does not apply to:

- Certain taxes if a return was not filed or was filed within two years before the petition was filed, or if the debtor filed a fraudulent return or willfully attempted to evade or defeat the tax
- Any amount borrowed that was based on false pretenses, a false representation, or actual fraud
- A creditor not listed on the debtor's schedules
- Any debt arising from fraud or defalcation while acting in a fiduciary capacity, embezzlement, or larceny
- Amounts owed to a spouse, former spouse, or child of the debtor for alimony, maintenance, or support
- Amounts owed for willful or malicious injury by the debtor to another entity or to the property of another entity
- A fine, penalty, or forfeiture that is payable to and for the benefit of a governmental unit, and that is not compensation for actual pecuniary loss, other than a tax penalty
- An educational loan made, insured, or guaranteed by a governmental unit
- A debt that arises from a judgment or consent decree entered in a court of record against the debtor, arising from the debtor's operation of a motor vehicle while drunk
- A debtor who waived discharge or was denied discharge.

The Bankruptcy Code provides for the conversion of a proceeding under one chapter to another chapter, the effect of which could have surprising results on the debtor and the creditors. A debtor who filed a Chapter 7 petition has an absolute and unconditional right to convert the case to Chapter 11, 12, or 13 at any time. Additionally, a case commenced under Chapter 12 or 13 can be converted to Chapter 7 at any time. However, if the case was originally commenced under Chapter 11, 12, or 13 and converted to Chapter 7, it cannot be converted back to one of the other chapters. Moreover, a waiver by a debtor of its rights to commence a proceeding under Chapter 7, 12, or 13 is unenforceable. The court, after receiving a request from any party with an interest or the trustee, and after notice of a hearing, can convert a Chapter 7 case to a Chapter 11 case or a Chapter 13 case to a Chapter 7, 11, or 12 case, although a Chapter 13 case cannot be converted to Chapter 7, 11, or 12 without the debtor's consent if the debtor is a farmer. If a case is converted from one chapter to another, the creditors and the trustee or debtor in possession are given an additional 60 days to assume or reject any executory contract or unexpired lease.

A Chapter 7 case can be dismissed only for cause and only after notice to the creditors and a hearing before the court. A Chapter 7 dismissal usually occurs if there have been unreasonable delays by the debtor that are prejudicial to the creditors or nonpayment of the required fees. The court may also dismiss a Chapter 7 case, if the debts are primarily consumer debts and the court determines that granting relief would be an abuse of Chapter 7. A Chapter 13 case can be dismissed because of an unreasonable delay by the debtor that prejudices the creditors; the debtor's nonpayment of filing fees or failure to file a plan in a timely manner; its failure to make payments pursuant to the plan in a timely manner; denial of confirmation; or a material default in a confirmed plan or the revocation of an order confirming a plan or the termination of a confirmed plan. A Chapter 12 plan must be dismissed at any time upon the request of the debtor. The court also has the authority to dismiss a case for cause on request of a creditor or a party in interest.

A Chapter 11 case can be dismissed after notice and a hearing on the request of a party in interest, if the court determines that there has been cause. Causes include:

- A continuing loss to, or diminution of, the debtor's estate
- The debtor's inability to effectuate a reorganization plan
- Unreasonable delay by the debtor that is prejudicing the creditors
- The debtor's failure to propose a plan within the time fixed by the court
- The denial of confirmation of several proposed plans
- Revocation of an order of confirmation
- The debtor's inability to substantially effectuate the consummation of a confirmed plan
- A material default by a debtor with respect to a confirmed plan
- The termination of a reorganization plan by reason of the occurrence of a condition specified in the plan
- Nonpayment of any fees.

If a case is dismissed, the debtor has the right to file a new petition and obtain a discharge in the later case. However, the dismissal lifts the automatic stay and voids any of the powers granted to the trustee or DIP under the Bankruptcy Code. The dismissal also vacates any order permitting the debtor to recover transferred property. Basically, when a case is dismissed, everything is restored to its status at the time prior to the filing.

PROTECTING THE DEBTOR'S ASSETS

Regardless of what chapter is utilized, whether the petition is filed voluntarily or involuntarily, whether the debtor is an individual or a business, and what the debtor's size and importance are, one of the most important purposes of the Bankruptcy Code is to protect and preserve the debtor's assets for the benefit of all the creditors. The intention of the Bankruptcy Code is to avoid a situation where the fastest or the largest or the most powerful creditor obtains payment on a claim to the disadvantage of the other creditors. Under the Bankruptcy Code, all creditors are equal except some are secured and some are unsecured. Accordingly, the Bankruptcy Code contains provisions that ensure that the value of the debtor's assets do not deteriorate or disappear during, or immediately prior to, the filing of the petition.

The Bankruptcy Code provides the bankruptcy court with extensive power to deal with and protect the debtor's assets. These powers provide the debtor's bankruptcy estate with the ability to maximize the value of the assets, which benefit all the creditors. These sections of the Bankruptcy Code provide the DIP or the trustee and the bankruptcy court with the discretion to deal with the debtor's property on an expedited basis and avoid a deterioration of the assets during the pendency of the bankruptcy proceeding.

Adequate Protection

The Bankruptcy Code permits the trustee or the DIP to take appropriate steps to adequately protect the estate's assets. Although the Bankruptcy Code does not define the meaning of the phrase *adequate protection,* the Bankruptcy Code does provide that when adequate protection is required to protect the interests of a particular creditor, the adequate protection may be provided by requiring the DIP or the trustee to:

- Make one or more cash payments to particular creditors that are adversely affected by the bankruptcy filing if the automatic stay or the use, sale, or lease of the assets or the granting of a lien results in a decrease in the value of property in which they hold an interest
- Provide an affected creditor with an additional or replacement lien to the extent that such stay, use, sale, lease, or grant results in the decrease in the value of such creditor's interest in the property
- Grant such other relief as will result in the realization by such creditor of the indubitable equivalent of such entity's interest in the property.

The three methods of providing adequate protection are not all-inclusive and can be adapted to suit the needs of the parties and the protection of the estate. Moreover, it has been determined that the term *indubitable equivalent* provides authority for the use of new methods of financing that are better suited to the particular facts or events of each situation.

The intention of Congress in enacting the Bankruptcy Code is that adequate protection should provide a secured creditor with protection while the creditor is unable to obtain its collateral. It should also preclude a creditor from being able to argue that the bankruptcy court is taking the creditor's property in violation of the Fifth Amendment to the United States Constitution, which prohibits the taking of property without compensation. The concept of adequate protection is supposed to protect those creditors having an interest in specific assets, including secured creditors, a co-owner, or a landlord. Moreover, adequate protection is not intended to protect unsecured creditors who do not have an interest in specific property. Adequate protection is intended only to protect the creditor against a reduction in the value of property resulting from the automatic stay; or the use, sale, or lease of the property; or the grant to a third party of the lien against the property. Adequate protection is not supposed to protect the creditor from a decrease in the property value caused by something other than those three items. Alternatively, if the secured party, the landlord, or the co-owner is not provided with adequate protection, then the DIP or the trustee will not be able to obtain the benefit of the automatic stay or the right to the use, sale, or lease of the property.

The need for, and adequacy of, the adequate protection depend upon a number of factors, including:

- The quality of the collateral
- The duration of the automatic stay
- Whether the value of the lien is increasing, decreasing, or remaining stable
- Whether tax and other required payments are being paid
- Whether the property is being kept free of statutory or mechanics' liens
- The likelihood of a successful reorganization.

In analyzing the payment methods of furnishing adequate protection, the issues to consider include the amount of the required payment and whether the adequate protection should be paid in a lump sum or through periodic cash payments. If the adequate protection is an additional or replacement lien, the relevant issue is the value of the additional or replacement collateral. If the additional protection is a guaranty, it would have to be from someone of unquestionable financial strength to provide the required adequate protection. The court's decision on adequate protection is one of fact that would be reversed only if clearly erroneous. If someone was to challenge the value of the collateral or the efficacy of an adequate protection order, that person would be obligated to bear the burden of showing that the court's decision was clearly erroneous.

Furthermore, providing a creditor with adequate protection is necessary only if the property affected diminishes in value during the pendency of the bankruptcy proceeding. Accordingly, as long as the value of the property exceeds the value of the lien, adequate protection is not necessary. In those instances where the value is in excess of the lien, the debtor's equity in the property serves as additional protection for the lienor. Similarly, there would be no need for adequate protection for a lienor holding a subordinate lien on property with a value at the time of the filing that is insufficient to pay the subordinate lien. In this event, the rationale is that the lienor would not be able to successfully terminate the superior lienor's interest in the property, and therefore the junior lienor would not have an interest that needs to be protected. The purpose of adequate protection is not to make certain that the creditor will receive either an asset or payment that equals its claim, but to be certain that the value of the asset does not decrease during the pendency of the bankruptcy proceeding to a value less than the amount the creditor would have received at the time the petition was filed. Finally, if the adequate protection granted to a secured creditor proves to be inadequate to protect the secured creditor, that creditor will receive an administrative claim in the bankruptcy proceeding with priority over virtually every other claim.

Automatic Stay

One of the best known and little understood aspects of the Bankruptcy Code is the automatic stay, which is the primary method utilized by the Bankruptcy Code to prevent the further deterioration of the situation, while the DIP or the trustee attempts to determine the most efficient and effective method of proceeding. The automatic stay goes into effect the moment the petition is filed and freezes all actions involving the debtor or property belonging to the bankruptcy estate, regardless of the harm or inconvenience that it may cause other parties involved with the debtor or the property.

The automatic stay provides the debtor with an opportunity to resolve its problems and attempt to liquidate or reorganize without pressure from any of its creditors. The automatic stay precludes any creditor from proceeding against the debtor's assets and allows for an orderly method of distributing the assets in such a way that all creditors of the same class are treated equally.

The filing of a voluntary or involuntary petition operates as a stay applicable to all individuals or entities and precludes the prosecution of any of the following acts:

- The commencement or continuation of a judicial, administrative, or other action or proceeding against the debtor that was or could have been commenced before the filing of the petition
- Recovery of a claim against the debtor that arose before the filing of the petition
- The enforcement, against the debtor or against property of the estate, of a judgment obtained before the filing of the petition
- Any act to obtain possession of property from, or exercise control over, property of the estate
- Any act to create, perfect, or enforce any lien against property of the estate
- Any act to create, perfect, or enforce any lien against property of the debtor to the extent that such lien secures a claim that arose before the filing of the petition
- Any act to collect, assess, or recover a claim against the debtor that arose before the filing of the petition
- The setoff of any debt owing to the debtor that arose before the filing of the petition
- The commencement or continuation of a proceeding before the United States Tax Court concerning the debtor.

The property of the estate includes all the following:

- Legal or equitable interests that the debtor has in property as of the filing of the petition
- All interests of the debtor and the debtor's spouse in community property as of the filing of the petition that is under the sole, equal, or joint management and control of the debtor
- Any interest in property that the trustee recovers
- Any interest in property preserved for the benefit of or transferred to the estate

- Any interest in property that would have been property of the estate if such interest had been an interest of the debtor on the date of filing of the petition and that the debtor acquires or becomes entitled to acquire within 180 days after such date by bequest, device, or inheritance
- Any interest in property acquired as a result of a property settlement agreement with the debtor's spouse
- Any interest in property acquired as a beneficiary of a life insurance policy
- Any proceeds, products, rents or profits of or from property of the estate
- Any interest in property that the estate acquires after the commencement of the case.

Nevertheless, the property of the estate does not include any power that the debtor may exercise solely for the benefit of an entity other then the debtor or any interest of the debtor as a tenant under a lease of nonresidential real property that has terminated at the expiration of the stated term of such lease before the filing of the petition. Additionally, the estate does not include a previously terminated lease.

Moreover, the debtor's interest in property becomes the property of the estate, notwithstanding a provision contained in any agreement that restricts or conditions transfer of such interest on the consent of the other party or debtor's not becoming involved in a bankruptcy filing. Accordingly, any contractual provision making a party's bankruptcy an event of default is invalid and unenforceable. Property to which the debtor holds legal but not equitable title upon the filing of the petition, becomes property of the estate only to the extent of the debtor's title to such property. The automatic stay applies to property that is owned by the debtor and property in which the debtor has a possessory interest.

Notwithstanding the foregoing, it should be noted that the following acts or events are not barred by the automatic stay:

- The commencement or continuation of a criminal action or proceeding against the debtor
- The collection of alimony, maintenance, or support from property that is not property of the estate
- Any act to perfect an interest in property to the extent that the trustee's rights and powers are subject to such perfection

- The commencement or continuation of an action or proceeding by a governmental unit to enforce that unit's police or regulatory power
- The enforcement of a judgment, other than a money judgment, obtained in an action or proceeding by a governmental unit
- Certain setoffs by a commodity broker, forward contract merchant, stockbroker, financial institution, participant in a repurchase agreement, or securities clearing agency
- The commencement of any action by the Secretary of Housing and Urban Development to foreclose a mortgage or deed of trust that or was insured under the National Housing Act
- The issuance to the debtor by a governmental unit of a notice of tax deficiency
- Any act by a landlord under a lease of nonresidential real property whose stated term expired before the commencement of, or during, the pendency of the bankruptcy
- The presentment of a negotiable instrument and the giving of notice of, and protesting dishonor of, such an instrument
- For 90 days after the filing of such petition, the commencement or continuation of certain legal actions that involve a debtor subject to reorganization and that were brought by the Secretary of Transportation or the Secretary of Commerce
- Setoff by a swap participant, of any mutual debt and claim under or in connection with any swap agreement.

The automatic stay can be released either by motion or at such time as the property is no longer property of the estate, or when either the case is closed or dismissed or the discharge is granted or denied. As noted, the automatic stay is one of the most all-inclusive powers possessed by the court under the Bankruptcy Code to protect the assets of the debtor for the best interest of the estate. In fact, even actions against third parties can be enjoined, where it is required to avoid harassment or interference with the operation of the debtor's business. Moreover, an act in violation of the automatic stay can be found to be either void or voidable. Additionally, the court is able to enjoin a violation of the automatic stay, and an individual injured by any willful violation of the automatic stay can recover actual damages and, in appropriate circumstances, punitive damages.

Nevertheless, a creditor can obtain relief from the automatic stay by filing a motion with a request for adequate protection. If the court determines that the creditor is being harmed by the automatic stay, the court can either lift or modify the stay or provide the creditor with adequate protection. To obtain relief from the automatic stay, a creditor must demonstrate a lack of equity in the action and show that the property is not required for the reorganization. Whether the property is required for an effective reorganization depends upon the likelihood that a reorganization plan is feasible.

Use, Sale or Lease of Property

To enable the debtor to continue to operate its business, the Bankruptcy Code permits the debtor to use, sell, or lease property that remains in its possession. The bankruptcy court's approval is not required for the use, sale, or lease of the debtor's property in the ordinary course of the debtor's business; however, the court's approval is required, after notice and a hearing, if the use, sale, or lease of the property is not in the debtor's ordinary course of business. Whether the use, sale, or lease of property is in the ordinary course of the debtor's business frequently depends on whether the proposed transaction creates an economic risk that is different from risks the debtor has taken in the past. The trustee has the right to use, sell, or lease property, notwithstanding any provision in a contract, a lease, or other agreement that provides the other party to the agreement with an option to forfeit, modify, or terminate the debtor's interest in such property.

Another issue that frequently arises has to do with the debtor's use of cash collateral. Cash collateral includes cash, negotiable instruments, documents of title, securities, deposits, or other cash equivalents (acquired at any time) in which the estate and another entity have an interest. Cash collateral includes the rents or profits generated by a property that are subject to a security interest. Neither the debtor nor the trustee can use, sell, or lease cash collateral unless the entity having an interest therein consents to the use or unless the court, after notice and a hearing, authorizes the use, sale, or lease of cash collateral. For the debtor to use cash collateral, the debtor must provide adequate protection for any secured creditor having an interest in the cash collateral. If the secured creditor is not adequately protected, the debtor cannot use, sell, or lease the property.

The trustee also has the right to sell property belonging to the debtor if the following conditions are satisfied:

- Applicable law permits the sale of such property.
- The trustee obtains the required consent.
- The price at which such property is to be sold is greater than the aggregate value of all liens on the property.

- The interest is in dispute.
- The entity could be legally compelled to accept a money satisfaction for such interest.

The trustee has the right to sell both the debtor's interest in the property and the interest of any co-owner even if the co-owner is not subject to the bankruptcy proceeding. However, to do this, the following conditions must be satisfied:

- The property cannot be partitioned among the estate and the co-owners.
- The sale of the estate's undivided interest in the property would realize significantly less for the estate than the sale of the estate's pro rata share of the proceeds of the sale of the property free of the interests of the co-owners.
- The benefit to the estate of a sale of such property free of the interests of co-owners outweighs the detriment, if any, to such co-owners.
- Such property is not used in the production, transmission, or distribution for sale, of electric energy or of natural or synthetic gas for heat, light, or power.
- Prior to the sale of property to a third party, the co-owner may purchase the property at the same price.

Immediately after the sale, the trustee is obligated to distribute to the co-owner, the co-owner's proportionate share of the proceeds of such sale, less the costs and expenses of such sale. The co-owner would not be charged with any compensation for the trustee.

Finally, the reversal or modification of an order authorizing the prior sale or lease of property will not affect the validity of a previously held sale or lease if the purchaser or tenant acted in good faith, unless the authorization for the sale or lease was stayed pending the appeal. The trustee can also void a sale if the sale price was controlled by an agreement among potential bidders.

Obtaining Credit

To retain the debtor's business and possibly improve it during the pendency of the bankruptcy proceeding, the DIP or the trustee must be able to operate the business with maximum efficiency. This frequently requires the operator of the business to obtain credit to acquire merchandise or to pay salaries to employees. The loss of credit inevitably occurred after the filing of the petition and, in many cases, caused the bankruptcy filing. Therefore, to facilitate the operation and possibly the sale of the business, the DIP or the trustee must have access to credit.

The Bankruptcy Code provides for the debtor's being able to obtain credit and incur debt after the petition has been filed. The kinds of credit a debtor can obtain include unsecured credit in the ordinary course of business, unsecured credit not in the ordinary course of business, secured credit, and credit with a special priority. A trustee who is authorized to operate the debtor's business is able to obtain unsecured credit and incur unsecured debt in the ordinary course of business and for ordinary operating expenses. This is referred to as postpetition debt and is treated as an administrative expense, which provides it with a priority over other claims against the estate. Moreover, the court can also authorize the trustee to obtain unsecured credit or to incur unsecured debt that is not in the ordinary course of the debtor's business, which also provides the new creditor with a priority over other claims.

If the trustee is unable to obtain unsecured credit allowable as an administrative expense, the court may authorize the trustee to obtain credit or incur debt with priority over any or all administrative expenses or secured by a lien on the property if it is not otherwise subject to a lien. Additionally, the court may authorize the trustee to obtain credit or incur debt secured by a senior lien on property if the trustee is otherwise unable to obtain credit and there is adequate protection for the holder of the existing lien on the property being secured.

Executory Contracts and Unexpired Leases

One area of bankruptcy practice that directly affects participants in real estate transactions has to do with executory contracts and unexpired leases. If the DIP or the trustee either owns real estate or is the tenant of a property, the other party to the transaction requires some assurances as to whether the DIP or the trustee is likely to fulfill its obligations under the agreement. Alternatively, the other party could be adversely affected by being forced by the automatic stay provisions to take no actions adverse to the estate while the bankruptcy proceeding is pending.

Accordingly, the trustee is permitted to use, sell, or lease property, notwithstanding any contrary provision in a contract, lease, or other document. Except in unusual circumstances, the other party to the agreement is unable to terminate the agreement due to the debtor's financial condition. However, the trustee has the authority to assume or reject any executory contract or unexpired lease of the debtor.

Unfortunately, because there is no definition of an executory contract, the first issue to be dealt with is determining whether an agreement is an executory contract. One definition describes an executory contract as a contract under which the obligation of both the bankrupt and the other party to the contract are so far unperformed that the failure of either to complete performance would constitute a material breach excusing the performance of the other.

A land sale contract has been held to be a lien rather than an executory contract, based upon the fact that the vendee was the debtor. Moreover, a security interest, even if it is in the form of a lease, is neither an executory contract nor a lease. There is an open issue as to whether an option agreement is an executory contract. It appears that a general partnership agreement is an executory contract, whereas a limited partnership agreement may not be an executory contract. The distinction may arise because the limited partners have no duty other than to supply capital, and the failure to make their capital contributions would not excuse the general partner from performing his or her obligation under the partnership agreement; it would only trigger the forfeiture of the limited partner's interest in the partnership. A similar issue involves defining a lease. The issue is whether an agreement that is called a lease is in fact a lease or a financing device.

The reason it becomes necessary to determine whether an agreement is an executory contract or a lease is that both an executory contract and a lease can be assumed by the debtor or the trustee and assigned to a third party for consideration. Alternatively, an executory contract and a lease can be rejected by the debtor or the trustee and are thereby nullified. The trustee has 60 days to assume an executory contract or lease, or it is deemed rejected. However, in Chapter 9, 11, and 13 cases, executory contracts and leases can be assumed at any time prior to the time that a plan is confirmed except that a nonresidential real property lease is deemed rejected unless it is assumed or rejected or the time extended within 60 days. Notwithstanding the foregoing, if the contract or the lease terminated prior to the filing of the petition, it cannot be assumed.

If a contract is no longer executory, it cannot subsequently be reinstated even if it is essential for the debtor's business. If the contract contains a cure period and the debtor files a bankruptcy petition before the expiration of the cure period, the debtor retains its right to cure the breach. However, if the contract or lease is actually terminated, the automatic stay does not prevent the landlord of nonresidential real property from proceeding to evict the debtor. In such a situation, the critical issue would be whether the lease or contract has actually terminated or whether it can still be revived under state law. If there is no further right to assume or revive the contract, the trustee cannot resurrect the lease or contract. However, if state law provides the tenant with a right to cure the default after the sending of the

the sending of the termination notice, then an intervening bankruptcy will make the termination notice irrelevant.

However, a clause in a lease or an executory contract that attempts to invalidate, terminate, or modify the lease in the event of insolvency or bankruptcy will be invalid. Likewise, a lease provision that limits assignments is invalid once a petition is filed. Nevertheless, the trustee may not assume or assign an executory contract or an unexpired lease, if applicable local law excuses a party other than the debtor to such contract or lease from accepting performance from, or rendering performance to, an entity other than the debtor. The contrary local law will be upheld regardless of whether the contract or lease prohibits or restricts assignments of rights or delegations of duties. This provision would include personal service contracts or contracts that require a nondebtor to approve the transfer where the nondebtor has a good business reason for not approving, or that require the approval of a public agency and the requirements have not been met, or that involve a government contract that contains a nonassignment provision.

The decision whether to accept or reject an executory contract or lease must be made in good faith. A brokerage agreement providing for the commission to be paid to the realtor who put the purchaser and seller together in a transaction would be subject to rejection even though the land purchase agreement is assumed, because they are separate agreements and not interdependent. Notwithstanding the foregoing, the entire agreement or lease must be assumed or rejected and not only a certain portion of it.

For the trustee to assume an executory contract or lease in which there has previously been a default by the debtor, the trustee must, at the time of the assumption:

- Cure or provide adequate assurance that the trustee will promptly cure such default
- Compensate the other party to the agreement or provide adequate assurance that the trustee will promptly compensate the other party for any actual pecuniary loss arising from such default
- Provide adequate assurance of future performance under such contract or lease.

The trustee is not required to cure a breach arising from the debtor's insolvency or financial condition. Therefore, the trustee is obligated to cure a default at the time the contract or lease is assumed even if it is a long-standing default. However, a default caused by the debtor's bankruptcy cannot be the basis of precluding an assumption.

There are special provisions for assuming shopping center leases. Although there is no precise definition of a shopping center, it usually refers to a property that was developed as a group of stores with different owners rather than a group of stores with a single owner. It is interesting to note that only shopping centers receive special protection, and not office buildings, to whom tenant mix may be just as important. The reason for the special provisions protecting shopping centers is that a shopping center's tenancy is usually carefully devised to attract a certain kind of shopper. This tenant mix is one of the most important characteristics of the center. Moreover, the success of the shopping center and all its tenants depends on the comfort given to the national creditworthy tenants as well as to the other tenants, and the expectation that the shopping center will continue to draw the correct mix of shoppers. In granting a lease to a particular tenant, the landlord considers the nature of the tenant's business, whether the business complies with the master plan of the shopping center and the provisions contained in the other tenants' leases, whether a particular lessee will generate sales at the location to assure the lessor of percentage rents, and whether a particular lessee's clientele will utilize the other stores in the shopping center or simply the limited parking facilities.

The adequate assurance of future performance of a shopping center lease includes providing assurances of the source of future rent payments. If the lease is being assigned, the assurances would include the financial condition and operating performance of the assignee. They would also include assurances that the tenant's guarantors will be similar to the financial condition and operating performance of the debtor and its guarantors as of the time the debtor became a tenant at the shopping center. Moreover, there must also be assurances that, notwithstanding the change in tenants, any percentage rent due under a shopping center lease will not decline substantially. The assumption or assignment of a shopping center lease is subject to all relevant lease provisions including, but not limited to, provisions relating to radius restrictions, location, use, or exclusivity provisions, and the new tenant cannot cause a breach in any similar provision contained in any other lease, financing agreement, or master agreement relating to the shopping center. Finally, the assumption or assignment of the lease cannot disrupt any tenant mix or balance in the shopping center. If there has been a default in an unexpired lease, the trustee cannot require the landlord to provide services or supplies incidental to such lease until the landlord is compensated for any services and supplies provided under the lease.

If the trustee does not assume or reject an executory contract or an unexpired lease of the debtor's residential real property or personal property within 60 days, such contract or lease shall be deemed rejected. However, in a Chapter 9, 11, 12, or 13 case, the trustee may assume or reject an executory contract or an unexpired lease of residential real or personal property at any time before the confirmation of a plan. The trustee is also obligated to perform all the obligations of the debtor under any unexpired lease of nonresidential real property until such lease is assumed or rejected. If the trustee fails to assume or reject an unexpired lease of nonresidential real property within the applicable time period, the lease will be deemed rejected and the trustee must immediately surrender such nonresidential real property to the landlord. Moreover, regardless of any provision in an executory contract or unexpired lease, an executory contract or an unexpired lease may not be terminated or modified after the filing of the petition solely because of the insolvency or financial condition of the debtor, the filing of the petition, or the appointment of or taking possession by a trustee. However, such limitations do not apply to an executory contract or an unexpired lease if local law excuses a party other than the debtor to such contract or lease from accepting performance from, or rendering performance to, the trustee or an assignee of such contract or lease. The decision to accept or reject a lease is left to the trustee's business judgment and will be reviewed by the court only when clearly erroneous or when there is an indication of wrongdoing. If the trustee does reject a lease, it is considered a breach, the lease can be terminated, and the landlord becomes a general unsecured creditor of the estate.

Additionally, regardless of any contrary provision or of a default in an executory contract or an unexpired lease, the trustee has the right to assign an executory contract or an unexpired lease only if the trustee assumes such contract or lease and adequate assurance of future performance by the assignee of such contract or lease is provided. The rejection of an executory contract or an unexpired lease of the debtor constitutes a breach of such contract or lease if such contract or lease has not been assumed immediately before the date of the filing of the petition.

Furthermore, if the trustee rejects an unexpired lease of real property and the debtor is the landlord, the tenant under such lease may treat such lease as terminated by such rejection. Alternatively, the tenant may remain in possession of the leasehold for the balance of such term and for any renewal or extension of such term that is enforceable by such tenant under applicable law. However, if the tenant remains in possession, such tenant has the right to offset against the rent under the lease for the balance of the term after the date of the rejection, any damages occurring after such date caused by the nonperformance of any obligation of the debtor under such lease.

Moreover, if a trustee rejects an executory contract of the debtor for the sale of real property under which the purchaser is in possession, the purchaser may treat the contract as terminated or may remain in possession of such real property. If the purchaser remains in possession, the purchaser must continue to make all payments due under such contract, but may offset against such payments any damages occurring after that date. The trustee must also deliver title to the property in accordance with the contract, but is relieved of all other obligations under the contract. Moreover, if a purchaser that treats an executory contract as terminated or a party whose executory contract to purchase real property is rejected by the debtor and the purchaser is not in possession, then the purchaser has a lien on the interest of the debtor in such property for the recovery of any portion of the purchase price that has previously been paid.

If the trustee assigns a contract or lease that has been assumed, the assignment relieves the trustee and the estate from any liability for breach of the contract or the lease occurring after the assignment. If an unexpired lease is assigned, the landlord has the right to require a deposit or other security for the performance of the debtor's obligation. However, such deposit or security must be substantially similar to what the landlord would have required upon the initial leasing to a similar tenant.

The decision as to whether to assume or reject a contract is a business decision for the debtor, which the courts will not overturn unless clearly erroneous. When a lease or a contract is assumed, the estate is fully liable as an administrative expense for all rent or other contractual obligations occurring under the contract or the lease. If the trustee does assume a lease, the landlord has the right to demand adequate assurance of future performance. Although there is no definition of *adequate assurance,* it has been interpreted to mean assurances that the landlord is given the performance that it contracted to receive and does not mean additional protection for the landlord or better terms in the lease. The trustee does not have the authority to alter the terms of the lease if it provides adequate assurance of future performance. Finally, neither the trustee nor the court can require the landlord to accept a subtenant if it is specifically precluded by the lease, and the landlord cannot be forced to subordinate its lease.

CREDITORS, THE DEBTOR, AND THE ESTATE

If a creditor is adversely affected by the rejection of an executory contract or an unexpired lease, it has the right to make a claim in the bankruptcy and will be treated as a prepetition creditor with regard to that claim. Likewise, any claim arising from the recovery of property or a claim that does not arise until after the filing of the petition for a tax that is entitled to priority, will be allowed or disallowed the same as if the claim had arisen before the date of filing. To a large degree, administrative expenses also have a priority. Administrative expenses include:

- The actual, necessary costs and expenses of preserving the estate
- Payment for services rendered after the commencement of the bankruptcy
- Any tax incurred by the estate
- Any compensation or reimbursement awarded to a trustee, an examiner, a professional, or the debtor's attorney for reasonable compensation for actual necessary services rendered or incurred by a creditor in an involuntary case
- Actual or necessary expenses for a creditor that recovers any property transferred or concealed by the debtor or a creditor.

The claims of secured creditors are separated into two parts. The secured creditor receives (1) a secured claim to the extent of the value of the collateral that is secured and (2) an unsecured claim for the portion of the creditor's claim in excess of the property value. Moreover, a creditor that holds security having a value in excess of the value of the claim will have the right to receive the reasonable fees, costs, or charges that are specified under the security agreement. Such claims will be considered secured claims to the extent that the value of the collateral exceeds the amount of the claim. However, the trustee has the right to recover from property that is subject to a security interest, the reasonable cost and expense of preserving or disposing of such property. If a lien secures a claim against the debtor that is not an allowed secured claim, the lien will be void. Postpetition interest, as well as reasonable fees and costs, are allowed on oversecured claims providing they are specified in the security agreement.

The following is the order of priority of claims and expenses in a bankruptcy filing:

1. Allowed administrative expenses and any fees and charges assessed against the estate
2. Unsecured claims by the creditors in an involuntary case
3. Unsecured claims for wages, salaries, or commissions earned by an individual, up to $2,000 per individual

4. Allowed unsecured claims for contributions to an employee benefit plan, up to $2,000 per employee less the aggregate amount paid to such employees under item 3, above

5. Allowed unsecured claims of persons involved in raising or storing grain or engaged as fishermen, up to $2,000 per individual

6. Allowed unsecured claims of individuals, up to $900 per individual, for deposits in connection with the purchase, lease, or rental of property or the purchase of services that were not delivered

7. Allowed unsecured claims of a governmental unit for a tax on income or gross receipts for a taxable year ending on or before the date of filing or assessed within 240 days before the date of filing.

Property of the Bankruptcy Estate

The bankruptcy estate is created upon the filing of the petition. The estate contains all the legal or equitable interests of the debtor in all property in which the debtor has either a legal or equitable interest, regardless of where it is located and who holds it. The estate also includes any interest in property that the trustee recovers, any cause of action the debtor has, any claim by the debtor that another party has been unjustly enriched, and liability insurance policies for officers and directors. The property of the estate does not include any power that the debtor may exercise solely for the benefit of an entity other then the debtor or any interest of the debtor as a tenant under a lease of nonresidential real property whose term has expired prior to the commencement of the bankruptcy.

Anyone holding property that belongs to the estate or that the trustee may have the right to use, sell, or lease, must deliver an accounting of the property to the trustee. Anyone owing a debt to the estate that is matured or payable on demand or on order must make the payment to the trustee unless there is a right of offset against the debtor. Anyone in custody of the debtor's property is precluded from making a disbursement from or from taking any action with regard to the debtor's property except to preserve the property. A custodian is required to deliver such property to the trustee and file an accounting of the property.

The trustee has the legal right and power to avoid any transfer of property by the debtor or any obligation incurred by the debtor. The trustee also has the right to avoid a statutory lien on the debtor's property, if it is caused by the debtor's bankruptcy or insolvency or is not perfected or enforceable on the date the petition is filed. Moreover, the trustee can avoid a statutory lien that is not perfected or enforceable at the time the case is filed with the same rights that a hypothetical bona fide purchaser would have if he or she purchased the property at the same time.

However, there are limitations on the trustee's avoiding powers. A trustee is unable to commence an action utilizing its avoiding powers more then two years after the trustee is appointed. Moreover, if someone has an unperfected interest in property when the trustee is appointed, and under local law that person has the right to perfect the lien against an intervening interest holder, then that person retains the right to perfect its lien against the trustee.

Rental Income

If no action to avoid a preferential or fraudulent transfer is brought within two years after the appointment of the trustee, the bankruptcy court does not have jurisdiction to subsequently hear the action. Additionally, a mortgagee who has a collateral assignment of rents, but has not petitioned the court for the appointment of a receiver to collect the rents or to otherwise obtain the rents, has not perfected its interest under state law.

The estate includes all property belonging to the debtor, including rental income arising from the debtor's property, even if the interest in the rents was assigned prior to filing of the bankruptcy petition. However, the postpetition rent may be the property of the estate even if the mortgagee had a perfected lien on the rents when the petition was filed. The trustee retains an interest in the postpetition rents and may attempt to avoid the mortgagee's interest in the rents. If the rents are not subject to an assignment of rents, the estate would have the absolute right to postpetition rents generated from the debtor's property regardless of whether the leases were executed before or after the filing of the petition.

With regard to rent, one of the biggest issues that will occur is whether the assignment of rents that the lender received from the debtor at the time the mortgage was executed continues to be valid. However, property acquired by the estate after the filing of the bankruptcy petition is not covered by a security agreement that is executed prior to the filing of the petition. The previously filed security agreement extends only to property that the debtor acquired prior to the bankruptcy filing and to the rents from such property that are acquired after the petition is filed. The main problem in the area of assignments of rents is determining the effect of an assignment under state law. Some states require the actual collection of the rents by the mortgagee after a foreclosure or the appointment of a receiver or a similar action that demonstrates a constructive taking of possession. The mortgagee's rights may also depend on the type of rent assignment that has been utilized and whether the mortgagee has actually been collecting the rent prior to the bankruptcy filing. Alternatively, the collateral assignment of rents, which is given as additional security for the mortgage, provides the least protection for the lender because it requires an affirmative act by the mortgagee after the mortgagor's default.

The trustee has the status of a judicial lien creditor that acquired its lien on the date the petition was filed. Therefore, the trustee is given the authority to avoid any transfer of property by the debtor that a judicial lien creditor could avoid. The trustee would also have priority over unperfected interests at the time the judicial lien creditor acquired its interest. The trustee also has priority over a mortgagee with an unperfected assignment of rents at the time the petition was filed. However, a mortgagee with an unperfected assignment, at the time the petition is filed, would be able to perfect the assignment only if the perfection would be retroactive under applicable state law. In that way, by recording the assignment after the filing of the petition, it would relate back to the period immediately prior to the filing and provide the mortgagee with priority for its assignment. Accordingly, if perfection was not retroactive under state law, then the trustee would receive a priority interest in the rents, even though the assignment of rents to the lender was executed prior to the bankruptcy filing. If the rent assignment was not perfected prior to the bankruptcy and the local courts do not permit postpetition perfection, then the mortgagee's interest in the rents will be the same as a general unsecured creditor.

Finally, the trustee may not utilize the rents even if the creditor has obtained a perfected interest in the rents. This is due to the fact that the rents would be considered cash collateral, so the trustee could utilize them only if the trustee or the debtor provided the creditor with adequate protection. In the case of rent, adequate protection could be an "equity cushion" if the creditor is oversecured. The trustee would have the right to utilize the rents for the maintenance of the property and to insure the continued operation of the facility, thereby assuring the continued payment of the rents.

Sale/Leaseback Transactions

One of the most popular forms of real estate financing over the last 20 years has been the sale/leaseback transaction. In such a transaction, the owner of real property sells it to a third party and simultaneously leases it back from the purchaser. In a sale/leaseback transaction, the seller is able to liquidate its investment in the property while continuing to maintain control over it, and the purchaser receives cash flow from the property and a reversionary interest at such time as the lease terminates. Unfortunately, the relationships between the purchaser and the seller can be recharacterized in bankruptcy as either a financing device (i.e., a secured loan) or a joint venture between the seller/lessee and the purchaser/lessor (see Example).

The problem arises in a sale/leaseback transaction because the relationship, which is based upon the lease and the financing aspect of the original sale, may involve purchase money financing. The trustee has the right to assume the lease without modification or to reject the lease. If the lease is rejected, the landlord has a claim in the bankruptcy for unpaid rent. However, because the purchase price in a sale/leaseback transaction was based on the projected rental income, the bankruptcy creates a particularly troublesome problem for the landlord/purchaser. Alternatively, if the relationship is characterized as a loan, the purchaser's problem would be greater. Lenders are treated in bankruptcy as either secured or unsecured and, if secured, the lender can either receive the collateral or have its interest recognized. If the secured lender is undercollateralized, the lender's claim will be limited to the value of the collateral and the balance of the claim will be considered an unsecured claim.

The sale/leaseback transaction could also be recharacterized as a joint venture. In such an event, the purchaser's interest will be in the joint venture that owns the property rather than the purchaser's actually being the owner of the property. Moreover, if the sale/leaseback was recharacterized as a joint venture between the seller and the purchaser, then the creditors of the seller, who are enjoined from proceeding against the seller due to the automatic stay, could attempt to proceed against the purchaser, as a nonbankrupt joint venturer.

EXAMPLE

Smith Seed Company owns a warehouse worth $5 million and requires operating capital but also requires the warehouse for its business operations. Smith sells the warehouse to Roberts Association for $5 million and agrees to lease it back from Roberts for 15 years at $500,000 per year. Although Smith is required to pay $7.5 million in rent, the rent is entirely deductible, Smith obtains the $5 million it needs, and Smith does not have to pay interest on the money it receives, unlike a loan, and does not need to pay it back. Roberts obtains a 10 percent return on its investment and the property at the end of the lease term and obtains depreciation deductions based upon the $5 million purchase price. The problem develops if either Smith, the tenant, or Roberts, the landlord, has financial difficulties and files a bankruptcy petition.

Unfortunately, if the trustee takes the position that the joint venture agreement is an executory contract, then the trustee also has the ability to accept or reject it.

Limitations on the Owner's Rights

The trustee and the DIP have been given a great deal of discretion under the current system of bankruptcy. Included within this authority is the ability to ignore or reverse a transaction. The trustee has the ability to ignore either the form or the substance of the transaction to further its objectives of gathering, protecting, and preserving the assets of the estate for the well-being of all the creditors.

Included within this authority is the trustee's right to avoid any transfer of an interest of the debtor if all the following conditions are satisfied:

- The transfer is to or for the benefit of a creditor.
- The transfer is on account of an antecedent debt owed by the debtor.
- The transfer is made while the debtor is insolvent.
- The transfer was made within 90 days before the filing of the petition or within one year before the filing of the petition, if the creditor was an insider.
- The transfer permits the creditor to receive more then the creditor would have received if the transfer had not been made.

However, the trustee is not permitted to void a transfer if the transfer was a contemporaneous exchange for new value given to the debtor or the transfer was in payment of a debt incurred by the debtor in the ordinary course of business or created a security interest in property acquired by the debtor and was perfected within 10 days after the debtor received possession of such property. Moreover, the trustee is not permitted to void a transfer for the benefit of a creditor if the transfer gave new value to or for the debtor. A payment by the debtor to a creditor and the creditor's simultaneous release of a valid lien within 90 days prior to the filing would not be considered a preference regardless of the value of the property securing the lien.

The trustee also has the right to avoid any fraudulent transfer or obligation, if it is made to hinder, delay, or defraud a creditor or if made for less than fair value at a time the debtor was or was about to become insolvent or was engaged in a business with an unreasonably small amount of capital or intended to incur debts that it could not repay. However, to be avoided, the transfer must be made within one year before the date the petition is filed. The trustee of a partnership debtor also has the right to avoid any transfer of an interest to a general partner in the debtor within one year before the filing of the petition if the debtor was insolvent on the date such transfer was made or an obligation was incurred or became insolvent as a result of such transfer or obligation. Nevertheless, if a transfer is made for value and in good faith, the transferee may retain the property. A foreclosure sale can be considered a fraudulent transfer if it occurs within one year prior to the filing of the bankruptcy petition. Whether the foreclosure sale can be set aside depends on local state law and, if it can be, the debtor or the trustee has the same right in the bankruptcy court.

Moreover, a creditor has a right to offset a mutual debt owing by such creditor to the debtor that arose before the commencement of the bankruptcy against the claim of such creditor against the debtor that also arose before the commencement of the bankruptcy. However, the creditor is not able to offset a claim against the debtor if:

- The claim of such creditor is disallowed.
- The claim was transferred by an entity other than the debtor to such creditor after the commencement of the bankruptcy.
- The claim was transferred within 90 days before the filing of the petition and while the debtor was insolvent.
- The debt owed to the debtor by the creditor was incurred by the debtor within 90 days before the filing of the petition while the debtor was insolvent and for the sole purpose of obtaining a right of setoff against the debtor.

If the creditor offsets a mutual debt owing to the debtor against the claim against the debtor within 90 days before the filing of the petition, then the trustee may recover from such creditor the amount so offset.

Plan of Reorganization

The plan of reorganization is the most important document in each bankruptcy proceeding that involves a reorganization or a rehabilitation of the debtor. The plan can be prepared by the debtor, the creditors, or the trustee. It basically is a blueprint for restructuring the debtor and provides the mechanism for the debtor to leave the protection of the Bankruptcy Code and again function independently.

The debtor has the right to file a plan of reorganization upon commencing the bankruptcy or at any time during the case. Only the debtor may file the plan for the first 120 days. Thereafter, any party in interest may file a plan. A plan of reorganization must:

- Designate classes of claims and interests
- Specify any class of claims or interests that will not be impaired (described below) under the plan
- Specify the treatment of any class of claims or interests that is impaired under the plan
- Provide the same treatment for each claim or interest of a particular class unless the holder thereof agrees to less favorable treatment
- Provide adequate means for the plan's implementation
- Provide for the inclusion in the debtor's certificate of incorporation of a provision prohibiting the issuance of nonvoting equity securities and providing appropriate distribution of power among various classes of securities
- Contain provisions that are consistent with the interest of creditors and equity security holders, and with public policy as to the selection of officers, directors, or trustees.

A plan may also impair or leave unimpaired any class of claims or interests; provide for the settlement or adjustment of any claim or interest belonging to the debtor; provide for the sale of all or substantially all the property in the distribution of the proceeds; and include any other appropriate provision.

The plan may include the following components:

- Retention by the debtor of all or any part of the property
- Transfer of all or any part of the property
- Merging or consolidation of the debtor with one or more entities
- Sale of all or any part of the property of the estate it is subject to or free of any lien
- Satisfaction or modification of any lien
- Cancellation or modification of any indenture or other instrument
- Cure or waiver of any default
- Extension of the maturity date or change to the interest rate of outstanding securities
- Amendment of the debtor's certificate of incorporation
- Issuance of securities by the debtor or of any other entity for cash, property, or existing securities or an exchange of claims or interest or for any other appropriate purpose.

Impairing a class of claims or interests means altering the legal, equitable, and contractual rights to which such claim or interest entitles the holder. Impairment also occurs if any contractual provision or applicable law entitles the holder of such claim or interest to demand or receive accelerated payment after a default. However, the plan should cure any default that occurred before the filing of the petition and reinstate the security of such claim or interest as it existed before the default. The plan should also compensate the holder of such claim or interest for any damages incurred as a result of reasonable reliance by such holder on such contractual provision. The plan would consider contractual rights of creditors or interest holders to be unimpaired even if there is a default, if the plan does not alter the legal, equitable, or contractual rights to which the holder is entitled; if the plan reinstates a claim or interest; or if the plan leaves the claim or interest unimpaired by paying its full amount other than in securities of the debtor, an affiliate of the debtor, or a successor to the debtor.

For the creditors, one of the most disconcerting aspects of a Chapter 11 filing by a debtor is the concept of a *cram down*. The secured creditors, most notably the mortgage holders, are concerned that the cram down will adversely affect the rights they have under their loan documents.

The cram down provisions permit the bankruptcy court to confirm a reorganization plan even though there are objections from a class of secured creditors. A cram down can occur if the class is unimpaired or if its members are going to receive under the plan property equal in value to the amount of their secured claims. The cram down can include discounting the full value of money owed over an extended term based upon the time value of money. Additionally, the plan can be confirmed over the objection of a class of unsecured creditors even if they have priority, if the creditors are unimpaired or will receive property of equal value to the allowed amount of their unsecured claims or if no class junior to such creditors shares under the plan. The court also has the ability to confirm a plan over the dissent of equity holders if the class is unimpaired or if these creditors receive their liquidation preference or redemption rights or if no class junior to such creditors shares in the plan.

A cram down occurs when, notwithstanding the fact that not every impaired class accepts the plan, the court confirms the plan. This occurs if the court determines that the proponent of the plan requests confirmation, the plan does not discriminate unfairly, and the plan is fair and equitable, and at least one impaired class of claims must accept the plan. Additionally, a nonvoting, nonobjecting creditor who is the only member of a class is deemed to have accepted the plan and permitted a cram down. Whether the plan discriminates unfairly depends on the classification and treatment of claims and interests of each set of creditors.

To be fair and equitable, the entire plan must be considered in the context of the rights of the creditors and the particular facts and circumstances. For a plan to be fair and equitable, junior creditors could not participate under the plan unless a senior rejecting class had been paid in full. A plan has been confirmed that included a three-year deferral of all payments on a first mortgage. Another cram down plan was approved in which the mortgagee received a note payable over 15 years out of one-half of the debtor's net operating profit with a cumulative interest rate of 10 percent per annum. In another instance, a cram down plan was approved that contained a substantial balloon payment at the end of seven years. Secured creditors can also be crammed down if they receive the indubitable equivalent of their claim, although there is no definition of indubitable equivalent of a claim.

Unsecured creditors also can be crammed down if the plan provides that no holder of a junior interest to the dissenting class of creditors will receive or retain any property under the plan. The current equity holders must be eliminated, even if their equity interests had no value, if the unsecured creditors were being crammed down. Alternatively, equity holders have been allowed to retain their equity interests if they contribute new capital even though the unsecured creditors are not paid their entire claims. Likewise, shareholders would be allowed to retain their equity interests if their additional contribution was found to be sufficient and essential.

Another issue to be considered in a plan is the value of the various claims. An undersecured creditor can elect to have its separate secured and unsecured claims allowed as a single secured claim for the full amount of the debt. Also, if a mortgagee is not classified in its own separate class, an election to have the claim treated as fully secured has to be made by the class as a whole and requires at least two-thirds of the claims in amount and more then one-half of the claimants in number to approve the fully secured treatment. This election can be made only when the collateral has consequential value or when the plan provides that the collateral will be sold free and clear of the secured parties' interests. If a class of secured creditors does not elect to have the claim treated as fully secured, the unsecured portion of each claim is recognized as an unsecured claim against the debtor even if it arose from a nonrecourse mortgage. Nevertheless, if the claim arose from a nonrecourse mortgage and the property was sold free and clear of the mortgage, no deficiency claim would be allowed. The abandonment of collateral to a secured creditor or a foreclosure sale by the creditor eliminates a nonrecourse debt to the creditor's deficiency claim.

CONCLUSION

The Bankruptcy Code offers the property owner protection while the owner restructures its obligations and relationships in the hope that a successful restructuring will benefit all the creditors. Additionally, the Code provides the debtor and creditors the ability to liquidate the debtor's assets and use the proceeds to pay the claims against the debtor in an orderly manner without favoritism or self-dealing. The system works effectively, particularly in real estate relationships, because the automatic stay precludes a secured creditor from moving forward to foreclose its lien to the detriment of the other creditors. It is possible that the debtor's assets can be efficiently utilized in such a way to maximize what everyone is receiving without unduly inconveniencing the secured creditor. Most importantly for the real estate owner, however, this respite provides it with the opportunity of salvaging the investment and the property.

11

Purchasing Distressed Property

An old adage states that the three most important factors in purchasing real estate are location, location, and location. However, that statement is not accurate. The three most important factors are location, timing, and price. Purchasing a parcel of real estate at the perfect location will not necessarily result in a successful acquisition if the purchaser overpaid for the property or made the purchase at the wrong point in the area's economic cycle. Although the purchaser has acquired property in the right location, because the timing was wrong or the purchaser overpaid for the property or is carrying an excessive amount of debt, the purchaser may not have the ability to retain the property until the market improves. Such circumstances present the perfect opportunity for the purchaser of distressed property to step in and acquire the distressed property at a bargain price, advance the necessary funds to rehabilitate the property or complete it, and reap the benefit of the perfect timing and price.

To avoid becoming a victim of the real estate cycle or other economic dislocation, the purchaser must carefully assess the situation before investing in a property. Although the purchaser will be represented by counsel, an understanding of the process by which the property is being acquired will enable the purchaser to assist in the acquisition. Moreover, an appreciation for the process of acquisition will provide the purchaser with a greater ability to advise his or her counsel as to the aspects of the transaction that are of particular importance to the purchaser. Protecting the purchaser is a three-step process, which includes (1) performing due diligence to ascertain that the purchaser knows what he or she is purchasing, (2) executing a contract that protects the purchaser's expectations, and (3) closing the transaction in such a way that those expectations are realized.

The initial step in acquiring distressed real estate is to identify the real estate to be acquired and develop an understanding of the reason for its problems. Identifying the property involves more than simply finding property that can be acquired inexpensively because it has problems. It also means determining that the property can be resuscitated economically or redeveloped or otherwise commercially exploited. The basis for the decision as to whether a certain property is capable of being economically reinvigorated is beyond the scope of this book. Although the various chapters of this book establish the problems that real estate can have, the actions that can be taken to prevent a deterioration of the property and a loss of the owner's investment, and the situations to be avoided, it is impossible to determine whether a property's problems can be eliminated at a cost that the purchaser can bear. Arguably, every problem can be solved, but the cost of solving the problem may be prohibitive for a particular owner or a particular property. This chapter explores the matters to be considered by the investor in determining whether to acquire a particular parcel of real estate, the salient portions of the contract, and the things to consider in closing the acquisition. It is by no means intended to replace the assistance of competent counsel.

In acquiring any property, one must first negotiate and execute either an agreement of sale or an option agreement to prevent someone else from acquiring the property. Either agreement will provide the purchaser with control over the property prior to the closing, although the option agreement is usually less costly and provides the purchaser with more flexibility. Alternatively, the parties can enter into a letter of intent, which is a preliminary, nonbinding agreement between a prospective purchaser and seller that reflects their desire to proceed to negotiate an agreement of sale. The purpose of the letter of intent is to ascertain that, prior to extensive negotiations, there is a clear understanding and agreement between the parties on the basic business terms involved in the transaction.

It should come as a surprise to no one that the purchaser would prefer executing a letter of intent, an option agreement, or an agreement of sale with sufficient contingencies to allow the purchaser to terminate the agreement if it decides not to proceed, whereas the seller would want to lock the purchaser into purchasing the property by having an agreement of sale executed. The ultimate resolution of this matter will depend on the purchaser's financial strength, the seller's weakness, and the amount of third-party interest that exists in the property. If there is a great deal of interest, the seller will not want to take the property off the market for even a brief time, and will therefore insist on a formal, unconditional agreement of sale. If there is little interest in the property, the seller will probably agree to the option in the hope that the purchaser will be convinced to acquire the property during the term of the option.

Regardless of the form of the agreement, it is in the best interests of both parties for the purchaser to expeditiously determine whether the property is satisfactory for the intended purposes. Only after the purchaser is satisfied that the property conforms to its needs and that it has the wherewithal to deal with the property's problems can both the purchaser and the seller be certain that their negotiations will result in a deal. Therefore, the purchaser must be given an opportunity to complete its due diligence regarding the property to ascertain that the property satisfies its needs. Depending upon the property, the due diligence investigation can take anywhere from several days to several weeks. However, notwithstanding the importance of the due diligence, the seller will not agree to keep the property off the market for an indefinite period of time. Therefore, eventually the purchaser will be required to reach a determination that it is more likely than not that the property is adequate and meets its expectations.

Purchasing distressed property involves five steps:

1. Identifying the property
2. Ascertaining that the property can be rehabilitated economically
3. Negotiating and executing the purchase agreement
4. Obtaining financing for the acquisition and rehabilitation, if required
5. Closing the acquisition.

These five steps can occur over a period of weeks or months or can be accomplished very quickly (almost simultaneously). Thus, the deal can close in as short a period as a few hours if the purchaser wants to take, or is required to take, a number of risks. The biggest risk in an accelerated closing is that the property may be unsuitable for economic rehabilitation. If that were to occur, the purchaser would then own the property and would have to determine whether it is economically feasible to put the property to some other use. The purchaser may decide to risk an expedited closing if speed is important, but in most instances, such an action could be a costly mistake. Even if the purchaser was making a mistake, however, unlike many other investments, the property would retain some value, which the purchaser could eventually liquidate. The purchaser would have a loss, but it is unlikely that the purchaser's entire investment would be lost.

While the purchaser is deciding whether to proceed with the acquisition, the parties could execute an option agreement, a letter of intent, or an agreement of sale. There are numerous advantages and disadvantages to both parties to each agreement. An option agreement provides the purchaser with the ability to acquire the property, but without an obligation to buy the property. The purchaser is granted a period of time during which the seller cannot sell the property to anyone else, while the purchaser decides whether to actually purchase the property. The option period provides the purchaser with the time to review the property, consider the ramifications of a purchase of the property, and do its due diligence, without forcing the prospective purchaser to risk its deposit. If the purchaser decides against acquiring the property, it has no obligation to proceed and no risk other than the cost of the option, if any.

It is common for a copy of the proposed agreement of sale to be included as an exhibit to the option agreement. In this way, there is no delay in executing the agreement of sale if the option is exercised. Although this procedure is beneficial if the option is exercised, it extends the negotiation process for the option agreement and is a waste of time if the option is not exercised. However, it is a valuable exercise because it precludes the seller from defeating the purpose of the option by creating obstacles to the execution of an agreement of sale after the option is exercised.

The option agreement also allows the purchaser to postpone its decision to purchase the property until it has had time to judge the real estate market and whether it will be able to maximize its return on the real estate investment. The only benefit to the seller from an option agreement is as an incentive for an undecided purchaser. The option is to the purchaser's benefit because, if, during the option term, the value of the property decreases, the purchaser will probably not acquire the property unless there is an appropriate decrease in the purchase price. However, the purchaser will most likely proceed with the acquisition of the property if its market value increases while the option is in effect. Although the seller is obligated to sell the property on specific terms, the purchaser is not obligated to purchase the property unless it exercises the option.

The second form of agreement, the letter of intent, is a preliminary understanding between the property owner and a potential purchaser that describes the business terms of a proposed agreement of sale. The letter of intent should be made specifically subject to the execution of a formal agreement of sale by the purchaser and seller. Basically, a letter of intent is a nonbinding outline of the salient terms that enables the parties to memorialize their understanding of the proposed transaction without being required to cover every point. The purpose of a letter of intent is to allow the property owner and a potential purchaser the ability to confirm early in the negotiation that they have the same understanding of the basic terms of the proposed transaction. The letter of intent avoids an extensive amount of time being taken up by the parties negotiating the finer points of an agreement, when the parties are not in agreement on the important, basic terms of the agreement. However, care must be taken in preparing the letter of intent. A problem can arise if all the elements of a contract are included in the letter of intent (i.e., price, property description, closing date) and the document is signed by both parties. In such an instance, the letter of intent could later be interpreted as a binding contract. The letter of intent should also provide that it will terminate if a formal contract is not executed by the parties within a specified number of days.

The third form of agreement is the agreement of sale, which is discussed in greater detail later in this chapter. Unlike the option agreement or the letter of intent, the agreement of sale binds both the purchaser and the seller to the specific terms and conditions of the transaction and, subject to specific contingencies contained in the document, commits the purchaser and seller to close the transaction. The agreement of sale establishes the exact parameters of the transaction and provides the conditions pursuant to which both parties must comply. However, this description assumes an unconditional contract or one without many contingencies. It is also possible for the agreement to be so conditioned that it is actually an option, with either the purchaser or the seller having the ability to terminate the agreement. Nevertheless, the traditional agreement of sale is unconditional and requires the purchaser to close if the seller delivers good and marketable title to the property. (See Example.)

EXAMPLE

The difference between an option, a letter of intent, and an agreement of sale can be explained as follows: Ross owns an office building that Daniels is interested in purchasing. If Ross and Daniels execute a letter of intent, they are describing their interest and the terms they are considering, but the document binds neither party. If they execute an option, Ross agrees to sell the property to no one other than Daniels during the term of the option, but Daniels is not obligated to purchase the property. If they execute an agreement of sale, Ross is obligated to sell the property to Daniels and Daniels is obligated to purchase the property from Ross on the terms and conditions indicated in the agreement.

DUE DILIGENCE

The due diligence investigation is the process by which a potential purchaser learns everything there is to know about the property and enables the purchaser to determine whether it has been told everything about the property and whether the property will be suitable for the anticipated use. The purchaser's due diligence investigation is one of the most important parts of the contract process and should commence as soon as the purchaser identifies the property to be acquired. Only through a thorough review can the purchaser understand sufficient facts about the property to enable it to identify the issues that should be negotiated and included within the agreement of sale. The purchaser must use this time to investigate the property and identify potential problems relating to the property.

Through an examination of the property and the documents relating to it, the purchaser can obtain a basic understanding of the property. This will enable it to gauge the risk that it is taking in acquiring the property. The documents to be reviewed include any promissory notes and mortgages encumbering the property (regardless of whether they are going to be satisfied at the closing); existing title reports or title policies; recent surveys; geologic and topographic studies; environmental reports, environmental impact studies; agreements with third parties that will remain in effect after the closing; the certificate of occupancy, if required by the local municipality; any lease; and, if existing improved property is being expanded or redeveloped, zoning and related information.

If the documents that are necessary to do the due diligence will not be available until after the agreement of sale is executed, then the agreement of sale should be conditioned upon the purchaser's receipt and approval of such documents within a reasonable period of time after the execution of the agreement of sale. This will protect the purchaser from unhappy surprises. To prevent the purchaser from being able to treat the agreement of sale like an option by allowing the purchaser too much discretion as to whether to proceed, the seller will want to limit the purchaser's ability to terminate the contract, or limit the amount of time within which the agreement can be terminated, or require that the purchaser's actions be reasonable. The seller will want to prevent the purchaser from having an unrestricted right to terminate the agreement of sale, which would make it a free option rather than a contract. The alternative is for the seller to be allowed to review the documents prior to executing the agreement of sale to reduce the likelihood that the purchaser will identify problems after the contract is executed.

Distressed property can be unimproved land, land in the process of being developed, land that has previously been developed and requires attention, or improved property that is ready for rehabilitation. It is easy to review documents for property that is totally vacant, because the only underlying documents to review are those relating to the condition of the property's title. However, if the property being acquired has already been improved, the purchaser must ascertain what its obligations will be under the agreements that will continue to affect the property, what rights will continue to be held by those having a continuing interest in the property, and what limitations there will be on the purchaser's use of the property. If the purchaser fails to make these determinations prior to acquiring title, it could pay a substantial amount of money for the property and find itself unable to solve the property's problems.

If the property being acquired is subject to existing financing, leases, or other rights to use or occupy the property, the purchaser should examine the documents reflecting the rights and obligations of the parties. Moreover, the relevant documents should be reviewed even if they are to be terminated by the seller prior to the closing, because this will enable the purchaser to ascertain whether the seller has the ability to terminate them. If the seller is unable to prepay the mortgage or terminate an unfavorable lease, or a tenant or third party has an option or a right of first refusal to purchase the property, which would interfere with the purchaser's rights, then the agreement of sale should provide that the purchaser not be required to proceed with its due diligence or seek its financing until the seller confirms that it has the ability to deliver the property in the condition that the purchaser expects to receive it. The purchaser should also obtain a title report as quickly as possible to ascertain if the seller is the owner of the property and whether anyone can defeat the purchaser's expectations with regard to the property.

If the property is being sold subject to mortgages, leases, or other operating agreements, those agreements could have a significant adverse effect on the purchaser. The documents must be analyzed regardless of what the purchaser intends to do with the property. The most important aspects of the documents are discussed in the following sections.

Leases

If the property being purchased is subject to operating leases, the purchaser should review each lease to determine the following:

- The term of the lease, especially the expiration date and any renewal options the tenant may have
- The base rent and any additional rent or percentage rent payable by the tenant

- The tenant's obligation to share in the cost of insurance, real estate taxes, common area maintenance, and overall repair costs
- Whether the calculation of the tenant's share of expenses will be affected by any change in the number of tenancies or size of the improvements
- Whether the tenant has any responsibility for repairs and maintenance to its leasehold or to the building or other common areas
- The tenant's ability to terminate its lease during the lease term for any reason
- The existence of any option or right of first refusal that the tenant may have to purchase the property
- The existence of any use restrictions relating to the balance of the property
- Any right the tenant may have to insist upon having its leased premises repaired, modified, or expanded by the landlord
- Whether the landlord has the ability to relocate the tenant to another section of the property to enable the landlord to put together a larger block of space
- The existence of any limitation on the use of insurance proceeds or condemnation awards
- Whether the lease is subordinate to the landlord's financing
- If the tenant has leased the entire property, whether the landlord has the ability to regain part of the property from the tenant
- Whether the landlord's anticipated use is incompatible with the tenant's current use.

Existing Financing

If the property is being purchased subject to financing, the purchaser should review the loan documents (including the promissory note, mortgage or deed of trust, assignments to the lender, and security agreement) to determine the following:

- The amount of the existing debt service, including any increases that could be caused by mandated adjustments in the interest or principal
- The maturity date of the financing
- Whether the loan is self-liquidating or requires a balloon payment

- The existence of any right the lender may have to share in future sales or refinancing proceeds
- Whether the financing contains a due on sale clause or due on encumbrancing clause
- The existence of any restriction on secondary financing
- The existence of any restriction on prepayment and, if so, whether there is a prepayment penalty
- The existence of any limitations on the owner's ability to develop the balance of the property
- Whether the financing encumbers the undeveloped portion of the property
- Whether the development of the balance of the property will require the lender's consent
- The existence of any right the lender may have with regard to insurance or condemnation proceeds.

Ground Lease

If the purchaser is acquiring a leasehold interest in the land, the purchaser must review the ground lease. This review is particularly important if the property requires financing, because the lender's inability to obtain a lien on the land will make obtaining financing for the development more difficult. The matters to consider in reviewing a ground lease include the following:

- The amount of rent that is currently being paid by the tenant, including a calculation of all likely increases during the balance of the lease term
- The existence of any right the leasehold tenant may have to purchase the land and, if it exists, the price at which the land can be purchased
- Whether the landlord has agreed to subordinate its interest in the land to the permanent financing
- Any limitations on the development of the property
- The term of the ground lease and any possible renewal options
- Whether the landlord owns adjacent land that could be added to the ground lease
- The existence of any limitation on the use of casualty or condemnation proceeds

- The existence of any interest the landlord has in increased rentals from the property
- The existence of any right the landlord has to limit to whom portions of the property can be subleased.

Title Report

A title report for the property should also be examined. The things to review in the existing title report include the following:

- The existence of any easements, encumbrances, or other restrictions on the transfer, use, or development of the property
- The existence of any continuing interest in the property by a third party
- Whether the entity from whom the purchaser is acquiring the property appears in the chain of title
- The existence of any discrepancy in the legal description of the property between what is contained in the title report and what the purchaser believes it is acquiring
- The existence of any exception in the title report that could increase the cost of title or other insurance
- The existence of any limitations on zoning or violations of existing zoning described in the title report.

Survey

The purchaser should also examine a survey of the property to make the following determinations:

- The exact area of the property and whether the portion being acquired by the purchaser contains the topography and area that the purchaser believed it was acquiring
- Any improvements that encroach onto the parcel being acquired or from the property onto adjoining property
- The location of all natural boundaries
- The existence of any wetlands area or other restricted area that could preclude a future development of the property
- The existence of any other feature that could inhibit the future development of the property
- Whether the property adjoins public roads or has other means of ingress or egress.

Demographic Study

Because location is the single most important factor in purchasing real estate, one of the first steps in purchasing the property is analyzing the demographics of the area in which the property is located to determine the likelihood of a significant change in the area. Any change will affect the property, regardless of whether it leads to its development, revitalization, or destruction. Understanding the demographics of an area entails a determination of whether the area is improving or deteriorating, whether the property being purchased is accessible to main roads, whether a limited number of large companies employ a large proportion of the area's workers, whether those employers are financially stable, and whether the decision by one of those employers to cease doing business in the area could cause a local economic recession.

The demographic study describes the age, education, marital status, religion, economic status, income, and background of the area's residents. It also indicates the employment statistics, major employers, and housing statistics of the area. A demographic study should indicate the best use of a particular piece of property and estimate the long-term viability of the use to which the property is being put or the intended use of the property. However, a demographic study should be read with a great deal of caution, because it can deal only with likely trends and cannot predict what effect a particular event may have on any area. The study cannot predict the effect on an area of over development, underutilization, or likely local and national economic cycles. Moreover, some events cannot usually be anticipated, such as a war, an oil embargo, a stock market crash, tax reform, the collapse of the savings bank industry, and the sudden influence of the homeless on particular areas of the country.

Engineer's Reports

The purchaser should also obtain an engineer's report for the property, which describes the condition of the improvements on the property and includes a geologic and topographic study of the property. If the engineer's report is not available prior to the execution of the agreement of sale, the agreement of sale should be made contingent upon the purchaser's receipt of a satisfactory engineering report within a reasonable period of time. In preparing the report, the engineer should physically examine the property, paying particular attention to:

- Soil
- Water
- Traffic conditions surrounding the property

- Structural portions of the improvements
- Roof
- Exterior walls
- Foundation
- Parking lot
- Water and sewer systems
- Heating, ventilating, and air conditioning systems
- Electrical and plumbing systems
- Parking and common areas.

The engineer not only should determine the current condition of these systems, but should estimate the useful life of the improvements and the cost to repair or replace the components of the systems.

An examination of components would entail making certain that they operate property, even if the systems have to be made operational to be tested. Special attention should be paid to the following:

- The roof needs to be checked for bubbling and buckling, and to see whether there have been extensive spot repairs in the past, indicating that a roof replacement might be necessary in the near future. The interior ceiling and walls need to be checked for discoloration, which indicates leaks and other serious roof problems.

- The parking area should be checked for a significant number of potholes or spot repairs and puddling. This may indicate a need for a new parking lot or better drainage facilities.

- The heating and air conditioning system should be turned on to confirm that it is in good condition.

- The electrical and plumbing systems should be checked by turning on all the power and water at the same time to confirm that the systems are adequate. The water should be tested for impurities and toxic material.

Insurance

The purchaser should also examine the casualty and liability insurance that the seller has on the property. This will enable the purchaser to determine if the coverage is adequate and whether insurance can be obtained at a reasonable cost for the property. It will also allow the purchaser to determine whether it is more efficient to assume the existing insurance after the closing. Because insurance has become more difficult to obtain than in prior years, it is important for the purchaser to determine whether comparable insurance will be available to it at the same or a better cost. Moreover, an examination of the seller's insurance coverage will indicate whether the property has a high history of claims. If the property has a higher than average number of insurance claims, the purchaser should investigate whether the property has more serious problems.

Environmental Report

Every property owner or purchaser must be concerned about air and water pollution and toxic wastes that are threatening the environment and that have led to the enactment of environmental laws by the federal government and most state governments. Each purchaser must be concerned with whether a property complies with all the existing statutory and regulatory requirements, as well as those requirements that are likely to be enacted in the future. Even if the state in which the property is located does not presently have environmental protection laws and regulations, it is likely that strict new laws will be enacted in the future. For purchasers to satisfy themselves that the property complies with the most stringent existing laws, the property must be inspected by an environmental engineer. The report should identify whether prior owners or tenants utilized the property in such a way as to create future environmental problems.

AGREEMENT OF SALE

The most important document in purchasing property is the agreement of sale, which should contain all the terms and conditions of the transaction. The purchaser must assume that anything it has been told or requires, is not true unless it is reaffirmed in the agreement of sale. There is no such thing in a real estate transaction as a ladies' or gentlemen's understanding. If it is not in writing and signed by the seller, then it does not exist. The words "trust me" simply do not take the place of a fully documented agreement of sale.

The purpose of an agreement of sale is to memorialize the purchaser's and seller's understanding of the terms of the agreement. However, the negotiation of those terms also forces the purchaser and seller to recognize their own requirements and obligations and those of the other party to the agreement of sale. The document assumes that there has been an agreement reached on the principal terms of the transaction. The purchaser should use the negotiation and execution of the agreement of sale as a way of obtaining written confirmation of what it has been told and promised about the property. The purchaser should use the period before the agreement is executed to learn as much about the property as possible. This review may alert the purchaser to facts about the property that make the transaction undesirable or unprofitable; however, this information will allow the purchaser to make an informed decision about the property and to decide whether to purchase the property, renegotiate the terms of the agreement, or terminate the negotiations or the agreement. If the seller insists that the agreement be executed prior to the completion of the purchaser's due diligence inquiry, then for the investigation to have any significance, the purchaser should negotiate for a provision allowing the purchaser to terminate the agreement if an issue is raised during the due diligence investigation, if the seller's representations and warranties are incorrect, or if any of the information the purchaser previously received is inaccurate.

Purchase Price

The purchase price is usually the first item to be negotiated. This price depends on many factors, including the market for similar properties, the potential for substantial appreciation in value, the competition for the property, the amenities included with the property, and the possibility that the seller will provide the purchaser with purchase money financing. The purchase price has to be specified for the contract to be valid. If the purchase price is not a specific amount, but is based on a formula that is dependent upon other factors, then the formula and the variable must be specified. If the purchase price is subject to adjustment, this should also be specified. The description of the purchase price should include the aggregate purchase price, including any mortgages on the property that are being assumed or being taken. The agreement of sale should also describe the amount of the deposit or earnest money; specify whether the deposit is to be held in escrow and, if so, who is to be the escrow agent; and state whether purchase money financing is being provided by the seller and, if so, its terms, the amount of the financing to which the property is subject, and the portion of the purchase price that is due at the closing. (See Example.)

Deposit

Even something that seems simple to resolve, such as the deposit, frequently involves numerous peripheral issues. Five deposit-related issues have to be negotiated:

1. The amount of the deposit
2. The form the deposit will take

EXAMPLE

The purchase price is not merely the amount paid for the property. If Cohen wants to sell his apartment house, the agreement of sale could provide that the purchase price is $6 million, which would mean that Kennedy, the purchaser, would have to pay $6 million at the closing. However, if the agreement of sale provides that the purchase price is $6 million, payable $250,000 on the execution of the agreement of sale, $2,250,000 on the closing of the title, $1.5 million by taking the title subject to an existing mortgage, and $2 million by the seller's taking back a purchase money mortgage payable with 10 percent interest over 5 years, then the purchase knows that he needs only $2.5 million with which to close.

3. Whether it is going to be held in escrow
4. The escrow agent
5. Whether the deposit is to be refundable.

The purpose of the deposit is to show the purchaser's good faith and to protect the seller from a loss in removing the property from the market after the contract is executed. The deposit also provides the seller with a source of damages in the event the purchaser defaults by not closing.

Many people do not understand that the deposit is not limited to cash being held in escrow, although cash is the seller's favorite kind of deposit. Purchasers are frequently able to negotiate the right to deliver an irrevocable bank letter of credit or a certificate of deposit or other security as a deposit. If the purchaser can give a deposit other than cash, it is not forced to tie up assets prior to the closing. If a letter of credit is used as a deposit, the seller will insist that the letter of credit be irrevocable and unconditional, drawn on a major national bank, and provide for the purchaser to supply a replacement letter of credit if the transaction does not close prior to the expiration of the letter of credit. The purchaser also gains from a noncash deposit because it takes longer for the seller to obtain the deposit after a contract breach, which provides the purchaser with added flexibility. The seller is able to obtain a cash deposit immediately after a purported default, but there is a delay for the seller to draw on a letter of credit. Moreover, even though the agreement frequently provides for an unconditional letter of credit, the bank usually requires a letter or affidavit from the seller that the purchaser has defaulted and the letter of credit can be negotiated.

Frequently, the purchaser will insist that the deposit be held in escrow. The seller will refuse, but may relent if the escrow agent is either the seller's attorney or the title insurance company. Therefore, the agreement should contain detailed escrow provisions describing the conditions under which the deposit can be released. The escrow agent will insist upon an indemnification provision, as well as specific instructions as to its responsibilities and obligations and, in the event of a dispute over the deposit, the right to deliver the deposit into court and be relieved of liability or responsibility. The contract should also specify a court with jurisdiction over disputes between the parties to avoid delays in the event of a dispute.

Another deposit issue is whether the deposit will be placed in an interest-bearing account and, if so, to whom the interest is to be paid. The deposit will usually bear interest if it is a substantial amount of money or if it is likely to be held in escrow for over 30 days. Typically, the agreement will provide that the interest will be paid to the party receiving the deposit. In that case, both the deposit and the interest earned will be paid to the seller if the transaction closes or if the purchaser defaults, or paid to the purchaser if the seller is unable to deliver title pursuant to the terms of the agreement. To obtain the interest on the deposit, the purchaser can argue that the seller is retaining the cash flow generated from the property prior to the closing and the purchaser is losing the ability to use the deposit.

Representations and Warranties

The representations and warranties provisions contained in the agreement of sale are extremely important to the purchaser. There are three reasons for insisting on receiving representations and warranties from the seller:

1. To provide the purchaser with confirmation of information it has received verbally
2. To provide the purchaser with information about the seller or the property that it could not otherwise obtain
3. To highlight the things that the purchaser should carefully review because the seller refuses to provide a representation or warranty regarding it.

The issue of representations and warranties raises several interesting issues in purchasing distressed property. The information is more critical for the purchaser of distressed property than of successful property because the purchaser needs to be able to accurately gauge the seriousness of the property's problems and its wherewithal to solve them. However, a representation and warranty from a potentially insolvent seller is probably not worth a great deal. Therefore, the purchaser should be concerned more with obtaining the information if it has executed an agreement containing a termination contingency, than with being able to sue the seller after the closing. Accordingly, it is imperative for the purchaser to obtain independent verification for everything it has been told or thinks about the property. In such circumstances, the representation and warranty section of the agreement is meant to preserve the purchaser's ability to terminate the agreement, rather than provide it with the basis for subsequent litigation.

From the time the purchaser learns about the property, the purchaser has been told many things by the seller, the broker, and third parties. This information has caused the purchaser to make certain assumptions about the property that may or may not be accurate. Therefore, the representations and warranties contained in the contract enable the purchaser to verify the information it has been told and provide additional information that the purchaser will have to verify prior to the closing. The alternative to obtaining the information in this fashion is that the purchaser must be certain that its facts about the property are accurate prior to executing the agreement of sale. Basically, the purchaser has four options in terms of gathering information:

1. Obtain representations and warranties that survive the closing
2. Obtain representations and warranties that do not survive the closing, and then obtain confirmation of the information prior to the closing, and then terminate the agreement if the representations and warranties are not accurate
3. Do the due diligence prior to executing the agreement if the seller provides no representations and warranties and no contingency period in which to obtain information
4. Obtain the right to terminate the agreement within a certain number of days after the execution if the due diligence is not satisfactory and the seller has not provided representations and warranties.

The seller is not obligated to provide the purchaser with any representations and warranties, notwithstanding their importance to the purchaser. A seller frequently refuses to provide representations and warranties because the seller does not want to be sued later over some incidental fact it accidentally overlooked. However, if the agreement of sale does not contain representations and warranties, the purchaser either should refuse to execute the agreement or can agree to waive its inclusion if the agreement contains a due diligence period that is long enough for the purchaser to make all necessary inquiries. If the seller does not want to wait, the purchaser either must have previously completed its due diligence or must proceed without a due diligence period or a contingency.

Once the seller agrees to provide the purchaser with representations and warranties, the parties must agree about how long they will survive. This issue frequently comes down to discussing whether the representations and warranties will survive the closing and, if so, for how long. The seller will not want them to survive closing, because the seller wants to forget about the property and not worry that several years after the closing the purchaser will sue, claiming that it was not told some salient fact about the property. If the seller adamantly refuses to allow them to survive the closing, the period in which they survive prior to the closing should be sufficiently long that the purchaser has an opportunity to confirm the information. If the seller allows them to extend beyond the closing, it would be highly unusual for a representation or warranty to survive indefinitely. A reasonable term for the representations to survive is one year after the closing. This provides sufficient time for dormant issues to arise and allows the purchaser with a period of time that encompasses every kind of weather condition, as well as situations that arise only periodically. However, if the seller is adamant against a one-year survival, then the purchaser should choose a length of time that is adequate for it to uncover any problems (at least 30 to 90 days). Nevertheless, the purchaser should act expeditiously to investigate everything that occurs that presents a problem. Finally, a conflict between the purchaser and seller over survivability can be solved by limiting the survivability only to certain items that are critically important.

At the very least, the purchaser has from the execution of the agreement of sale to the closing to investigate the truth of the seller's representations and warranties. If the representations are false or inaccurate, the purchaser can declare a default in the agreement of sale and receive a refund of its deposit. If the seller is unprepared to allow the representations and warranties to survive the closing, it would be difficult for the seller to object to the purchaser's right to terminate the agreement of sale, if the information the seller supplied turns out to be false. Although the seller may argue against this proposal, because the termination of the agreement of sale would be limited to the seller's failure to provide accurate information, the seller's fears should be reduced.

Representations and warranties should be included in the agreement of sale, even if the purchaser has agreed to acquire the property in an "as is" condition. This inclusion enables the purchaser to terminate the contract and receive a refund of its deposit if the property is not as represented.

Finally, the purchaser can agree to proceed with the purchase without any representations or warranties. However, the purchaser should not consider doing this unless it is absolutely certain as to the accuracy of the information it would receive, or the facts and circumstances are such that the prior owner's information is irrelevant or the purchaser's potential benefit from the transaction is so large and the risk so small, that the purchaser is willing to assume the risk. Nevertheless, it is not a risk that should be taken without a great deal of knowledge about the property and experience in the real estate business.

Specifically, the representations and warranties should describe any matter that could adversely affect the property after the closing. It is not mandatory that every agreement of sale contain reference to every conceivable representation or warranty. Some will not be necessary or relevant, and others the seller will not be willing to provide. Generally, the agreement of sale should include the representations and warranties discussed in the following section.

Environmental Conditions. The agreement of sale should indicate whether the property has ever been used for toxic wastes or other environmental hazards or is in a wetlands or other restricted area. The agreement should also state whether any prior attempt has been made to obtain approvals to develop or to actually commence development of the property.

Liens and Encumbrances. The agreement should describe any easements, mortgages, leases, ground leases, encumbrances, or liens that will continue to burden the property after the closing. It should state that such agreements are in full force and effect, not in default by either party, and that the agreement of sale and the sale will not create a default under the terms of the agreement.

Mortgages. The agreement should indicate the current unpaid balance, the maturity date, and whether the indebtedness self-liquidates or there is a balloon payment due for each mortgage on the property.

Condition. If the property is improved, the agreement of sale should specify whether there are structural defects to any improvements on the property, including the roof, foundation, and exterior walls, and should indicate whether the heating, plumbing, air conditioning, and electrical systems are in good working order.

Litigation. The agreement of sale should disclose any litigation involving the property or the seller's title to the property, as well as the seller's knowledge of any threatened condemnation proceedings or the property's violation of municipal, state, or federal laws, rules, or regulations. If there are preexisting litigations, the purchaser will have to determine whether they affect only the seller or they could ultimately jeopardize the purchaser's title to the property, result in a claim against the purchaser, or otherwise limit the purchaser's use or development of the property.

Condemnation. The agreement of sale should state whether the seller has knowledge of any pending or threatened condemnation of all or part of the property.

Preexisting Building Code Violations. The agreement of sale should disclose any known building code violations. The purchaser will have to determine that they have been cured by the seller and whether the violations are a warning sign that the property has far worse problems.

Title and Authority. The seller should represent that it owns the property (or has a contract to purchase the property) and that the seller has the requisite authority to enter into the contract and convey the property to the purchaser without the consent of a third party. If the seller is a contract vendee, the purchaser should examine the seller's contract to acquire the property and seek notice from the owner if, for any reason, the seller is not going to be able to close or the seller's vendor is unlikely to close.

Unpaid Tax Assessments. The agreement of sale must state whether there are unpaid tax assessments. The purchaser may be required to pay for work affecting the property that was required by local regulations and that has been completed.

Employees. The agreement of sale should specify all employees that the purchaser will have to hire, as well as any contracts involving the property with which the purchaser must comply after the closing.

Insurance. The agreement of sale must state whether the property is within a flood zone and whether the seller has received notice from any insurance company that would adversely affect the insurability of the property. In either case, insurance premiums would be increased or work would have to be done to the property. These representations would alert the purchaser that the ownership of the property entails an additional insurance cost and that there is an additional risk that the property could have long-term problems.

Brokers. The agreement of sale should represent which broker or brokers, if any, are responsible for the transaction and should indicate which party is to be liable for the brokerage commission. Each party should also indemnify the other party against claims made by any other brokers. The amount of the commission is not usually described in the agreement of sale, but is contained in a separate agreement that is referred to in the agreement of sale.

Income and Expenses. If representations regarding the property's income and expenses have been made to the purchaser, then the agreement of sale should describe them.

Sellers frequently object to providing representations and warranties, not from a desire to hide some horrible fact about the property, but either because the seller does not have the information on which to base the representation or because the seller wants to limit its obligation to the purchaser after the closing. This concern can be handled by merely requiring the seller to represent that, "to the best of seller's knowledge," the condition does or does not exist. Alternatively, the agreement of sale can provide that the seller has not received notice that a particular situation exists or a specific event has occurred. Thus, the seller is representing only those facts of which it has knowledge. The purpose of the representation and warranty section of the contract is to provide the purchaser with the same knowledge that the seller possesses, so the purchaser can make an intelligent decision. The representations and warranties are not intended to replace due diligence.

Closing Adjustments and Expenses

Because of the need to pay closing expenses, the amount of money purchasers pay and sellers receive at the closing is not the exact amount described in the agreement of sale as the cash purchase price. Based on local law or custom, these closing expenses could include transfer taxes, deed stamps, mortgage recording taxes, survey costs, and title insurance costs. Another reason the payment fluctuates at closing is that the price is adjusted to reflect operating expenses that were prepaid by the seller (adjustments in favor of the seller) or accrued by the seller for future payment (adjustments in favor of the purchaser). The agreement of sale should specify which operating expenses will be adjusted at the closing and the method that will be used to make such adjustments. The agreement should also indicate which party will pay each of the closing expenses.

Closing expenses are usually allocated between the parties based upon the local custom where the property is located. Alternatively, the parties could agree to each pay half of the closing costs. Traditionally, the purchaser pays the mortgage recording tax for purchase money financing and the deed stamps, and the seller pays the other expenses. If the agreement of sale is silent on these matters, then local custom prevails. Closing adjustments usually include rent, interest on mortgages that will continue to encumber the property after the closing, utility charges, real estate taxes, premiums for preexisting insurance that will remain in force after the closing, employee wages and benefits, taxes, fuel, building supplies, management fees, and sewer and water charges. The purpose of closing adjustments is to enable the purchaser to reimburse the seller for any prepaid expenses, and the seller to reimburse the purchaser for expenses that accrued while the seller owned the property, but for which payment is deferred until after the purchaser has acquired title. The agreement of sale should specify the expenses to be adjusted and the method of adjustment.

Unpaid Assessments

The agreement of sale should also deal with the manner of handling unpaid tax assessments. An assessment is a fixed charge by the community that is payable like real estate taxes, except that it is payable in installments and is meant to reimburse the government for an improvement that benefits a particular property. If the assessment is due and payable at, or prior to, the time of closing, then, like real estate taxes, it is the seller's responsibility to pay. If the assessment is payable in fixed installments over an extended period of time and assessments are due after the closing, the purchaser should argue that the assessment is for an improvement that the purchaser is already paying for through the purchase price and should not be required to pay twice for the same item.

Condition of the Property

The property should be in the same condition at the closing as it was when the agreement of sale was executed. The word *condition* refers to the relationship among those having an interest in the property, as well as the physical structure of the property. The agreement of sale should require the seller to continue to operate the property in the same manner as the property had been operated prior to the contract's execution. The seller should not take any action that would adversely affect the property, the tenants, or the mortgagee of the property. This provision ensures that the seller will maintain the property until the closing. However, complications can occur if the tenant is in default and the seller is able to and wants to fill the vacancy as quickly as possible. The purchaser may want the vacancy to be left unfilled so the purchaser can be certain of maximizing the rent with a different tenant, or the purchaser may insist that the vacancy be filled so that it can obtain the cash flow it bargained to receive. If the purchaser requested that the space be left vacant, then the seller should be reimbursed for the rent it does not receive prior to the closing. The agreement of sale should provide how each of these situations is to be handled.

The agreement of sale should also obligate the seller to continue to maintain the property in the same manner as before the contract was executed and to perform all necessary repairs to the property. The purchaser will want to receive immediate notice of any significant change affecting the property. Few purchasers will want the seller to change any of the leases or to take any action or forebear from taking any action that would cause a default in any lease, mortgage, easement, or lien on the property. The purchaser would also want the seller to maintain the good will of the tenants, mortgagees, and other third parties having an interest in the property, as well as employees and tradespeople.

TITLE INSURANCE

Title insurance protects the purchaser and the lender against the risk that the seller and borrower do not have good title to the property. Title insurance also insures that:

- The title to the property is as described in the title commitment
- There are no defects to the title to the property that is being conveyed
- There are no encumbrances on the title or the property other than those disclosed in the title commitment and acknowledged by the purchaser
- The title to the property being conveyed to the purchaser is "good and marketable."

The title insurance premium is paid at the closing and remains in effect as long as the property is owned by the same party. Title insurance should always be obtained; the risk insured against is huge compared with the insignificant cost of the insurance.

The primary purpose of the title search is to ascertain that the person or entity attempting to sell the property actually owns the property. However, the title report discloses a great deal of additional information about the property. The title report describes each document that has been recorded as an encumbrance against title to the property, including deeds, mortgages, leases, grants or reservations of easements, restrictions on use, deed restrictions, judgments, and tax liens. Documents are recorded to provide notice to the world that someone other then the owner of the property has an interest in the property.

Title reports usually contain a legal description of the property, the name of the property owner, the instrument through which the owner acquired title to the property, the date of acquisition, real estate taxes, and assessments and payments. Any of the following items that are relevant to the property are also itemized: unsatisfied mortgages and assignments, federal tax liens, recorded leases or memoranda of leases or installment, sale contracts, restrictions, notice of pending legal actions that could affect the title to the property (i.e., "lis pendens"), foreclosures, mechanics' liens, building code violations, judgments docketed against the owners, and unpaid franchise taxes. Every document described in the title report must be reviewed separately.

A title objection is an exception to title that is a lien against the property and described in the title report that is not permitted by the agreement of sale. If the agreement of sale does not specify the permitted title exceptions, then any exception that prevents the purchaser from acquiring good and marketable title can preclude the sale. Title objections include, but are not limited to, the following as they relate to the prior ownership of the property: a break in the chain of title; violations of covenants, conditions, or restrictions that are liens on the property; rights of heirs; defective descriptions in prior transfers; disputes in boundary lines or dimensions; possessory rights; significant encroachments by improvements; judgments; liens; unpaid taxes; the absence of a certificate of occupancy; building code violations; and lis pendens. These objections do not necessarily prevent the purchaser from acquiring the property; they are simply things of which the purchaser should be aware. If they are described in the agreement of sale as permitted exceptions, the purchaser has already been warned about them, and their existence should not adversely affect the purchaser's ability, desire, or obligation to close. The problem arises if the agreement of sale does not refer to these objections, and the objection effectively limits the purchaser's use and enjoyment of the property.

There are five kinds of title insurance policies, which are described as an owner's policy, a leasehold policy, a lender's policy, a leasehold lender's policy, and a construction lender's policy. Although each policy insures against a different kind of ownership interest, each policy also insures against the following problems:

- Loss or damage arising from the items covered by the insurance, and covers the claim against the property, as well as attorney's fees and expenses even if the amount exceeds the amount of the insurance

- A title defect that renders the title unmarketable and is not an exception to the coverage
- The unenforceability or invalidity of the lender's lien
- The lack of a lien's priority due to unrecorded construction or mechanics' liens.

However, the title insurance policies exclude or limit coverage in the following instances:

- Loss or damage resulting from government regulations and police powers, including items relating to zoning, environmental protection laws, and related regulations
- Loss or damage arising from the government's exercise of its right of eminent domain, unless the public record indicates that the government is contemplating such a taking at the time the insurance is issued.

Lender's policies exclude coverage for the validity or enforceability of a mortgage that is insured if the loan secured by the mortgage violates the usury law or any other consumer protection law. Lender's policies also exclude coverage of mechanics' liens for work started after the policy is issued and is not financed from the loan proceeds.

The title insurance policy limits the title company's obligation to defend a claim, and provides the procedure for making claims, limitations on its liability, arbitration and subrogation, and other related matters. The title policy contains coinsurance protection, so that the owner must defend a claim if the amount of insurance is less than 80 percent of the property value. Title insurance companies provide a varied number of endorsements for the title insurance policies they issue, which should be of particular interest to those contemplating acquiring distressed property. The endorsements include the following:

- Street Assessment Endorsement (ALTA (American Land Title Association) Form 1) insures lenders that any tax assessments for street improvements under construction prior to the loan will be subordinate to the lender's mortgage.
- Truth-in-Lending Endorsement (ALTA Form 2) insures lenders from a loss of good title due to the exercise of a right of rescission pursuant to the Federal Truth-in-Lending Act.
- Zoning Endorsement (ALTA Form 3) is used when undeveloped land is being purchased or financed and provides an owner or lender with

assurances with regard to the zoning of a particular piece of property, including the zoning classification and the permitted uses under that classification. ALTA Form 3.1 is used for permanent financing or the acquisition of property containing completed improvements and provides the same insurance as Form 3, as well as insuring against loss or damage from a judicial decision prohibiting a permitted use of the property or improvements located thereon or requiring the removal of the improvements located thereon. The endorsements insure against violations regarding the area, width, or depth of a building site; or the floor space of the improvement; or the setback or height of the structure.

- Condominium Endorsement (ALTA Form 4) insures against the failure of the condominium unit and the common elements to be part of the condominium, the failure of the condominium to be a valid condominium, violations of restrictive covenants, the lien priority of the condominium charges over the lien of a mortgage, the failure of the condominium to be separately assessed for taxes, the encroachment of a condominium unit on the common elements, and any loss due to the exercise of a right of first refusal contained in the condominium documents.

- Planned Unit Development (PUD) Endorsement (ALTA Form 5) provides protection that the restrictive covenants in the PUD documents do not cause a forfeiture or reversion of title and that any liens created by the restrictive covenant do not have priority over an insured mortgage and also protects against the forced removal of any improvement on the property due to encroachments onto adjoining property.

- Variable Rate Mortgage Endorsement (ALTA Forms 6, 6.1, 6.2) protects lenders when making a loan based on an interest rate other than a fixed-rate, level-payment, self-liquidating loan. The endorsement precludes difficulties due to negative amortization, compound interest, accruals, and fluctuating interest.

- Manufactured Housing Units Endorsement (ALTA Form 7) protects mobile homes or movable housing units.

- Environmental Protection Lien Endorsement (ALTA Forms 8 and 8.1) protects against the absence of priority of an insured mortgage over environmental protection statutes in effect when the policy is issued.

- Construction Loan Mechanics' Lien Endorsement protects lenders from mechanics' liens for work done prior to the mortgage, when state statute does not require that the mechanics' lien has to be recorded prior to the mortgage.

- Bring-Down Endorsement is used in construction loans as each advance is made under the original construction loan.

- Comprehensive Endorsement is used to protect against loss due to any covenants, conditions, or restrictions that may result in a lender's mortgage being eliminated or subordinated or any present violation of a restrictive covenant or an encroachment by any improvements, as well as future violations of any covenant, condition, or restriction, and provides indemnification for damages caused by an easement holder's exercising a right to maintain or use an easement and indemnifies the insured to the effect that it can maintain improvements on encroaching land.

- Commercial Inflation Protection Endorsement provides for the automatic increase of insurance coverage as inflation increases the value of the property up to 150 percent of the original insurance.

- Assignment of Policy Endorsement makes the purchaser of a loan the insured under the original insurance coverage.

- Interior Contiguity Endorsement is insurance that protects against any gap between several contiguous parcels and provides that they are all contiguous.

- Public Road Contiguity Endorsement provides that the property has direct access to public streets.

- Assignment of Rents Endorsement provides for the priority of a collateral assignment of leases, rents, and profits to a lender as additional security for a mortgage.

- Land Survey Endorsement provides insurance that the property described in the legal description is the same land shown in an attached survey or map.

- Option Endorsement protects an optionee's right to purchase the property as contained in a written option agreement.

- Imputed Knowledge Endorsement insures that the insured will not lose its protection due to knowledge of a defect that is imputed to it.

Affirmative insurance is a special form of title insurance coverage that provides that, notwithstanding the existence of a cloud on the title, if the cloud is enforced, it will not defeat the purchaser's title to the property or prevent its current use of the property. Affirmative insurance may also provide that a violation of a restriction or a building encroaching part of an easement will not cause the building to be removed. In affirmative insurance, the title company is taking the risk that if a third party attempts to enforce its rights, the third party will not require a change that will adversely affect the building or the use of the property.

Title insurance is of particular importance to the purchaser of distressed property because of the possibility that the seller's financial problems have provided an atmosphere in which liens and encumbrances can and have been placed against the property. The purchaser must carefully examine the title report for distressed property and obtain updates of the information contained in the report immediately prior to the closing.

PLANNING FOR THE CLOSING

Planning for a closing requires a careful analysis of what will be required to expedite the closing. The seller and the purchaser should begin to obtain the required material as soon after the execution of the agreement of sale as possible. Some material needed for the closing will be readily available, whereas other material will not be available at all. The party required to supply the latter material will have to do whatever is required to obtain it in time for the closing.

One of the first things to do in preparing for the closing is to identify the things that have to be done or obtained for the closing. The earlier the list is prepared, the more time the parties will have to accomplish the necessary tasks prior to the closing. In a typical transaction, the following things must be accomplished:

Seller

1. Order title report and survey
2. Request estoppel letters and consents
3. Obtain copies of original leases, notes, mortgages, and other relevant documents
4. Prepare closing documents
   a. Deed or assignment of ground lease
   b. Assignment of leases
   c. Bill of sale for personal property
   d. Assignment of warranties, guaranties
   e. Assignment of licenses and permits

    f. Assignment of union contract

    g. Transfer of security deposits

5. Arrange for payoff letters and satisfactions of existing indebtedness
6. Prepare rent schedules
7. Prepare files for transfer
8. Obtain copies of certificate of occupancy, permits and licenses, and other municipal documents
9. Prepare notification letters to tenants, mortgagees, contractors, and suppliers
10. If corporation is seller, prepare corporate resolution to sell and obtain good-standing certificate from Secretary of State
11. If partnership is seller, obtain certified copy of partnership agreement and consents from partners, if required
12. Prepare transfer affidavits
13. Prepare affidavit of title
14. Prepare apportionments
15. Cancel insurance, if it is not being assigned to purchaser.

Purchaser

1. Arrange for payment
   a. Review loan commitment for requirements
   b. Review loan documents—note, mortgage, collateral assignments of leases and rents, guaranty, affidavits, security agreement and financing statements
   c. Obtain balance of purchase price from investors
2. Review title report and advise seller's attorney of objections in writing
3. Read survey and compare with legal description in the title report
4. Set up purchasing entity (e.g., corporation, partnership)
5. Review seller's closing documents
6. Arrange for casualty and liability insurance coverage for the property
7. Inspect the property
8. Arrange for environmental study of the property

9. Arrange for fuel delivery and utilities
10. Prepare notification letters to tenants, mortgagees, and suppliers.

If the property is being sold encumbered by one or more mortgages or deeds of trust that are to be satisfied with the closing proceeds, the seller must advise the lender and obtain payoff letters for the closing. Alternatively, if the property is being sold subject to the existing financing or the purchaser has agreed to assume the existing financing, the lender has to be supplied with financial information regarding the purchaser so that it can make its credit decision. The lender will take this opportunity to reanalyze the loan to make certain that the interest rate is still favorable and that the loan-to-value ratio has not deteriorated. If the market for interest rates is significantly higher, the lender may want to increase the interest rate as a precondition to giving its approval to the transfer of the property. Alternatively, the lender may ask for a fee as a condition for giving its approval to the transaction. However, as long as the mortgage does not contain a due on sale provision, the lender cannot preclude the closing, only delay it.

Estoppel letters or certificates are notices from the tenant of an operating lease, the lessor of a ground lease, a mortgagee, or a guarantor that the lease or mortgage is in full force and effect and not in default. The purchaser must insist on receiving it to ascertain that the property being purchased is subject to effective leases and mortgages. The estoppel letter not only should indicate the absence of a default, but should describe the lease or mortgage, so the purchaser knows that it has seen the correct documents. This can be done by reference to the date and parties to the mortgage or lease, as well as the salient terms of the document, such as the principal balance of the indebtedness, interest rate, debt service, and maturity date of a mortgage, and the rent, percentage rent, and termination date of a lease. The tenant estoppel letter should also state that any preconditions to the lease commencement contained in the lease have been satisfied and that the lease has not been assigned by the other party to it or the rents prepaid.

The estoppel letter should be obtained within 30 days prior to the closing so that it is not outdated by the time the closing occurs. If the seller waits too long to obtain the estoppel letter, which describes a problem at the property, the seller will not have adequate time to correct the problem prior to the closing. The other problem that can arise with estoppel letters is the format of the letter. The purchaser should insist on a detailed estoppel letter, specifying the absence of any defaults or other problems with the property. However, the tenant will want to provide as little information as possible to avoid an argument with the new landlord at a later date that the tenant waived all lease problems by issuing the estoppel letter. Additionally, when the property requires repairs at a later date, the tenant will not want the landlord to use the estoppel letter to challenge the tenant's right to have the repairs made. The landlord could claim that the tenant should have specified the possible need for the repairs in the estoppel letter.

The seller should also obtain the consent of third parties, if required. The purchaser should review the leases, mortgages, and other title documents to determine whether any third party must consent to the transaction. The seller may also be required to obtain from a third party a waiver of a right of first refusal to obtain the property from the seller on the same terms and conditions.

CLOSING

The closing is the time when the purchaser and seller meet and complete the conveyance of title to the property. The purchaser and seller, their attorneys, lenders (if required), and the representative of the title insurance company meet in one place at one time and resolve any problems and close the transaction. The attorneys examine the closing documents, and the representative of the title insurance company calls the recorder's office to get a current update on the condition of the title to the property. Once the title company is convinced that the seller has the right to convey the property and the documents reflect the conveyance, the closing documents are executed and acknowledged, the money paid, and the transfer completed.

The representative of the title company will also want to ascertain that the seller is conveying to the purchaser the seller's entire right, title, and interest to the property and will also want to see proof that the seller is in good standing, if it is a partnership or a corporation, and that the person representing a partnership or corporation has the authority to execute the closing documents and sell the property. The seller will also be required to satisfy the title company that any title exceptions can be removed.

The seller then executes the deed or assignment of ground lease and the lease assignments, if any, and the purchaser executes the purchase money note and mortgage and collateral assignment of lease, if required. The signatures on the original documents are then acknowledged by a notary public, and the originals of the deed, assignments, and purchase money mortgage are delivered to the representative of the title company for recording. The original promissory note is delivered to the seller. If additional things have to be completed, the parties will deliver the closing proceeds and the documents to the representative of the title company, who will execute an escrow agreement and agree to deliver the checks and documents at such time as the conditions are satisfied. Once everything has been completed, the parties leave.

Based on the kind of transaction involved, the closing agenda could include the following items:

- Execute deed or assignment of ground lease
- Execute assignments and assumption of leases
- Execute bill of sale for personal property
- Execute notification letters to tenants and supplies relating to the sale
- Execute assignment of warranties and guaranties
- Execute reaffirmation of contract representations and warranties that survive the closing
- Execute assignment of permits and licenses
- Execute purchase money promissory note, if applicable
- Execute purchase money mortgage, if applicable
- Execute collateral assignment of leases and rents, if applicable
- Execute Uniform Commercial Code financing statements (UCC Form 1), if applicable
- Execute security agreement or chattel mortgage, if applicable
- Deliver original leases
- Deliver certificate of occupancy
- Deliver permits and licenses
- Deliver plans and specifications for improvements
- Deliver "as built" survey
- Deliver tenant security deposits
- Deliver tenant files
- Deliver copy of preclosing insurance policy
- Provide evidence of authority of person executing closing documents
- Deliver certified copy of a corporate seller's certificate of incorporation and bylaws or partnership seller's partnership agreement and partner consents
- Provide estoppel certificate for commercial tenants and mortgagees

- Provide consents to the sale and waivers of right of first refusal from those having such rights
- Provide a satisfaction of any preexisting mortgages, that will not remain a lien on the property
- Prepare closing adjustments or prorations
- Update and issue title insurance policy
- Prepare transfer tax forms
- Pay for title insurance and transfer taxes
- Pay balance of purchase price
- Pay brokerage commissions
- Deliver keys.

Closing Adjustments

Closing adjustments are intended to reimburse each party for income and expenses that should be paid to or by the other party. The seller is required to reimburse the purchaser for expenses that accrued while the property was owned by the seller but have not as yet been paid. The purchaser is obligated to reimburse the seller for expenses that cannot be terminated on the closing date but that the seller paid. Expenses that can be stopped on the closing date and then restarted after the closing date (e.g., utility charges) need not be prorated because the third party will bill the seller for the services through the closing date and will bill the purchaser for services provided after the closing date.

Rent Adjustment

Rent is usually payable monthly in advance on the first day of the month. If the closing occurs during the month and the rent is paid in advance, then the seller owes the purchaser rent for the portion of the month in which the purchaser owns the property (see Example below).

If the rent is payable in arrears, the purchaser would owe the seller the rent for the portion of the month in which the seller owned the property (see Example on page 283). If rent is paid quarterly or annually, the adjustment is still made, although the period of time and the size of the rent adjustment will change.

EXAMPLE

If the rent is $3,000 per month, the seller will be required to reimburse the purchaser $1,600 if the closing occurs on the fifteenth day of a 30-day month, in which case there are 16 days left.

EXAMPLE

> Therefore, the purchaser would owe the seller $1,400, because there
> are 14 days between the beginning of the first day and the end of the
> fourteenth day.

If the tenant pays percentage rent, the percentage rent for the year the
conveyance occurred is calculated when it is received in the following
year rather than at the closing. The purchaser is then obligated to forward
to the seller a pro rata portion of the payment based on the fraction of the
year that each party owned the property, assuming that the sales upon
which the rent was calculated are made equitably over the year. Additional rent based upon the operating expenses or upon a fluctuation in a
consumer price index or other criteria would be adjusted after the end of
the year for the expense that accrued in the prior year, and each party
would receive a portion of the additional rent from the purchaser based
upon the portion of the year that the party owned the property.

Security Deposits

If the seller is holding a tenant's security deposit, the seller should deliver
to the purchaser the deposit plus the interest earned on the deposit. Although the purchaser could take a credit against the cash purchase price,
it is better for the seller to deliver the deposit and interest to the purchaser
by separate check marked accordingly or by delivering the segregated
bank account to the purchaser with new signature cards. In this way, there
can be no question at a later date as to the amount received by the purchaser or whether the transfer was made.

Real Estate Taxes

If the owner pays the real estate taxes for the property, the taxes would be
adjusted based upon the tax year or the lien year according to which party
owned the property for which portion of the year in question. If the property is located within several different taxing jurisdictions (school district, village or town, county, and possibly state), each tax will have to be
separately adjusted. If the taxes are assessed a year in arrears or if the tax
assessment is being challenged by the seller when the closing occurs, the
tax calculation is complicated. Taxes that are assessed in arrears are prorated based upon the prior year's assessment, with the seller's having a
continuing obligation to pay the difference between the prior year's tax
and the current year's assessment if it is higher, when the current tax bill is

received, for the portion of the year in which it owned the property. The seller should have the right to proceed with actions to reduce the tax assessment for years prior to the year of sale and to retain the portion of the refund attributable to years in which it owned the property. However, the refunds that are received for the year of sale should be divided between the purchaser and the seller based upon the portion of the year in which each party owned the property.

Water Charges

Water use can be charged to the owner of the property as a fixed charge based upon a formula or as a varying charge based upon the amount of water actually used. If the water charges are calculated using the first method, the adjustment is based upon the ratio of the portion of the year each party owns the property. Water charges that are based upon a meter reading require that the meter be read immediately prior to the closing. The seller pays for the water used at the property prior to the closing, and the purchaser pays for all water charges after the closing. If the municipality does not read meters other than at the end of the period, the adjustments can be based upon the cost per day pursuant to the last meter reading with an estimate made as to the cost of the next meter reading. If the water charges are paid by the tenants, the water charges do not have to be adjusted at the closing unless portions of the premises are not leased at the time of the closing.

Insurance

Premiums for casualty and liability insurance have to be adjusted at the closing only if the insurance is transferable and is retained by the purchaser after the closing. The insurance adjustment is usually made based upon the premium for the year of the closing, and the proration is based upon the portion of the year that each party owns the property. If the insurance carrier pays dividends at the end of the policy period, which reduce the aggregate cost of the insurance, the purchaser would deliver to the seller a pro rata portion of the dividend when it is received.

Payroll and Related Expenses

If the seller of the property employs people at the property who will become the employees of the purchaser, an adjustment must be made for the current payroll expense, as well as the fringe benefits, vacation allowance, and other similar expenses. The purchaser should have its accountant review the seller's records prior to the closing to certify the accuracy of the seller's tax reports and payments that have previously been made. The seller should also execute a survival agreement providing that its obligation to pay such taxes shall survive the closing.

Index